The Complete Book of Bathroom Design

THE HOMEOWNER'S LIBRARY

THE COMPLETE BOOK OF BATHROOM DESIGN

**Barb Machowski and the Editors
of Consumer Reports Books**

CONSUMER REPORTS BOOKS
A DIVISION OF CONSUMERS UNION
YONKERS, NEW YORK

The publisher would like to thank the following photographers for permission to reproduce their work in the 8-page color insert appearing between pages 58 and 59. Page 1: *top right, center,* Stephen Cridland; *bottom,* Karen Bussolini. Page 2: *top left and right,* Jennifer Jordan; *bottom,* Karen Bussolini. Page 3: *top right,* Jennifer Jordan; *center,* Elizabeth Heyert; *bottom,* Robert Perron. Page 4: *top,* Jennifer Jordan; *bottom,* Keith Scott Morton. Page 5: *top left, center, right,* Keith Scott Morton; *bottom,* Jeff McNamara. Page 6: *top left,* Keith Scott Morton; *bottom left,* Tim Street-Porter; *bottom right,* Jennifer Jordan. Page 7: *top and bottom,* Tim Street-Porter. Page 8: Jeff McNamara.

Library of Congress Cataloging-in-Publication Data

Machowski, Barb.
      The complete book of bathroom design   / Barb Machowski and the
editors of Consumer Reports Books.
          p.   cm. — (The Homeowner's library.)
      Includes index.
      ISBN 0-89043-590-1
      1. Bathrooms—Remodeling.   2. Bathrooms—Design and construction.
3. Consumer education.   I. Consumer Reports Books. II. Title.
III. Series.
TH4816.3.B37M33   1993
643'.52—dc20

          93-25295
          CIP

Designed and produced by Jonathan Press, Cannon Falls, Minnesota
    Director: Al Gutierrez
    Writer: Barb Machowski
    Senior Editor: Gary Branson
    Copy Editors: Kathy Wachendorf, Cheryl Clark
    Illustrator: Sharon Doucette

First Printing, September 1993
This book is printed on recycled paper ♻
Manufactured in the United States of America

The Complete Book of Bathroom Design is a Consumer Reports Book published by Consumers Union, the nonprofit organization that publishes *Consumer Reports,* the monthly magazine of test reports, product Ratings, and buying guidance. Established in 1936, Consumers Union is chartered under the Not-for-Profit Corporation Law of the State of New York.

    The purposes of Consumers Union, as stated in its charter, are to provide consumers with information and counsel on consumer goods and services, to give information on all matters relating to the expenditure of the family income, and to initiate and to cooperate with individual and group efforts seeking to create and maintain decent living standards.

    Consumers Union derives its income solely from the sale of *Consumer Reports* and other publications. In addition, expenses of occasional public service efforts may be met, in part, by nonrestrictive, noncommercial contributions, grants, and fees. Consumers Union accepts no advertising or product samples and is not beholden in any way to any commercial interest. Its Ratings and reports are solely for the use of the readers of its publications. Neither the Ratings nor the reports nor any Consumers Union publications, including this book, may be used in advertising or for any commercial purpose. Consumers Union will take all steps open to it to prevent such uses of its materials, its name, or the name of *Consumer Reports.*

Contents

Introduction

The bathroom is changing more rapidly than any other room in the home. It has evolved from a utilitarian space to a *designed* room, a room planned to meet individual and family needs. The bath has become a multipurpose room equipped for relaxing, exercise, entertainment, and complete personal grooming, from bathing to dressing. The bath may be an extension of the master bedroom; it may include a laundry.

Because of the changes in both style and function, the bathroom has become the most frequently remodeled room in the '90s. Each year, approximately 2.7 million new baths are installed and another 5 million are remodeled. New homes often are built with $2\frac{1}{2}$ baths; older homes are catching up to that number through bathroom remodeling projects and bathroom additions.

CHANGES

A number of changes in bathroom design are emerging:

1. Universal design trends emphasize easy-to-use bathrooms for all generations, from children to aging adults. Wider doorways may be incorporated to accommodate wheelchairs or walkers, for example. Faucet levers and lighting controls that can be activated easily are helpful to the very young as well as those with arthritis or a disability.

2. Bathrooms are designed to fit the human body. Bathroom designers and manufacturers of bathroom equipment are borrowing from the study of *ergonomics,* a method of designing equipment and space based on the range of motion of the human body. These designers pay attention to such

features as the amount of elbowroom needed between the sink and the wall, and the optimum location of storage cabinets, considering the variations in the human reach.

Designers working with body-smart principles may recommend a raised vanity cabinet with sink for the tall individual, or a high-rise toilet that suits the limited range of sitting and standing for the elderly. For the multigenerational family, grab bars at the tub and shower can be planned for the height and reach of all family members.

3. Bathroom design at its best is personalized design. The bath is planned to meet the specific needs of those who use it, whether the design is for a working couple, children, the elderly, or the multigenerational family.

Consider the working couple who use one bath, for example. The partners may require both shared and private space in the bathroom. A personalized plan might include a separate tub and shower, a vanity with two sinks for shared space, and a toilet with a privacy wall. A family with elderly members may add features for low vision to the bath, such as enhanced lighting levels at the mirror, strips of minilights to illuminate steps to a whirlpool, white cabinet interiors, and a light color scheme throughout the bath.

4. Conservation concerns have extended to the bathroom. Methods for conserving water and using electricity efficiently have affected the design of bathroom products. For example, low-flush toilets require only 1.6 gallons (or less) of water per flush, compared to 3.5 for a "water-saver" toilet; low-flow showerheads reduce water consumption to 2 to 3 gallons per minute (gpm), compared to 5 to 8 gpm. Compact fluorescent bulbs, which produce more light for less energy than incandescent bulbs, can now fit right into standard incandescent fixtures.

5. Safety issues have affected bathroom planning and product development. The current thinking on safety is that *everyone* needs safety devices in the bathroom. Nonslip surfaces and grab bars in the tub and shower are vital for accident prevention for people of all ages. Children as well as older adults benefit from specially-designed soft tubs and antiscald faucets, for example. And GFCI (ground fault circuit interrupters) are required in all electrical outlets to reduce the hazard of electrical shock.

6. New standards for bathroom design professionals have become increasingly sophisticated. Since 1989, the National Kitchen and Bath Association (NKBA), a major trade organization of kitchen and bath specialists, has offered specialized training that leads to the designation of Certified Bathroom Designer (CBD). Certification, however, is not always a guarantee of competence.

In addition, the NKBA published in 1992 a comprehensive planning reference, The Bathroom Industry Technical Manuals (BITMs). For the first time in the industry, the publications are designed to equip professionals with a standard technical guide to bathroom equipment, mechanical systems, building materials, and construction methods.

Developed over a period of three years with the assistance of designers, manufacturers, and technical and academic advisors, the manuals also address problems of contemporary bathroom design, such as controlling water use, universal or multigenerational design, and safety.

TAKING THE FIRST STEPS

These changes in bathroom planning make it an exciting time to begin a bathroom remodeling project. Perhaps your family has already begun the remodeling process. You may have made a list of what is outdated in the bathroom and a list of features you want. Floor plans may have been created, and discussions begun about how family needs will change in the future. You may have pictured luxury features and considered the remodeling budget.

We provide accurate, up-to-date information gathered from bathroom designers, architects, interior designers, contractors, plumbers, electricians, lighting designers, tile distributors, fixture manufacturers, and building code and safety officials. And there are many experts we would like you to "talk" to, so lists of resource organizations and helpful publications are included in Appendices A and B.

We believe that the practical advice included in these chapters will enable your family to complete the bathroom remodeling process — *with confidence.*

Part One

GETTING READY TO REMODEL

☐ **REMODELING SCOPE** ☐ **BATHROOM INVENTORY** ☐
☐ **COSTS** ☐ **PAYBACK** ☐ **CHOOSING THE PROS** ☐

1

Getting Started

THE ASSIGNMENT:
Identify the scope
of remodeling, take a bathroom
inventory, and research
products and designs.

Arriving at the best possible remodeling plan is a *process* in which *ideas about design, style, and products are refined according to such factors as personal preference and budget.* Doing the homework suggested here is a first step in refining your own ideas about design and communicating them to a designer.

To do your homework, follow these steps:

■ **Identify the scope of the remodeling project.** How much needs to be done? Should fixtures be replaced? Does the entire room need redesigning?

■ **Take a bathroom inventory.** What is wrong with the present bath? What does the family need, now and in the future?

■ **Research bathroom products and designs.** Collect magazine pictures of baths you like. Survey products available.

TYPES OF REMODELING PROJECTS

Remodeling projects may be divided into three categories:

■ **The face lift,** the least expensive remodeling plan, includes changing surface materials such as wallcovering, flooring, cabinet finish, and countertops. Adding new faucets, medicine cabinets, mirrors, and/or lighting fixtures updates the bath.

■ **The replacement** or **minor remodeling** (also called a **change-out**), in which surface materials are changed and new fixtures are installed close to, or in, their old location. Relatively minor structural changes may be made, such as relocating a doorway, replacing windows, adding a skylight, altering all or a portion of a partition (nonbearing) wall.

■ **The major remodeling** (includes the **room addition**), the most expensive alternative, in which the entire bath is redesigned; new surface materials and fixtures are installed; fixtures may be relocated; structural, electrical, and plumbing changes may be made.

The categories may overlap. For example, a face lift may involve the replacement of a fixture or cabinet. On the other hand, in some minor remodeling projects, not all fixtures will be replaced.

THE BATHROOM FACE LIFT

The best candidate for a face lift is a bathroom in which the floor plan is workable and the space is

MAJOR REMODELING

Before remodeling, the bath is long and narrow with adequate counter space, but the tub is too small.

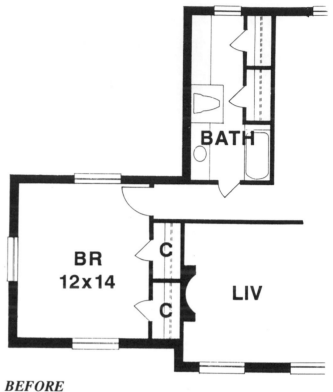

BEFORE

adequate. However, surface materials, such as walls, flooring, counters, and cabinets, may be worn or out of date.

There are several situations in which a face lift may be the best remodeling solution:

■ **For the home that will be sold.** Without investing a large amount of money, the bath can be updated with a face lift. However, it is important not to invest too much in a face lift when a home is sold because the new owner may redecorate according to personal taste. (See Chapter 2, "Money Matters," for a discussion of payback on the remodeling investment.)

■ **For the bathroom that is relatively new** — ten years old or less — chances are that a face lift will renew the bath satisfactorily.

■ **For the homeowner who will do some of the remodeling work,** the face lift is the easiest remodeling to tackle. Wallpapering and painting, for example, are within the reach of homeowners with moderate do-it-yourself experience. Installing a new countertop or lavatory faucets are other tasks the homeowner may wish to complete.

A relatively low-budget face lift produces economic options. Low-budget options include:

■ **Reface cabinets** with a durable hardwood veneer instead of buying new cabinets.

■ **Remove the old countertop and install an**

attractive laminate, about $100 for a 48" length.

■ **Trade an aging wall-hung sink for a graceful pedestal lavatory,** starting at $150.

■ **Re-porcelain a tub** instead of replacing it. (See Chapter 11, "Fixtures: Tubs and Showers," for details.)

■ **Replace plastic tile with ceramic,** which starts at about $3 per square foot.

■ **Paint, hang new wallcovering, and add a window treatment;** the quickest, least expensive change.

Choose quality fixtures or materials such as these:

1. Exchange stock vanity cabinets finished with a wood veneer with sleek European style laminate cabinets trimmed with handsome hardware. As a matter of practicality, laminate is easy to clean too.

2. Add a feature that looks custom made, such as the sinks with floral designs that appear to

After an addition, the bathroom has more than doubled in size. Amenities include a whirlpool, shower for two, and expanded wardrobe and linen storage. For guests, a powder room is added.

be hand-painted, and coordinate counter, walls, and flooring colors.

3. Build the bath around a focal point, such as a tile mural or stained glass window.

THE REPLACEMENT (MINOR REMODELING)

The most common reason for remodeling is to replace outdated bathroom fixtures, according to industry surveys. That makes the replacement project, or minor remodeling, a popular home improvement choice.

The replacement project or minor remodeling — also called a **change-out** — usually costs more than the face lift. Buying and installing a new bath or whirlpool, vanity, sink, toilet and/or shower adds significantly to the budget. Minor structural changes of bathroom layout, such as closing a door opening, will certainly boost remodeling costs.

Additional costs may result if one or more fixtures are repositioned and minor plumbing modifications are required. For example, a toilet often

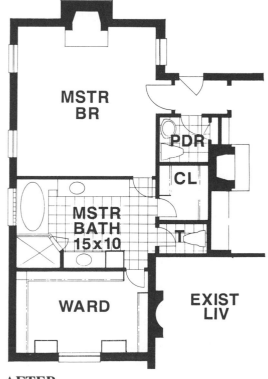

AFTER

BATHROOM INVENTORY CHECKLIST

FIXTURES (fill in name of fixture)
- ❑ Stained/damaged _____
- ❑ Style/color outdated _____
- ❑ Have plumbing problems _____
- ❑ Lack storage/shelving nearby
  _____
- ❑ Other_____

SYSTEMS

Water
- ❑ Water pressure inadequate
- ❑ Hot water supply inadequate
- ❑ Water heater inefficient
- ❑ Other_____

Electrical
- ❑ Inadequate outlet for shaving
- ❑ Inadequate outlets for hair drying/styling
- ❑ Inadequate lighting at mirrors
- ❑ Lacks lighting over shower
- ❑ Fixtures outdated/unattractive
- ❑ Overall lighting levels inadequate
- ❑ Other _____

Heating/Venting
- ❑ Damage from inadequate venting
- ❑ Lacks ventilating fan
- ❑ Lacks supplemental heat at shower
- ❑ Inadequate heat
- ❑ Other _____

Septic
- ❑ Deteriorating system
- ❑ Larger septic needed
- ❑ Drainage field required

- ❑ Septic does not meet building codes
- ❑ Other _____

Windows
- ❑ Inadequate daylight
- ❑ Window frames deteriorating
- ❑ Placement does not offer privacy
- ❑ Other _____

WATER CONSERVATION
- ❑ Lacks water-conserving showerhead
- ❑ Lacks water-conserving faucets
- ❑ Lacks water-conserving toilet
- ❑ Other _____

SAFETY
- ❑ Lacks grab bars at shower/tub
- ❑ Lacks safety glass shower/tub door
- ❑ Lacks safety glass windows
- ❑ Lacks ground fault circuit interrupter outlets
- ❑ Lacks temperature-controlled faucets to prevent scalding
- ❑ Other _____

STORAGE

Vanity Counter
- ❑ Counter space inadequate
- ❑ Material/color outdated
- ❑ Other_____

Vanity Cabinet & Mirror
- ❑ Lacks adequate storage
- ❑ Mirror surface deteriorating
- ❑ Mirror too small
- ❑ Mirror too far away for grooming
- ❑ Finish worn/damaged

❑ Cabinet material/color outdated

❑ Other _____

Storage Cabinets

❑ Inadequate storage

❑ Finish outdated/damaged

❑ Inconvenient location

❑ Other _____

Towel Racks

❑ Inconvenient location

❑ Inadequate number of racks

❑ Other _____

Which items lack storage or have inadequate storage space?

❑ Cosmetics

❑ Shaving equipment

❑ Hair grooming aids

❑ Medicine

❑ Other personal hygiene aids
_____

❑ Linens

❑ Cleaning supplies & equipment

❑ Other _____

WALLS/FLOORING

❑ Walls/ceiling mildewed/stained

❑ Wall color/material outdated

❑ Flooring color/material outdated

❑ Tile stained/damaged

❑ Grout stained/deteriorating

❑ Other _____

FLOOR PLAN

❑ Inadequate space

❑ Space poorly utilized

❑ Inadequate room around fixtures

❑ Inadequate room at vanity

❑ Inadequate room for two users

❑ Other _____

BATHROOM USES

Space

❑ Master bath planned

❑ Family bath planned (multigenerational)

❑ Children's bath planned

❑ Guest bath planned

❑ Bath measurement ____ x ____

❑ Need more space for:
_____

❑ May expand into:
_____

❑ May build addition

❑ Other _____

Primary Users

❑ Adults

❑ Children

❑ Guests

❑ Disabled; aging with special needs

❑ Number who prefer showering ___

❑ Number who prefer bathing ___

❑ Two will use room together ___

❑ One at a time will use room ___

❑ Number storing grooming aids ___

Planned Activities

❑ Bathing

❑ Bathing children

❑ Showering

❑ Shaving

❑ Hairstyling

❑ Makeup application

❑ Relaxing in whirlpool/sauna/steam

❑ Exercise

❑ Listening to radio/TV/VCR

❑ Hand laundry

❑ Machine laundry

may be moved several inches from the original location and reconnected to existing plumbing. Pipes in older structures may need replacing; in fact, codes may require modifications to pipes during a remodeling. However, a replacement project usually does not require major plumbing changes.

The minor remodeling may be a good idea if:

■ **You plan to live in your current home for several years or if you anticipate changes in family size or makeup,** such as more children, children nearing the teen years, the addition of an aging parent, frequent guests

■ **The current bathroom lacks water conservation, safety products and equipment**

THE MAJOR REMODELING

Some bathrooms are too small, too outdated, or too poorly arranged to fill the needs of the users. These rooms call for a major remodeling — the most expensive of all remodeling projects — in which surface materials, fixtures, and structures are changed.

The major remodeling is a good choice for bathrooms with:

■ **Damage,** such as a wallboard deteriorated from exposure to moisture; missing or loose ceramic tile

■ **Inefficient floor plan**

■ **Inadequate space**

■ **The need to accommodate an aging relative or young child**

■ **Fixtures that are stained, pitted, or cracked**

■ **Plumbing and electrical systems that do not comply with current codes**

■ **Space for expansion**

In the major remodeling, the bath is often enlarged by "borrowing" space from adjacent areas. For example, space is added from a clothing or linen closet next to the bath; a portion of a bedroom may be incorporated. Two small bathrooms may be combined into one large room. Enlarging the bath even a few square feet can improve the efficiency of the floor plan.

Now take the time to consider which of the three remodeling projects (refer to page 5) best suits your bathroom and your pocketbook.

THE BIG QUESTION

Are you ready for a remodeling project?

How well does the household handle the dust, disruption, and inconvenience of a remodeling project? If there is a low toleration for the inevitable messiness encountered in a remodeling project, the family may wish to keep the project as simple as possible. A face lift usually involves the least disruption of all remodeling projects; a replacement project may be extremely irritating for a family with a low tolerance for living in the midst of construction.

Consider the inconveniences of living without a tub, shower, or toilet. Is there another tub to use during the remodeling? Is there more than one toilet? What about showering and bathing? If there is a second bathroom, can a schedule be arranged for the entire household to use it conveniently?

Creative designers and experienced contractors can find solutions to minimize disruption. One method is to stockpile remodeling materials and supplies until all are received, which helps minimize construction delays and returns the new bathroom to use quickly.

Another strategy: If there is only one toilet, it is possible, in some situations, to remove and reset the toilet several times as construction proceeds by stages on plumbing and adjacent areas.

Take time to assess the family attitudes about living with a remodeling project. When discussing the project with design and building professionals, be frank about needs in this area.

TAKING A BATHROOM INVENTORY

To help put remodeling goals in focus, you will need to take an inventory of bathroom problems. You may do this by using the checklist, drawing a floor plan, or by keeping a diary.

The Checklist

Evaluate the responses to the checklist. Determine if there are so many problems that a major remodeling looks like the best solution. Find out if

BATHROOM PLANNING LIST

	NEED	WANT	STYLE/COMMENTS
REPLACE:			
Sink/faucet			
Tub/faucet			
Shower/valve			
Vanity counter			
Vanity cabinet			
Mirror			
Toilet			
Flooring			
Wallcovering			
Other _____			
ADD:			
Storage cabinets			
Private toilet area			
Bidet			
Whirlpool			
Steam shower			
Separate tub/shower			
Shower for two			
Water conservation equipment			
Safety features			
Mirror lighting			
Overhead lighting			
Shower lighting			
Night light			
Heating			
Ventilating fan			
Clothing closet			
Laundry equipment			
Exercise equipment			
Other _____			

problems are limited to certain areas, such as aging fixtures or inadequate storage. Evaluate whether a minor remodeling can correct these inadequacies. The inventory also is a useful communication tool. Take it to the initial meeting with a bathroom designer or builder.

Drawing a Floor Plan

A second way to learn about bath problems and needs is to draw a floor plan of the existing bathroom. Taking the measurements for the plan is an excellent way to focus on space requirements for fixtures. Make notes on the plan about the areas and features which are inadequate.

Prepare a floor plan by drawing the existing room on grid paper, using a scale in which 1" equals 1 foot. Indicate the location of all fixtures, cabinets, doors, windows, and lighting.

Buying a room planning kit is an alternative to making a floor plan. The kit includes a plasticized floor grid and self-sticking templates for bathroom fixtures, cabinets, windows, etc. Mark the room size on the grid, then place the templates on the plan. Later in the remodeling process, use this kit to develop new floor plans.

One advantage of the room planning kit is that templates may be lifted and repositioned, which allows experimentation with many floor plans. Kits are available at selected bookstores and home center stores. Or make your own kit on graph paper by drawing the existing room and, on a separate sheet of paper, drawing fixtures, cabinets, and windows. Cover both with transparent adhesive paper. Home design computer programs are available so you can easily input your existing bath specifications and alter them to suit your remodeling ideas. They often provide clip-art for bathroom fixtures, which can be positioned and rotated anywhere on your plan. Look for these programs where computer software is sold.

The Diary

Keep a notebook or clipboard in the bathroom. Ask those who use the bath to write comments about inconveniences and problems as the room is used during one week. Encourage all household members to contribute ideas.

Note the busy times of the day, such as the morning rush when it is time to prepare for school and for work. How about bedtimes? What are the use patterns at night? What else do you notice about using the bath?

RESEARCH

The final part of the remodeling homework assignment is to research bathroom products and design. Collect magazines, books, product brochures, and clippings of appealing concepts. It is an old idea, but it is still a good one for forming a visual record of your likes.

Two other sources in print: Trade association publications for consumers, listed in Appendix A, and manufacturers' literature. (Call 800-555-1212 to ask for toll-free consumer lines for major manufacturers.)

This is the time to do some legwork, to get out to stores and homes to see current trends in bathroom design. Here are twelve ways to enjoy your research on bathroom design and products:

1. Visit model homes

2. Visit homes for sale in the neighborhood

3. Attend home tours sponsored by clubs or the local builders association

4. Survey products at home center stores

5. Survey products at major manufacturers' showrooms

6. Survey products at specialized retail outlets, such as those for windows, lighting, cabinets, mirrors, and plumbing supplies

7. Visit showrooms of bathroom designers and builders

8. Visit outlets where products are fabricated, such as a cabinet shop or ceramic tile studio

9. Attend remodeling seminars at home center stores

10. Attend classes at community education facilities

11. Attend design seminars at home furnishings stores

12. View TV programs on bathroom remodeling or borrow remodeling videos from the library

And now that the homework is done, you should have a clearer picture of the kind of remodeling project you need, whether it is a face lift, a minor remodeling, or a major remodeling. Use the chart, "Bathroom Planning List," to keep a record of your ideas.

WORTH REPEATING

1. Decide which level of bathroom remodeling suits your needs and budget:

The face lift, the least expensive, in which surface materials are altered.

The replacement, minor remodeling, or change-out, to update fixtures and materials, which may include minor structural, electrical, and plumbing changes.

The major remodeling, or addition, the most expensive, in which fixtures and materials are replaced, and structural, electrical, and plumbing changes may be made.

2. Take an inventory of bathroom design problems. The inventory helps you select the level of remodeling most appropriate for your bathroom.

3. Complete the Bathroom Inventory Checklist.

4. Draw the existing floor plan.

5. Keep a family diary of problems in bathroom design.

6. Research bathroom products and materials. Visit homes, stores, and attend classes. View bathroom remodeling tapes to expand your knowledge of bathroom design.

7. Record your design ideas on the Bathroom Planning List.

2

Money Matters

*Getting a quality bathroom
within your budget is one of the
goals of remodeling.*

How much will it cost to get a quality bathroom? That's the question that needs to be addressed early in the process of planning a remodeling project. Until the last tile is laid and the construction debris is hauled away, money matters are an ongoing concern.

Square-foot costs for bathroom remodeling are usually higher than for any other room in the home. The price tag is so high for two reasons. First, remodeling a bathroom is a labor-intensive project. Many skilled tradespeople are required, including a carpenter, electrician, plumber, tile setter, and drywall hanger. Second, this small room accommodates two to four fixtures, which boost square-foot costs significantly.

Money matters break down into several dollars-and-cents issues:

■ Setting the budget
■ Estimating cost of fixtures and materials
■ Finding ways to cut costs
■ Evaluating the payback on your bathroom remodeling investment

SETTING THE BUDGET

One simple idea to remember about setting the remodeling budget: **Be realistic.**

It is possible to spend $5,000, $10,000, $30,000 (or more for luxury materials) to get a new look for the bath. But the extent of the remodeling, and the fixtures and materials selected, will make the $30,000 bath look quite different from the $5,000 project.

Remodeling costs range widely, depending on the size of the room, the scope of remodeling, the regional cost of labor, and the materials and fixtures selected. The extent of the changes to the structural, plumbing, and electrical systems is also significant in the remodeling bill.

To set a realistic budget, answer these questions:

■ What portion of financial resources can be committed comfortably to the project?

■ If financing is needed, how much debt can the household budget carry?

■ How long will it take to pay for the bath?

■ Will additional major expenses arise as the remodeling is paid for?

■ Are other remodeling projects anticipated in the near future? How much do you expect them to cost?

■ How long will the family live in the home?

■ Will the improvement add to the value of the home? (See the discussion on "Payback" in this chapter.)

Finally, a working relationship between the bathroom planner and client is enhanced if the budget figures are realistic. Don't feel that it is necessary to impress a designer with a large remodeling budget. On the contrary, experienced designers are skilled at designing attractive baths in a wide variety of price ranges. In fact, it is their job to find the design solutions that fit the budget.

ESTIMATING COSTS

Every item in the bathroom — fixtures, hardware, cabinets, and surface materials — are available in moderate, upgraded, and deluxe styles. That is one reason why estimating costs is a difficult job.

But there are several measures to help owners arrive at a ballpark figure for their project. *Surveys of annual remodeling costs* provide one measure; *comparisons of fixture and material costs* yield another value.

Average Remodeling Costs
Sources of average remodeling costs are:
- Surveys tabulated annually by several trade associations

ESTIMATING BATHROOM COSTS

PRODUCT	BASIC	MODERATE	LUXURY
TOILET	$80-125	$125-300	$300-700
TUB			
Standard	$250-325	$325-600	$600-1,000
Whirlpool	$450-650	$650-1,500	$1,500-3,000
Faucets/fittings	$75-150	$150-275	$275-600
SHOWER			
Shower enclosure	$175-275	$275-450	$450-1,000
Showerhead/valve	$30-75	$75-125	$125-300
VANITY			
Cabinets	$250-500	$500-1,500	$1,500-2,000+
Counter (per linear foot)	$25-75	$75-150	$150-275+
Laminate		$10-25	
Tile		$5-40	
Solid-surface		$15-50	
Granite/marble		$40+	
Sink	$75-150	$150-275	$275-500
Faucet/fittings	$75-125	$125-200	$200-400
Pedestal sink	$150-250	$250-350	$350-750
FLOORING/ WALLCOVERING			
Vinyl flooring (per sq. ft.)		$3-$10	
Tile (per sq. ft.)	$5-10	$15-25	$25-40
Wallcovering (per roll)	$10-15	$15-35	$35+

STANDARD MASTER BATH COSTS

Description	Quantity	Man-hours	Material
Partition wall for shower stall, 2" x 4" plates & studs, 16" O.C., 8' high	152 L.F.	2.3	49.66
Rough-in frame for medicine cabinet, 2" x 4" stock	16 LF.	0.5	5.23
Drywall, 1/2" thick on shower stall walls, water resistant, taped & finished 4' x 8' sheets	2 Sheets	1.1	24.78
Flooring, underlayment grade, hardboard 3/16" thick 4' x 4' sheets	3 Sheets	1.1	32.52
Painting, ceiling, walls & door, primed & 1 finish coat	330 S.F.	2.6	35.94
Vanity base cabinet, 2 door, 72" wide	1 Ea.	2.4	471.90
Vanity top, plastic laminate	1 Ea.	2.0	226.51
Lavatory with trim & faucet, porcelain enamel on cast iron, 18" round, white	2 Ea.	5.0	304.92
Fittings for lavatory	2 Ea.	13.9	214.78
Shower stall with door and trim, fiberglass 1 piece, 3 walls, 32" x 32"	1 Ea.	6.7	408.98
Bathtub, recessed, porcelain enamel on cast iron, w/trim, mat bottom, 5' long	1 Ea.	3.6	340.01
Fittings for tub and shower	1 Set	7.7	117.60
Medicine cabinet, center mirror, 2 end cabinets, 72" long	1 Ea.	1.4	294.03
Walls, ceramic tile at tub, thinset, 4-1/4" x 4-1/4"	12 S.F.	1.1	26.86
Flooring, vinyl sheet goods, backed, .093" thick	50 S.F.	1.8	78.65
Toilet, tank type, vitreous china, floor-mounted, 2 piece	1 Ea.	3.0	166.98
Fittings for toilet	1 Set	8.3	103.64
Towel bar, stainless steel - 30" long	2 Ea.	0.7	42.59
Toilet tissue dispenser, surface mounted, stainless steel	1 Ea.	0.3	19.36
Trim, baseboard, 9/16" x 3-1/2" wide, pine	16 L.F.	0.5	15.49
Totals		66.0	$2980.43

This typical standard bath includes: white tub, white two-piece toilet, fiberglass shower stall, standard 72" vanity with laminate top and two cast-iron bowls, 72" medicine cabinet, 12 square feet of ceramic wall tile and vinyl flooring. Cost, including fittings: $2,980.43. Installation savings include plumbing lines installed in the wall between tub and shower for both fixtures; vinyl sheet flooring is installed in one piece. The experienced handyperson may install tile and flooring to reduce costs.

Project Size	8' x 10'	Contractor's Fee Including Materials	**$7023**

Key to Abbreviations
C.Y. - cubic yard | Ea. - each | L.F. - linear foot | Pr. - pair | Sq. - square (100 square feet of area)
S.F. - square foot | S.Y. - square yard | V.L.F. - vertical linear foot

■ Reference books on pricing that contractors consult to determine remodeling project charges. Check your library's reference section for *Dodge Square Foot Cost Data* or *Architects, Contractors and Engineers Guide to Construction Costs*

Trade groups that conduct annual cost surveys are the National Kitchen and Bath Association (NKBA) and the National Association of Home Builders (NAHB), among others. Typically, the trade association membership is surveyed, and reports about remodeling projects are collected.

A recent NKBA Trends Survey, for example, concluded that the **average bathroom cost was $9,700.** More than 40 percent ranged in size from 35 to 75 square feet; 26 percent measured 75 to 100 square feet.

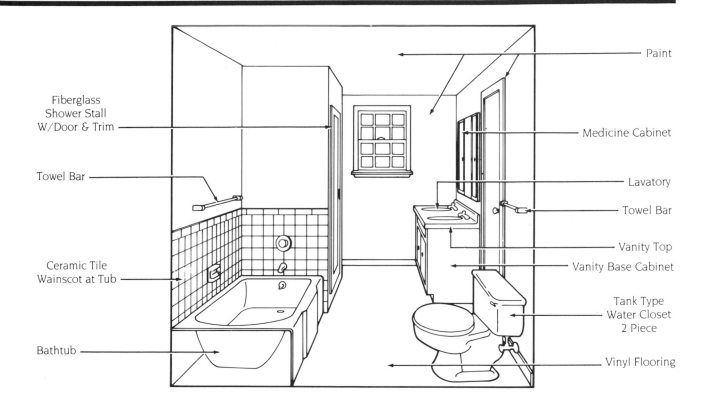

The survey profiled design features too. Half of the bathrooms were designed for use by more than one person at a time; separate tubs/showers and more than one lavatory were installed in 33 percent of the bathrooms. Whirlpool tubs were installed in 29 percent of the projects. Only 3 percent included luxury features such as a steam shower, sauna, exercise equipment, or a video/stereo/TV center.

Other bathroom features in the survey:

■ The number-one color choice in the overall design was basic white (60 percent).

■ Wooden cabinets were the popular choice (63 percent); oak was the favored wood (61 percent).

■ 40 percent of cabinets were custom made.

■ Laminate was the top material for the counter (35 percent), followed by solid-surface counters resembling marble, (27 percent), and cultured marble (24 percent).

■ Almost half of the homeowners (48 percent) selected ceramic tile flooring; vinyl flooring was used by 39 percent.

■ Bathroom walls were finished with wall-covering (37 percent), paint (35 percent), and tile (20 percent).

So what does this mean to you? The NKBA survey is not intended to be a guide to costs for all bathroom remodeling. However, if your project resembles the survey averages, your costs may be close to $9,700. Nevertheless, detailed information about the installation of fixtures and the alterations to structural, electrical, and plumbing systems is needed to obtain accurate costs.

Price reference books for contractors are also available to consumers, either in the library or bookstore. These aids to cost estimating give line-by-line prices for every aspect of remodeling — from electrical wiring to carpentry, from fixtures to hardware. References are updated annually to reflect changing costs for materials and labor.

These books are useful for obtaining a rough estimate of costs before meeting with a bathroom designer or reviewing a contractor's bid. The book

DELUXE MASTER BATH COSTS

Description	Quantity	Man-hours	Material
Partition wall for shower stall, 2" x 4" plates & studs, 16" O.C., 8' high	152 L.F.	2.3	49.66
Rough-in frame for medicine cabinet, 2" x 4" stock	16 L.F.	0.5	5.23
Drywall, 1/2" thick on shower stall walls, water resistant, taped & finished, 4' x 8' sheets	5 Sheets	2.7	61.95
Painting, ceiling, walls & door, primer & 1 coat	330 S.F.	2.6	35.94
Deluxe vanity base cabinet, 2 door, 72" wide	1 Ea.	3.4	660.66
Vanity top, cultured marble, 73" x 22" double bowl	1 Ea.	3.0	423.50
Fittings for lavatory	2 Sets	13.9	429.55
Shower stall, terrazzo receptor, 36" x 36"	1 Ea.	8.0	641.30
Shower door, tempered glass, deluxe	1 Ea.	1.3	187.55
Bathtub, recessed, porcelain enamel on cast iron, w/trim, mat bottom, 5' long, color	1 Ea.	3.6	340.01
Fittings for tub & shower	1 Set	7.7	117.60
Medicine cabinet, center mirror, 2 end cabinets 72" long, lighted	1 Ea.	1.4	294.03
Walls, ceramic tile, shower stall & wainscoting, thin set, 4-1/4" x 4-1/4"	170 S.F.	15.1	380.55
Flooring, porcelain tile, 1 color, color group 2, 1" x 1"	40 S.F.	3.5	166.98
Toilet, tank-type, vitreous china, floor mounted, 1 piece, color	1 Ea.	3.0	657.51
Fittings for toilet	1 Set	8.3	103.64
Towel bar, stainless steel, 30" long	2 Ea.	0.7	38.72
Toilet tissue dispenser, surface mounted, stainless steel	1 Ea.	0.3	22.99
Totals		81.3	$4617.37

Project Size 8' x 10'

Contractor's Fee Including Materials **$10,788**

Upgraded bath includes: color tub, color one-piece toilet, ceramic tile shower stall with terrazzo base, deluxe 72" vanity with cultured marble top and two integral bowls, 72" medicine cabinet, ceramic tile wainscoting throughout, and porcelain tile flooring. Cost, including fittings: $4,617.37. Installation differences: 15.3 additional hours were required to complete the bath, including fourteen hours for installing ceramic tile and shower.

Key to Abbreviations
C.Y. - cubic yard   Ea. - each   L.F. - linear foot   Pr. - pair   Sq. - square (100 square feet of area)
S.F. - square foot   S.Y. - square yard   V.L.F. - vertical linear foot

guidelines may also help you decide if a contractor's bid is realistic.

Some rules of thumb: Expect labor costs to equal 40 to 60 percent of the remodeling bill; fittings and fixtures account for almost 30 percent more. If possible, set aside 10 to 15 percent of the estimated project cost for additions or surprises.

Comparing Fixture and Material Costs
Bathroom fixtures and materials come in an increasing array of materials, colors, and styles. Choices in sink faucets, for example, range from a basic chrome ($75) to a sculptural gold-tone model that discharges water in a mini-waterfall ($400 to $600). Sinks include a graceful shell-shaped vanity with hand-painted roses (about $400) to a simple, white style ($75 to $150).

Every component of the bathroom — from hardware and fixtures to cabinets and countertops — is available in *basic, moderate,* and *luxury models*.

The rich array of products makes it difficult to pin down which ones will fit your budget. But by keeping the three price groups and your budget estimate in mind, you can select specific fixtures and materials.

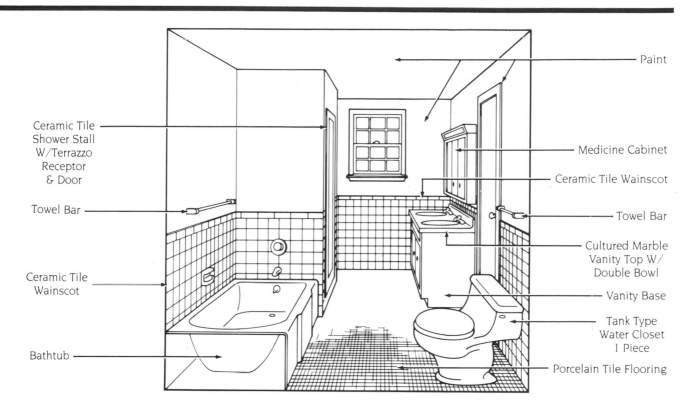

Paint

Ceramic Tile Shower Stall W/Terrazzo Receptor & Door

Towel Bar

Ceramic Tile Wainscot

Bathtub

Medicine Cabinet

Ceramic Tile Wainscot

Towel Bar

Cultured Marble Vanity Top W/ Double Bowl

Vanity Base

Tank Type Water Closet 1 Piece

Porcelain Tile Flooring

PAYBACK

What is the return on the remodeling investment? That's what "payback" is all about. If a major bathroom remodeling costs $10,000 in a $160,000 home, will the home then be worth $170,000?

No, probably not. But year after year, reports from trade associations and home publications show that the professional bathroom remodeling project typically increases a home's value by 60 to 80 percent of the job cost. These cost-recovery values are most applicable when the new bath is in keeping with the character and style of the home.

And real estate professionals will attest that a well-designed bath is a selling point in the home market.

The Danger of Overimproving

While homeowners wish to increase the value of the home with a bath remodeling, it is possible to *overimprove* the property. Overimproving means the house now has features worth more than other houses in the area. People willing to pay for such

features may want to live in an area surrounded by more expensive homes.

Let's say that homes in one neighborhood are about 15 years old and are valued between $150,000 to $180,000, and that most of these neighborhood homes have three bedrooms and 2½ bathrooms. Assume one homeowner puts on a home addition with two more bedrooms and 1½ baths. But if that house goes on the market, a buyer may not be willing to pay a price that is out of line with the typical homes in the neighborhood — the homeowner may not recover all the costs of the improvement.

Now, let's look at an older, smaller home with three bedrooms and 1½ baths in the same neighborhood. An addition with at least one bath will bring this home closer to the standards of the neighborhood. This homeowner is more likely to get back the value of the remodeling investment.

And how about the case of an inexpensive home that gets a luxury bathroom remodeling? Consider a simple three-bedroom ranch in an aging suburb,

Bathroom Remodeling Checklist

Everything needed for the bathroom remodeling is listed below. It provides one more way to think about bathroom costs.

FIXTURES
- ❑ Toilet (water-saving)
- ❑ Bidet
- ❑ Tub/whirlpool
- ❑ Tub skirt
- ❑ Whirlpool platform
- ❑ Tub/whirlpool faucet and fittings (temperature control)
- ❑ Tub/whirlpool wall surround
- ❑ Shower surround
- ❑ Shower floor (nonslip surface)
- ❑ Showerhead and valve (low-flow, temperature control)
- ❑ Shower door (safety glass)
- ❑ Tub/shower grab bars, textured surface
- ❑ Sink
- ❑ Sink faucet and fittings (low-flow)

SPECIALIZED EQUIPMENT
- ❑ Sauna
- ❑ Sauna heater
- ❑ Steam shower
- ❑ Steam generator
- ❑ Exercise equipment
- ❑ TV/video/stereo
- ❑ Hot tub

CABINETRY
- ❑ Base cabinet
- ❑ Wall storage cabinet
- ❑ Wall-hung cabinet with mirror
- ❑ Small storage cabinet
- ❑ Storage cabinet accessories
- ❑ Countertop
- ❑ Countertop backsplash
- ❑ Countertop end treatment

ELECTRICAL
- ❑ Ventilating fan
- ❑ Ventilating fan/light combo
- ❑ Ventilating fan/light/heat
- ❑ GFCI circuits
- ❑ Heat lamp
- ❑ Shower light
- ❑ Mirror lighting
- ❑ Ceiling fixture

---

valued at $125,000. The owners decide to install an ultracontemporary bath with whirlpool for two, separate shower, vanity with two sinks, custom cabinetry, and marble tile on the walls and floor. They expand into a closet and build a sauna. The price tag for this kind of project could equal one-fourth to one-third the value of their home; on this overimprovement, payback would fall below the 60 to 80 percent figure, as explained earlier.

Payback is important not only when a home goes on the market, but also when it comes time to appraise the home for a home equity loan. If the home is over-improved, the lender may not base the loan on the full value of the home plus the cost of the remodeling.

The level of remodeling that nets the most profit for the homeowner will vary from region to region, from neighborhood to neighborhood. To get an idea of the kind of remodeling plan that will add value to your home, consult with a real estate agent who knows the area. That agent has up-to-date information on home values and amenities. Another strategy is to hire an appraiser to value the home and estimate the payback on the proposed improvement.

❑ Heating system alteration

❑ Water heater installation

FLOORING

❑ Vinyl/tile/stone (nonslip surface)

❑ Baseboard

❑ Underlayment

WINDOWS

❑ Replacement (safety glass)

❑ Skylight

❑ Window casing

❑ Window treatment

DOORS

❑ Solid core (open outward)

❑ Bifold door

❑ Pocket door

❑ Door casing

WALLS

❑ Wallcovering

❑ Tile

❑ Laminate

❑ Paint

ACCESSORIES

❑ Towel bars/rings

❑ Mirror

❑ Tub soap dish

❑ Shower soap dish

❑ Sink soap dish

❑ Hamper

CONSTRUCTION

❑ Electrical

❑ Electrical, supplies

❑ Plumbing, rough-in

❑ Plumbing, modifications

❑ Plumbing, supplies

❑ Carpentry, demolition

❑ Carpentry, reconstruction

❑ Carpentry, supplies

❑ Tile setter

❑ Tiling, supplies

FEES/PERMITS

❑ Design fee

❑ Engineering/architectural fee

❑ Plan fee

❑ Inspection fee

❑ Construction supervision

❑ Building permits

❑ Loan fees

❑ Trash removal

❑ Job site cleanup

10 WAYS TO CUT COSTS

What if the plan comes in over budget? Don't immediately scrap it. Instead explore ways to trim project costs without sacrificing the bath you want. Here are ten ways to save.

1. Avoid extensive structural changes. Taking down or moving a partition wall — the type of wall that separates one room from another — is usually a moderate expense. On the other hand, if the plan involves a change in a load-bearing wall — the wall that supports the roof — the remodeling tab gets bigger because the structural support provided by the bearing wall must be replaced.

2. Keep the plumbing where it is. A toilet must be located within 18" of the waste stack, a pipe which connects the toilet to the sewer. If the toilet is moved, there is a charge for each additional foot of pipe needed to connect it to the stack. Sometimes relocating the toilet means that a new vent stack must be installed at considerable expense. However, there is good news about plumbing; there are options for repositioning a sink in a vanity cabinet without incurring a big plumbing bill.

3. Select materials and bath fixtures that fit the budget. There is a wide range of prices for products, so select the materials that will not strain the budget. White fixtures, for example, are often less expensive than colored fixtures. Vinyl flooring is a fraction of the cost of a tile floor. And make *tradeoffs*. An expensive custom touch, such as a backsplash of hand-painted tile above the vanity, may fit the budget if a moderately priced vinyl flooring is selected. Want a whirlpool tub and new vanity cabinet, but buying both will break the budget? One solution is to select a whirlpool and update the cabinets with refacing, painting, or elegant faucets.

4. Avoid adding on by stretching the existing space. Visually expanding the available space is an alternative to the more-expensive prospect of expanding the bath with an addition. Strategically placed mirrors can dramatically enlarge a room. Consider a pedestal sink for the small bath instead of a cabinet, which has more volume and takes up more floor space; install an attractive shelf above the sink to replace some of the cabinet storage area.

5. Update rather than replace. Select an attractive solid-surface counter — a polyester or acrylic that resembles marble — or a standard-size granite or marble top for about the same money, instead of investing in a new cabinet and sink. Or dropping in a new colored sink and faucets can make a big difference when the cabinet is in good shape. Got plain white tile on the walls? If the tile will remain, add an accent strip of colorful tile above the white tile.

6. Stick to the plan during construction. Changes made during construction are expensive and time-consuming, especially if the changes involve alterations to plumbing, electrical, or structural systems. Delays may be encountered while new materials are shipped and construction crews

are rescheduled. Of course, some minor aspect of the design may not work well in even the most carefully planned remodeling, and a correction must be made. But demanding many changes may eventually strain relations among the client, designer, and builder.

7. Limit or avoid custom-made features. There is nothing like a custom-made feature to provide a focal point in the bath, but a whole list of one-of-a-kind touches dramatically boosts the remodeling bill. The designer has ways to personalize the bath without customizing. For example, stock cabinets can be joined to create a wall storage unit with a custom look. Accent tiles, such as diamond shapes set into the wall or floor, or trim molding that tops the wall, may be combined with ceramic wall and flooring tiles to create unique looks at a low cost.

8. Do some of the work yourself. Tasks such as painting, wallpapering, removing old equipment, installing storage accessories in cabinets, and staining window trim or baseboards may be within the skill of the homeowner. Some homeowners are skilled enough to tackle tiling or installing vinyl flooring. Leave the complicated work to the carpenter, electrician, plumber, and other skilled trades.

9. Hire the right pro for the job. It is usually possible to hire a contractor for straightforward improvements, but a skilled designer or architect may be desirable for a major remodeling job that involves structural changes and new fixtures. What's more, the experienced planner is well versed in cost-cutting strategies.

10. Suit yourself. Don't plan a top-of-the-line bath with all the amenities, thinking that the new bath will quickly attract a buyer to the home. The new bath may in fact be an overimprovement and will not pay back what it costs. And if the family doesn't like the new room, everybody loses. Instead, shop for a bath that is within the budget, one that fills the family needs.

WORTH REPEATING

1. Understand bathroom fixture and material price categories: basic, moderate, and luxury. Make tradeoffs using a top-of-the-line material for one purpose, a lower-priced material for another.

2. Consult contractors' reference books on cost estimating (such as *Dodge Square Foot Cost Data* or *Architects, Contractors and Engineers Guide to Construction Costs*) to get an idea of realistic remodeling costs. Ask the librarian for help.

3. Consider payback, or the return on the remodeling investment. Bathroom remodeling usually adds value to the home; 60 to 80 percent of remodeling costs are often recovered when the home is sold. But an overimprovement, adding a bath that is worth more than baths in other homes in the area, usually will produce less than a 60 to 80 percent recovery of investment.

4. To cut costs, avoid major changes. One of the most significant ways to manage costs is to keep changes in structural and plumbing systems to a minimum. To minimize plumbing changes, do not relocate fixtures. Avoid alterations in load-bearing walls; changes in partition walls are less expensive.

3

Working with the Pros

*How to pick a top-quality
lineup of professionals for
the remodeling team.*

Although the bath is the smallest room in the house — 85 percent of baths in the U.S. are 6′ X 8′ or less — remodeling it is a big job. Planning a small space well is an art.

The pro's job is to stay abreast of trends in products, technology, safety regulations, and building codes. This should save the client time and money, and ensure a new bathroom that suits the client's lifestyle.

WHICH PROS FOR THE TEAM?

There are many qualified professionals who are trained in bathroom design and installation: architects, interior designers, kitchen and bathroom design specialists, design/build firms, and general contractors.

Both the design and construction branches of the bathroom industry sponsor education programs that lead to professional credentials. For example, remodelers and designers may have credentials as Certified Remodeler (CR), Certified Bathroom Designer (CBD), or American Society of Interior Designers (ASID), among others.

It is important to understand the language of professional credentials. The credentials mean that the professional:

■ Received specialized training from an industry organization

■ Passed a qualifying examination and/or completed required course work

■ Practices in the field and obtained the required years of services

■ Subscribes to a code of ethics or professional standards

■ Has opportunities for continuing education and/or professional growth through meetings and course work

The education and experience required for the most common professional affiliations in the bathroom industry are outlined in detail in the chart on pages 26-27. (Appendix A contains information on additional design organizations.)

Keep in mind that many competent professionals do *not* have credentials granted by industry associations. But these individuals should be prepared to demonstrate their expertise by giving a prospective client information on their training and experience, samples of many well-designed projects, and referrals to satisfied customers.

Remember, too, that professional qualifications are always changing. In 1989, for example, the National Kitchen and Bath Association introduced the Certified Bath Designer credential. This specialty developed in response to the growth in bathroom remodeling and the need for professional standards in bathroom design and technical education.

Generally speaking, the role of each professional is as follows:

The **architect** has a three-fold task for both remodeling and new construction projects: to provide construction drawings and specifications of materials on which bids are based, to ensure that the new design will provide adequate structural support, and to design the new structure so it blends with the existing home.

The **interior designer,** once known as an expert in selecting furnishings and fabrics, has an expanded role. Working with contractors and architects, the interior designer plans the complete remodeling project. Interior design training also includes courses in technical areas such as home heating, ventilation, and electrical systems.

The **bathroom design specialist** is often employed by a **kitchen and bath dealer**, a retailer who maintains a showroom and sells products of selected manufacturers. There are also independent kitchen and bath designers who specialize in bath design without a showroom who are capable of supervising a general contractor. Bathroom design specialists (and some kitchen design specialists with bathroom design experience) develop the bathroom plan with the client, provide floor plans, and sometimes provide elevations, detail drawings, and electrical plans. The bathroom specialist assists in fixture and material selection from the manufacturers represented by the showroom as well as other products.

The **general contractor** reviews the project drawings and specifications, then bids for the remodeling project. The contractor awarded the bid will hire and schedule all subcontractors. The contractor supervises the construction crew, ensuring the project is built according to plans.

The **design/build contractor** provides both design and construction services within the same general contracting company. The staff designer draws plans and writes clear specifications for the contracting side of the business.

WHICH PRO FOR THE JOB?

For a major remodeling. An architect may be an important team member if the project involves extensive work such as breaking through exterior walls, altering windows, modifying the roof line, or planning an addition that blends with the existing home. Major remodeling projects require construction drawings which can be prepared by an architect.

Not all jobs with structural changes, such as moving a partition wall, require architectural drawings. Yet an architect may be hired for any bathroom remodeling job, if the client wishes. The decision depends on client needs and remodeling goals.

For a minor remodeling. If the job involves interior changes with the purposes of maximizing space and using it efficiently, a designer with substantial experience in bathroom remodeling is suitable. The client may select a kitchen and bath dealer with a bath design specialist on staff, an interior designer with remodeling expertise, or a contractor who provides both design and building services.

For a face lift. Any of the design pros mentioned above will be able to handle this job. Be sure to select someone with experience in bathroom remodeling.

Two Pros or One?

Many professionals are willing to **collaborate** with each other, which may result in a team strong in both design and construction skills. **An architect**, for example, might plan an addition, then work with a **bathroom design specialist** or **interior designer** to supply fixtures and materials. That architect may also inspect the construction, working as a team member with the **contractor.**

A kitchen and bath dealer may have its own specialists, such as countertop fabricators and installers; the dealer may turn over other work to a qualified **contractor**; others may build cabinets in their own workshops. (Note that some dealers may act as general contractor in remodeling projects or

PROFESSIONAL CREDENTIALS

CREDENTIAL	SPONSORING ORGANIZATION	EDUCATION & EXPERIENCE	EXAMINATION/ CERTIFICATION
AIA, Associate AIA — American Institute of Architects	American Institute of Architects	Must attend school accredited by National Architecture Accrediting Board; 5 to 8 years of graduate/undergraduate study; serve a 3-year internship with an architectural firm.	4-day state-administered exam; every state has its own examination. Earns designation as registered architect. (Need not be AIA member to be a registered architect, but all registered architects must take state exam.) AIA associate member has not yet taken exam.
ASID, Allied ASID — American Society of Interior Designers	American Society of Interior Designers	B.A. or M.A. in interior design or architect registration, plus 2 years full-time work in interior design; or 3 years education plus 3 years work experience; or high school education plus 6 years work experience.	Exam administered by National Council for Interior Design Qualifications (NCIDQ). ASID allied member (practitioner) is fulfilling requirements and has not yet taken the NCIDQ exam. Some states provide state certification.
CBD — Certified Bath Designer	National Kitchen and Bath Association, Council of Societies (NKBA)	Either 7 years in design, planning, and supervising installation of baths, 4 years experience and NKBA Bathroom Correspondence Course, or NKBA bathroom seminars, or college course work in design/architecture and work experience; plus documentation of experience, knowledge, and ability in planning and installing bathrooms, including 2 client references, 2 professional affidavits, 2 work samples with complete drawings.	1-day examination administered by NKBA; formal study of Bathroom Industry Technical Manuals prior to exam is recommended.
CKD — Certified Kitchen Designer	National Kitchen and Bath Association, Council of Societies (NKBA)	Either 7 years in design, planning, and supervising installation of kitchens, 4 years experience and NKBA Kitchen Correspondence Course, or NKBA kitchen seminars, or college course work in design/architecture and work experience; plus documentation of experience, knowledge, and ability in planning and installing kitchens, including 2 client references, 2 professional affidavits, 2 work samples with complete drawings.	1-day examination administered by NKBA; formal study of Kitchen Industry Technical Manuals prior to exam is recommended.

CREDENTIAL	SPONSORING ORGANIZATION	EDUCATION & EXPERIENCE	EXAMINATION/ CERTIFICATION
CGR — Certified Graduate Remodelor™	National Association of Home Builders, Remodelors™ Council (NAHB)	5 years general management experience in residential and/or commercial remodeling, plus course work in general remodeling, business management, and remodeling design and construction. Continuing education required to retain certification.	Certification after completing Remodelors™ Council education program; valid for 3 years; take additional courses to continue certification.
CR — Certified Remodeler	National Association of the Remodeling Industry® (NARI®)	At least 5 years in remodeling industry, plus documentation of training in remodeling, education, and business management.	1-day examination prepared by University of Illinois on construction and business practices. Formal study of NARI® Examination Study Guide Manual prior to exam recommended. Registration for certification required annually.

manage their own construction crew.) The range of services varies greatly from dealer to dealer. Be aware that kitchen and bath dealers may attempt to sell you unnecessary products.

The independent designer, a design professional unaffiliated with a design firm or a kitchen and bath dealer, often has very flexible arrangements with other professionals. For example, the trained independent may draw floor plans for a client, then team up with a **kitchen and bath dealer** to supply the materials and fixtures. Shopping for bathroom products with the client also may be a service of the independent designer; the client then buys design and construction services from other pros.

If you are considering hiring two professionals to collaborate on the job, find out if they have a successful record of working together. How well have the designs been translated into reality? Spell

out exactly the services that may be expected from each professional.

On the other hand, buying design and installation services under one roof — from a design/build firm or from a full-service kitchen and bath dealer, for example — may simplify the communication process for both the professional and the client. This may be a good option for those planning a remodeling project for the first time.

In some areas where design services or kitchen and bath showrooms are not available, the homeowner may work directly with a contractor. In this case, the homeowner would bring design ideas to the contractor, who would both draw the plans and complete the remodeling job. Also, large home center stores often provide free design services as well as discounted products. Check the credentials and experience of the design professional. If you have a relatively simple job, this type of service may be an economical choice. Be aware that the products available are usually more limited than those offered by a kitchen and bath dealer.

PICKING THE PROS

Pay as much attention to selecting the professional remodeling team as you do to selecting fixtures and materials for your new bathroom.

Locating professionals for the remodeling project is not difficult. Consider these sources:

■ **Get recommendations from friends and neighbors** who have completed a bathroom remodeling job

■ **Read newspapers and regional home magazines** for examples of remodeling work

■ **Contact the local chapter or national office of professional organizations** such as NKBA, ASID, etc., for qualified professionals in the area

■ **Talk to real estate agents;** these professionals view hundreds of homes each year and often have information on bathroom designers and remodelers

■ **Identify teachers of community education classes in interior design and bathroom planning;** these individuals are often professional designers looking for clients

Put together an initial list of at least three or four designers and/or contractors to interview. Narrow down the list as the interview with each pro is completed.

WHAT TO LOOK FOR

Some people claim that, in selecting a bathroom remodeling pro, compatibility and trust are more important than professional credentials. Play it safe, and look for compatibility as well as expertise. Seek a professional who is easy to work with, as well as knowledgeable about products, technical matters, and design trends.

As you search for the right pros, follow these steps:

1. Visit the designer's and/or builder's showroom. Bring along your ideas, clippings, floor plans, sketches, photos — the results of the home-

The Showroom Visit

During the initial interview, ask to talk to the individual who will design your project. This is the time to discuss the services offered, budget, contract, and scheduling.

1. What is your impression of the showroom? Is it neat and clean? Do the displays embody creative designs? Are different styles represented?

2. Assess your comfort level as you talk to the designer. Is the professional listening? Do you feel he or she will work with you to achieve the desired result, instead of dictating a design? The bathroom is such a personal space that it is important to feel at ease with the design pro.

3. Is the individual willing to answer questions? If during the interview there is something you don't understand, ask for clarification. Does the person explain the answer

in a way that you can understand?

4. Discuss the plan. Does the designer seem knowledgeable about products, technical matters, and installation? Discuss budget too. If the client has done a good job describing what is wanted, the designer should be able to offer an estimate of remodeling costs.

5. Confirm the services offered. If complete services (design and construction) are not available, will referrals be made to other professionals? Discuss fees, contracts, and the payment plan. Go over scheduling too. How busy is the firm? Do they have the capacity to take on your work?

6. Schedule a visit to a recently completed remodeling project, if you have developed a favorable impression of the designer and the company.

The Site Visit

Make at least one site visit for each designer or design/build firm you are considering. Select a project similar in scope and design to the one you are considering. Ask the homeowner these questions:

1. What is the quality of the work? Were all the jobs completed as stated in the contract?

2. Were there any major obstacles in design and/or construction? How were they resolved?

3. How long did the job take? How well was the work scheduled? How well were the materials scheduled? Were there delays?

4. Were workers reliable? Were they on the job daily? Were they courteous? Did they clean the job site every day?

5. Was the project completed within the contract price? If not, why? Were workers called back to redo any work?

6. How good was the communication among the designer, builder, and client? Would you work with the designer or builder again?

After the site visit, if you are still impressed, sign an agreement for services with the designer and/or contractor, and prepare for a **home visit.** At that time, the professional hired will take measurements of the existing bathroom and conduct an in-depth interview about the homeowner's needs and wants for the remodeled bathroom. Next the designer draws a preliminary plan. Then you are really on your way to a new bath.

---

work you completed in Chapter 1. There should be no charge for this initial consultation. (See "The Showroom Visit" in this chapter.)

2. Find a specialist in bathroom design. There are thousands of excellent designers and design/build contractors, yet not all are equally experienced in bathroom design. Find out how many years of design experience the individual or firm has and the number of bathrooms they have completed.

3. Review the professional portfolio. Also make site visits to finished jobs; look for craftsmanship and creative solutions to design problems. (See "The Site Visit.")

4. Ask for sample plans from current remodeling projects. A professional's ability to execute plans varies widely; some are easy to read, others are not. The plan is an essential tool of communication among the client, designer, and builder; make sure that the pro is an expert in drafting floor plans, elevations, detail drawings of features such as a custom tub platform or shower base, and electrical plans.

5. Ask for references and check them out. Ask for at least three references for recent projects that are similar in scope and budget to yours. Verifying a professional's skill in designing a deck or finishing a basement does not indicate equal competence in bathroom remodeling. Visit at least one project.

6. Ask about professional degrees, education, licensing, and certifications.

7. Ask about membership in professional organizations. Being an active member of an organization does not guarantee the individual's ability, but it does indicate an interest in maintaining professional standards.

8. Ask about basic business facts. These facts should be available to clients: business address, phone number, number of years in business. For contractors, inquire about proof of licensing, insurance, bonding (if needed), and certification of insurance covering workers' compensation, property damage, and personal liability. It is the client's right to verify this information with insurance providers.

9. Ask for bank references. This is a way to check the financial stability of the company. Once the references have been given, check them out.

10. Determine if there are complaints against the company. Contact the Better Business

Bureau or state Consumer Affairs Office. Ask if there are outstanding complaints, whether the complaints have been resolved, and any other relevant file information.

11. Request literature. Company brochures are sales tools, but they should include a clear and detailed statement of the firm's qualifications and experience.

FEES

The ways in which contractors and designers charge for their services is sometimes confusing to homeowners. There are several ways to set fees.

Design Fees

A fixed fee or flat fee. There is one charge for the planning service; the plans become the property of the homeowner, and he or she may give them to a contractor to complete the project.

An hourly fee. If only minimal services are needed, the fee may be figured on an hourly basis; a minimum number of hours may be required. For example, a design fee may be charged on an hourly basis.

A percentage of costs. An architect, who draws plans for a major remodeling, may also inspect the job progress for compliance with building codes

---

SAMPLE DESIGN AND CONSULTATION SERVICE AGREEMENT

Agreement to provide bathroom design services for:
(name)_____
(address)_____
_____
_____

1. INTERVIEW. An interview will be conducted regarding the scope and goals of the project and to assist you in personalized planning.

2. JOB SITE VISIT. Your designer will visit the job site to obtain field measurements, study traffic patterns, survey structural considerations, and consult with you. In the case of new home construction, this information will be obtained from your house plans but must be field verified by the cabinet supplier after the framing is in place.

3. PRELIMINARY PLAN. A preliminary floor plan will be prepared to outline the possibilities, present conceptual ideas, and form the basis for discussion and revision.

4. FINAL PLAN. The final plan will include the floor plan and details, along with perspective views prepared with strict adherence to the guidelines prescribed by the National Kitchen and Bath Association for such drawings. You will receive copies of the final plan when approved.

5. PRICING AND EQUIPMENT SPECIFICATIONS. We will furnish complete specifications and prices for products supplied by us.

For new home construction, we will prepare an electrical plan for outlets, appliances, and task lighting, and a plumbing plan, at no additional charge, after the order has been placed.

THE PROFESSIONAL FEE FOR THE ABOVE LISTED SERVICES IS DETERMINED BY THE COMPLEXITY OF THE PROJECT.

FEE (PAYABLE IN ADVANCE) $_____

IF THE OWNER PURCHASES THE BATHROOM FROM THE DEALER WITHIN SIX MONTHS FROM THE DATE THIS AGREEMENT IS SIGNED, THE FEE IS CREDITED TOWARD THE PURCHASE PRICE.

and job specifications. The inspection charge is often based on a percentage of the project cost, usually 10 to 20 percent.

A retainer fee. A fee for design services varies, depending on the size and complexity of the job. It may range from a few hundred dollars to one thousand dollars or more. In this case, the client will own the completed plans. If the client elects to have the same company install the project, all or part of the retainer may be credited against the total job; the part that is not credited is considered to be a design fee.

There is no set method by which design fees are paid. Many designers require a percentage payment before work begins and a final payment when work is completed.

Contractor Fees

Contract. A contractor's bid on remodeling plans and specifications includes costs for materials and labor, plus a percentage for contractor profit. These costs are written into a contract for the successful bidder.

Contractors typically receive an **initial payment**, then a **"draw"** against the total at prearranged times during the remodeling; **the final payment** is made when both client and contractor agree that the job is complete.

It is vital to discuss fees at the *beginning* of the project, during the initial visit, before the first sketches are made, and long before the contractor's truck pulls up at your door.

DOING THE WORK YOURSELF

Some homeowners want to do part of the remodeling work themselves, usually to save money and/or to use their do-it-yourself skills. Others consider taking on the big job of general contractor. Before you make this commitment, ask yourself two important questions:

1. What are your skills and construction knowledge? *Realistically* assess your DIY (do-it-yourself) skills. It may cost you money to attempt jobs at which you are not qualified.

If you are a novice do-it-yourselfer, limit your participation to tasks that usually do not carry a large risk, such as demolition (done with care), trash hauling, or job site cleanup. Other jobs such as installing vinyl flooring tiles, painting, hanging wallcoverings, and staining windows and woodwork are within the reach of the average DIY homeowner.

Plan two days' work for priming and wallcovering, or laying vinyl tile. That means two days in which no one else is working in the bathroom.

Do you know enough about electrical work and plumbing to act as general contractor? Do you have the patience and management skills to hire and schedule subcontractors? Can you assume financial responsibility for workers' compensation insurance, or liens against your property because a subcontractor has not paid for materials?

2. When will your work be scheduled? How will it fit with the contractor's schedule? *Realistically* assess your schedule, especially if you work full-time. If you decide to undertake part of the remodeling project, be prepared to work *as scheduled* by the contractor. It will cost you money if workers must wait or be sent to another job while you finish your portion of the project.

If you are considering acting as general contractor, do you have time to be on site daily to oversee construction, receive materials, handle problems? Can you be available for inspections? A general contractor must be familiar with building codes.

Acting as general contractor is basically a full-time job. If you don't have the time and experience to do it yourself, you will probably save money by having a professional do it for you.

WORTH REPEATING

1. A designer or contractor with a professional certification has obtained the education and experience required by the industry organization that sponsors the certification program.

2. Major design credentials include membership in the American Society of Interior Designers (ASID) and the American Institute of Architects (AIA), as well as Certified Bathroom Designer (CBD), a program of the National Kitchen and Bath Association (NKBA).

3. Major construction certifications include Certified Graduate Remodelor™ (CGR) from the Remodelors™ Council of the National Association of Home Builders (NAHB), and Certified Remodeler (CR), sponsored by the National Association of the Remodeling Industry® (NARI®).

4. Specific experience in bathroom design and construction is a prerequisite for hiring a designer and/or contractor.

5. To select a quality professional, visit the designer and/or contractor showroom and inspect a finished remodeling job similar in scope and budget to the one you are planning.

6. Design fees vary widely, from a flat fee to a percentage of the total project. Obtain a contract outlining the fee agreement and payment schedule at the beginning of the remodeling project. There are no set methods for paying design fees; consult the designer for his or her particular practice.

7. Contractor's fees are indicated in the bid and written into the remodeling contract. An initial payment is made and a regular draw is taken at specified times. A final payment is made when the client and contractor agree that the work is complete, which is usually worded in the contract as "substantial completion."

Part Two

CREATING A BATHROOM PLAN

☐ **DESIGN PROBLEMS/SOLUTIONS** ☐
☐ **STRUCTURAL ISSUES** ☐ **PLUMBING** ☐
☐ **DESIGN NOTEBOOK** ☐ **UNIVERSAL DESIGN** ☐

4

Problem-Solving Floor Plans

How to plan functional, flexible bathroom space for your family.

Consider yourself a *partner* in the bathroom design process. The information that you, the client, bring to the design table is the raw material from which the bathroom is planned. Understanding the role of both the client and the designer is the first order of business in the design process.

Next consider three aspects of space planning:

■ **Function** — How well does the new bathroom design "fit" the users? Is it comfortable? How well does the plan meet with clients' needs?

■ **Aesthetics** — How does the bathroom look?

■ **Plumbing considerations** — How does the structure of the plumbing system affect changing fixture locations? Which fixture changes are economical to make?

These planning principles are illustrated in three "Design Problems."

CLIENT/DESIGNER PLANNING ROLES

In the design process, the client contributes:

■ A **bathroom inventory** that defines current problems and indicates the extent of the remodeling (face lift, minor remodeling, major remodeling, or addition); some familiarity with bathroom products and materials. (See Chapter 1, "Getting Started.")

■ A **preliminary budget.** (See Chapter 2, "Money Matters.")

■ **Knowledge of bathroom design and construction services.** (See Chapter 3, "Working with the Pros.")

The design professional's role is to:

■ **Listen** to client input.

■ **Help the client set specific remodeling goals** based on the bathroom inventory and budget. For example, increase storage with floor-to-ceiling cabinets, find room for separate tub and shower, improve lighting with a skylight and mirror fixtures, provide a private toilet compartment, design a tub platform finished with ceramic tile.

■ **Provide information** on bathroom products and materials.

■ **Offer several design solutions** for the bath, considering remodeling goals and budget.

■ **Prepare a final plan** that meets client needs and budget.

■ Help the client to **understand the plan.**

PLANNING APPROACH

Planning should begin with function, rather than aesthetics. The functional approach deals with the fixtures first, which may be organized in three zones, or centers of activity:

1. **Bathing/showering zone**
2. **Sink/grooming zone**
3. **Toilet zone**

The tub, shower, toilet, and sink locations are based on the exact size of the fixture, how many people will use the fixture, and at what time of the day. Recommended clearances at each fixture must be allowed. For example, the floor space in front of the shower must be adequate for drying. (For further information, more details follow in Chapter 11, "Fixtures: Tubs and Showers" and Chapter 12, "Fixtures: Sinks and Toilets.") Traffic should flow in and out of the room, and from center to center, without congestion.

The location of adjoining bedrooms is an issue in fixture arrangement and traffic patterns. In fact, a trend in new construction is to locate bathrooms so that a bath is accessible from each bedroom without walking through a hallway. The typical arrangement in an older home is that the bath is accessible from the hall and serves several bedrooms; others may be sandwiched between two bedrooms with hall access. The newer approach is to locate a guest bath in the guest bedroom; the master bath is ideally accessible only from the master bedroom for privacy.

The designer may begin by brainstorming many floor plans, weighing the pros and cons of each with the clients, then selecting several for refining. Insist on seeing *several* bathroom plans. Some design pros present plans in a good-better-best format, from the least expensive bathroom with the fewest plumbing, electrical, and structural changes, and fixtures and materials of moderate cost, to the most luxurious bathroom with the most changes.

As you evaluate the plans, ask as many questions as necessary to understand the design. Ask for additional floor plans if those offered do not meet your needs. Visualizing the plan from a relatively small, two-dimensional drawing is difficult for some. Elevations — drawings of each wall, viewed straight on — add detail.

Other visual aids include enlarging the plan on several sheets of graph paper, or asking the designer to do this for you. Or draw the plan with chalk — in actual size — on the basement floor, patio, or driveway; use boxes to simulate locations of fixtures, cabinets. Walk around in the "room" to study clearances, convenience of fixtures, and cabinet placements.

PLUMBING CONSIDERATIONS

The home plumbing system has a significant effect on bathroom design because its structure dictates where fixtures should be located and which new fixtures should replace old models. First consider how the plumbing system is structured and then the factors in fixture changes.

Water Supply System

A home plumbing system has two basic components: **the supply lines,** which carry water into the home from the city water system or well, and delivers the water to fixtures; and the **drain/waste/vent (DWV) system**, which removes waste and sewer gasses.

In the water supply systems, the main supply line (1" in diameter) delivers water to two sets of pipes that run *horizontally* through the floor joists or slab, called **supply branches** (³/₄"). One supply branch runs to the water heater, called the **hot water branch;** the second is the **cold water branch.** When the pipes run *vertically* through the wall to a second story they are called **supply risers;** some two-story homes may have additional branch lines between the second-floor joists.

At the end of each hot and cold water pipe is a **tee** that goes through the wall to which a **shutoff valve** is attached. The shutoff allows the water to be cut off from that single fixture for repairs. When remodeling, every fixture should have a shutoff. Showers and bathtubs should have an access panel to make future repairs easier.

Water pressure is affected by several factors: the number of outlets the system serves, use of

DESIGN PROBLEM 1
Finding Space: Enlarging the Small Bath

The average bath in a home built before the '70s measures 5' X 7' (35 square feet) to about 6' X 10' (60 square feet). No wonder most homeowners are searching for more bathroom space. Some of the best ways to enlarge the bath are:

1. "Borrow" from adjacent areas. Consider the linen closet, hallway, laundry chute, even the bedroom or adjacent bath. This solution is especially appropriate for "Empty Nesters" who have bedrooms available because their children have grown up and left home.

2. Unify divided space. Tear down partition walls, yet ensure privacy by providing a separate area for showering, bathing, and grooming. **Eliminate doors** that break up walls; open a door in another area, or install a pocket door.

3. Expand up and out. Raise the ceiling to the roof to add volume to the room. Add a greenhouse window or a cantilevered miniaddition, such as a bay window or a window seat with storage beneath.

4. Downsize fixtures. Exchange a tub for a shower. Consider corner fixtures of every type, including tub, whirlpool, shower, toilet, wall-hung or pedestal sink; consider a corner vanity cabinet fitted with a Lazy Susan for storage. A small whirlpool is available that fits in a standard tub space, 30" X 60 inches. Extend the countertop over the back of the toilet — called a banjo top — for more counter space without the bulk of a cabinet.

5. Visually expand space. A glass block wall can replace a partition wall. **Use the same colors on walls and floors. Stick with white**; white tile can be very inexpensive and works well with colored tile accents. **Use mirrors;** place two perpendicular to each other on the wall at the end of the cabinet.

6. Install a pedestal sink or a wall-hung sink to eliminate the vanity cabinet and be sure to include more storage with wall cabinets and shelving. **Select a glass shower stall. Add natural light,** especially a skylight. Use strategic lighting, such as cove lighting, installed high on the wall near the ceiling, to give the illusion of expanded space. (See Chapter 15, "Good Looks with Lighting.") Enlarge window(s), replacing the old ones with energy-efficient double- or triple-pane styles, but be sure that you can keep your privacy.

And remember that the little luxuries don't take up much space. Consider an electric towel warmer, wall or floor models; lighted magnifying makeup mirror; "rain bar," a gentle water spray for the shower; built-in hair dryer at the grooming center so you'll never have to plug in a small appliance again; a built-in soap dispenser for sink and shower, which eliminates cleaning the soap dish.

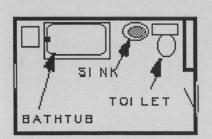

BEFORE

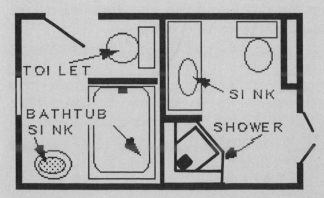

AFTER

THE PROBLEM: Find space for a master bath and a guest bath in a 200-year-old home with only one bathroom and plumbing dating from 1900.

THE SOLUTION: Rework plumbing and create two baths, each about 5 1/2' X 7'. In the guest bath (right), a corner shower (38" X 38") saves space; a vanity with a sink set near one end is an adequate 42" long. In the master bath (left), a short but wide tub (48" X 32"), pedestal lavatory with storage shelf above, and new door create a functional yet compact bath.

outlets at the same time, the length of the piping run, and the number of turns the piping makes, among other factors.

Building codes specify the diameter of the supply line to each fixture. The standard tub, shower, and one-piece toilet usually must be supplied by ½" pipes; but if a whirlpool tub or a shower with multiple heads is installed in a remodeling project, a higher volume of water is required and ¾" pipe usually is needed. Remember that codes specifying supply line sizes vary from region to region.

The diameter of the supply pipe also determines how many fixtures may be supplied. Codes specify that two fixtures may be served on a ½" branch line, three on a ¾" line; four fixtures usually require a 1" pipe. If fixtures are rearranged in a remodeling project, plumbing costs will be reduced if the supply lines serve the same number of fixtures for which they were originally intended.

Drain/Waste/Vent System

These pipes slope slightly downhill to carry water and waste **via gravity** to a single sewer line that carries the waste to the municipal sewer system or septic tank. For economy, fixtures should be grouped around a central area where the main soil stack (vertical waste pipe) is located. This accounts for the arrangement of a bathroom directly above a kitchen or back-to-back bathrooms.

The **drain system** works together with a **trap** in each fixture. The trap, a P-shaped pipe that connects the fixture and the drain, prevents sewer gas from backing up into the home. When the water is draining from the fixture, the P-trap never empties completely; the water in the trap forms a seal against sewer gas.

In the **waste system,** pipes running horizontally are **lines; stacks** run vertically. The toilet discharge pipe, for example, is a soil stack; the bathtub discharge pipe is a waste line.

Waste line diameters vary depending on the fixture, so fixture changes may require installation of new waste lines. For example, a standard bath and sink require 1½" diameter waste lines.

Whirlpools and shower stalls require 2"; showers with multiple heads, 3"; and toilets 3 to 4 inches.

The location of **vent lines** is also a consideration in remodeling. These lines **bring air into the system** so liquid waste flows freely and **vent sewer gas out of the system.** Each trap must be tied to the venting system; the vent line extends to the **vent stack** which exits through the roof.

Maximum distance between the P-trap and the vent is established. For example, the distance for a bathtub or sink using 1½" drain pipe must be no more than 30"; if the distance is greater, a larger drain pipe may be needed—then it is time to consult the plumbing contractor.

PLUMBING CHANGES

If fixture locations are unchanged, then plumbing costs will be minimal. On the other hand, an immovable plumbing system limits design possibilities. A compromise is the selection of fixture changes that can be made with modest plumbing alterations.

At the vanity cabinet. *Reposition the sink* up to 12" to the right or left by installing flexible water supply lines; the waste and vent lines remain in the same location within the cabinet. This technique makes possible a change such as adding a longer vanity cabinet to allow more storage and counter space.

Adding a second sink to create a double vanity in the same location may be possible with the addition of a flexible supply line; both sinks may be plumbed to the existing DWV system.

At the toilet. *The toilet waste can be offset 2" by means of a flange that fits over the drain. Those two little inches can produce two big results, without installing a new soil stack:* (1) *The toilet can be turned to face in another direction,* or (2) *a space-saving corner toilet can be installed.* Moving the toilet may free space for a privacy wall or pocket door to create a private toilet compartment.

At the tub/shower. *Replace a standard 30" X 60" tub with a shower.* In many cases, the existing vent pipe and supply lines (½") can serve the shower, but it requires a 2" drain line rather than the

1½" drain for the tub. Adding a shower is often feasible by adding supply lines and tapping into existing drain and vent lines.

Another possibility: *separating the tub and shower*, but placing the shower at the end of the tub so plumbing can be shared between the two fixtures. When replacing the shower, the drain in the new shower pan or base should be compatible with the location of the old drain. The drain in a square or round shower pan is usually located in the middle of the pan; in a rectangular pan, the drain usually is located off to one side.

ABOUT SEPTIC SYSTEMS

Some homes are served by a septic system for sewage disposal rather than the municipal water system. The septic system has two parts: a **tank** which receives waste, and a **drain field** (or leach field) of gravel and earth through which the waste water (effluent) is dispersed.

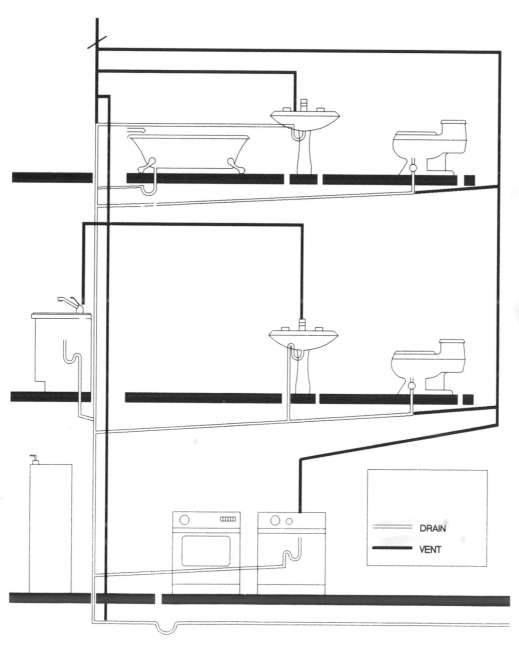

DRAIN/WASTE/ VENT LINES. The drain/waste/vent system (DWV) removes wastes and gasses. Waste and vent lines are grouped around a central soil stack which carries waste water to the municipal sewer system or to a septic tank. Then vent lines exit through the roof and allow toxic gasses to escape.

EDUCATE YOUR EYE

Aesthetics play a role in planning. Look for these design features as you evaluate floor plans, products, and materials:

1. Color. Whites and neutrals enlarge the bath, especially when the same color (monochromatic color scheme) is selected for walls and floors. Many tile manufacturers provide matching floor and wall tile. Whites and neutrals reflect light, thereby brightening the bath and aiding those with low vision. Choose fixtures of the same color for continuity. Use accent colors (contrasting colors that add visual interest) for tile border trim, lighting fixtures, faucet handles, linens, and bathroom accessories, for example. Select warm accents — reds, oranges, yellows, browns — or cool accents — blues, greens and purples.

2. Coordinate. The work is done for you by groups of manufacturers which cooperate to provide matching lines of fixtures and materials. For example, select tile and countertops from a coordinated line of surfacing options. Or choose fixtures from colors that are coordinated with vinyl flooring.

3. Size. The bathroom must "fit" just like clothing. Recommended space in the shower, for example, is a 30" turnaround; for a large, tall person this may not be enough. A person 5′ tall will have difficulty reaching the top of floor-to-ceiling cabinets. Fixtures must fit too. Try out the whirlpool tub and bend over the lavatory in a showroom.

4. Line. Notice what a ceiling molding, a chair rail, or a baseboard does to a room; it provides consistent **horizontal lines,** maintains design continuity, creates a feeling of stability, and widens space. Key bathroom lines to consider include the top of a mirror, which may line up with the top of a window; and a tile backsplash at the vanity counter which may be extended along the entire wall. **Vertical lines** (such as vertical tile patterns) draw the eye upward; they add visual height to the bath. **Curved lines** (such as rounded edges on countertops) soften space; **diagonal lines** (such as wall covering) are dramatic, and create a feeling of action or movement. Also, if the budget allows, "eliminating" lines by tiling the floor and entire walls visually enlarges the bathroom.

5. Focal Point. The focal point is the visual "center" of the room or the most eye-catching feature. Some examples of focal points are a curved whirlpool, a tile pattern or tile mural, a large vanity mirror lighted with subtlety, a custom window, an antique pedestal sink. Even the smallest bath can have a focal point.

6. Style. What theme appeals to your family — contemporary, traditional, country, period, or a combination? Every material in the bath can help define the style. An ultracontemporary bath, for example, emphasizes shape and simplicity. Laminate cabinets, high-gloss finishes, solid-surface or stone counters, geometric or abstract patterns on wallcovering, and accents of chrome and glass can contribute to the contemporary look. Identify your style, then talk to the designer about specifics to achieve this look.

7. Volume. Simply, what takes up space. The smaller fixtures and cabinets appear, the larger the bath seems. A pedestal sink is a good example of reduced volume in a fixture, compared to the bulk of a vanity cabinet. But even a vanity cabinet can look smaller by "raising" it off the floor; the "floating" vanity is secured to the wall several inches above the floor.

Sewage flows from the home to the tank by gravity, the solid waste sinks to the tank base, and anaerobic bacteria begin to break it down over a period of three to five days. Liquid sewage flows to the drain field where it is further broken down by anaerobic bacteria and dispersed through the soil.

(Some systems use pumps to move the waste from the household to the tank to the drain, but most rely on gravity and have no moving parts.)

Both the septic tank and the drain field are sized to handle a certain amount of waste water per day, based on an estimate of the total water used by all persons in the household per day. But the daily household water use may change when:

■ **The number of people living in the home increases**

■ **Water consumption increases**

■ **Bathroom fixtures are added**

■ **Fixtures with a high water consumption such as a whirlpool are added**

If the amount of waste water produced by the household each day increases beyond the capacity of the tank and drain field, then problems may result. For example, waste may be pushed out of the tank by incoming waste in less than the three to five days recommended to begin the settling and decomposing process; the tank eventually may become clogged with waste solids. Also, the drain field may become saturated, which prevents the effluent from percolating through the soil.

To prevent these problems when a bathroom is remodeled, it is important to determine whether the original capacities of the septic tank and drain field is adequate to handle any changes in water consumption. First, determine the capacity of the septic tank and drain field when they were installed.

It is important that your septic system have enough capacity to handle the waste water flow from your new bathroom. Experts may estimate the flow of waste water at 100 gallons per person living in the house. But extra capacity should be built into the septic system to handle waste water from a garbage disposal, automatic washer or whirlpool.

Minimum sizes for septic tanks are usually set according to the number of bedrooms in the house, with a minimum of 750 gallons for a house with up to two bedrooms, 1,000 gallons for three bedrooms, and a 1,200 gallon tank for a four bedroom house. Allow an extra 150 gallons of tank capacity for each additional bedroom above the four bedroom size. Be aware that the size and type of septic tank and drain field needed will depend on the absorption or "percolation rate" of the soil. Loose, sandy soil can easily absorb waste water, while clay may have a poor percolation rate. Check with your plumber and local building inspector to be sure your septic system is adequate for your area.

Estimate, with the help of the designer or plumbing contractor, the household water consumption after remodeling. For example, adding a whirlpool may add 20 to 100 gallons of water per use; on the other hand, some fixtures such as the low-flush toilet and low-flow showerhead reduce water consumption. Several chapters contain details on fixtures and water consumption: Chapter 8, "Using Water Wisely;" Chapter 11, "Fixtures: Tubs and Showers;" and Chapter 12, "Fixtures: Sinks and Toilets." If the existing septic system is undersized, it may be time to install a new one.

Another factor in septic systems and bathroom remodeling is the age of the septic system. Tanks made of fiberglass or concrete have an almost unlimited life. A drain field is usually sized and designed to last 20 to 30 years. And because the system usually has no moving parts, its life is extended.

If your local building codes require a building permit for your bathroom renovation, an inspector will also inspect your septic system to ensure it meets all codes and capacities.

ABOUT ADDITIONS

In some cases, an addition is the best answer to finding space to expand the bathroom, especially when:

■ **The family is growing and changing** with the addition of a child, an aging relative, or one or more children entering the teen years

■ **A master suite is desired**, or no master bath exists

■ **Enhanced guest space is desired** for families that regularly entertain family and friends

■ **No interior space can be sacrificed**

An addition can be as small as a 4' X 6' space that can hold a tub or as expansive as a master suite with a generous bathroom and bedroom space. But as soon as an addition is considered, expenses start adding up, beginning with a new roof and possibly a new foundation. When your property is reassessed by the municipal assessor, its value may rise, as a result of the addition, and therefore the property

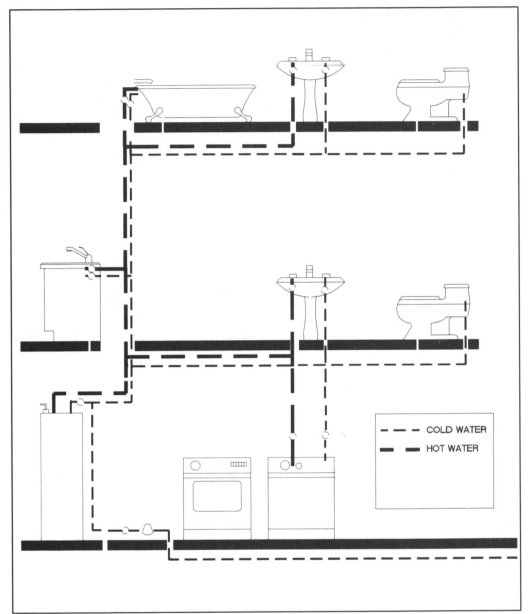

WATER SUPPLY LINES. Supply lines carry water into the home from the municipal water system or well and deliver it to bathroom fixtures. Notice the main supply line below the floor at the bottom of the illustration and the hot water line from the hot water heater.

- - - - COLD WATER
- - HOT WATER

taxes will increase. Ask these questions to decide if an addition is suitable for your home:

■ **How will it look from the outside?** How can the addition blend into the existing architecture?

■ **What is the best location, considering the building site** and factors such as view, privacy, shape of lot, soil type, existing yard structures, and yard use?

■ **What is the best location, considering interior factors**, such as floor plan, traffic patterns?

■ **To what extent can existing mechanical and plumbing systems be shared** in the addition?

ABOUT THE BASEMENT BATH

The once-popular basement recreation room of the '50s and '60s, complete with powder room or even a bath with a shower, has given way to the main-level family room. Yet there are situations in which a lower-level bath is desired:

■ **An aging bath exists** that is due for remodeling

■ **The area is used for a playroom or entertainment**

■ **The family regularly uses the space** for a home office/hobby area

■ **An exercise suite is planned**

■ **Guest accommodations are needed**

■ **Bedroom/bath for growing family**, extended family, rental space

■ **Lower level is a walkout basement** — one side opens to ground level — so it is living space with natural light

■ **Newer home with lower level designed to be finished after purchase**; includes full height (8′) ceilings, rough-in plumbing, or capped water supply lines.

Locate the bath outside of the traffic patterns to and from the stairs, laundry, etc. Position the bath towards one end or side of the basement so the living space is not carved up into small areas.

Installing the plumbing may require removing part of the concrete floor for a new drain line; if a laundry is present, consider tapping into the existing drain/vent system. Supply lines will be necessary for the new fixtures too. A toilet designed for below-grade applications, called an upflush toilet, is available.

Ventilation. The fan must be ducted and the warm, moist air discharged outside. (See fan ducting principles in Chapter 16, "Clearing the Air: Ventilation.") One option is to install the ventilation fan duct horizontally along the floor joists in the basement ceiling, then vertically through the exte-

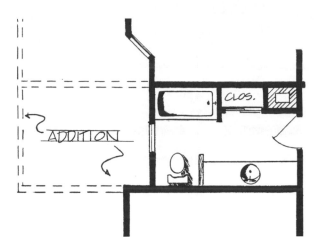

BEFORE

ADDITIONS. A two-story addition, including a family room below and a master suite above, added about 65 square feet to this 7¹/₂′ X 10′ bath, creating room for a whirlpool bath, double vanity, separate shower, and storage.

The existing bath was gutted — plumbing fixtures, plaster, wiring, rough plumbing, mudset tile floor, and millwork were removed. The flat ceiling and existing rafters were also removed, and a new ceiling was installed to match the cathedral ceiling of the addition. Other roof work included a skylight installation to bring light into the shower area of the long, narrow bath.

AFTER

DESIGN PROBLEM 2
Planning a Family Bath: Balancing Private Space/Shared Space

The issue: Several people use the bathroom at the same time. Shared spaces and private spaces are needed in this bath. Creating privacy with such features as a toilet compartment or separate dressing area may be balanced with shared space such as a vanity with two sinks.

1. Plan for physical differences. For people of varied heights, install a hand-held shower-head, which is attached to the water supply line by a flexible tube. The hand-held spray may be hung on a vertical slide bar at any height. Consider two sinks at different heights, whether they are set into a counter, pedestal sink, or wall-hung style.

2. Provide privacy. Compartmentalize, especially at the toilet. Or compartmentalize at the shower by adding its own dressing room. Separate the vanity sink by installing a decorative panel perpendicular to the vanity cabinet that extends from the floor to ceiling or from the top of the counter to the ceiling.

3. Provide separate fixtures and grooming areas. Install two separate vanity cabinets, each with a sink, or one with a sink and the other with a sit-down grooming center. Or try a double vanity with two sinks. Plenty of storage is a must with wall cabinets, cabinets recessed between wall studs. (See Chapter 13, "Bathroom Storage," for details.) Separate tub and shower for use by two people at the same time.

4. Create two baths with one or more shared fixtures.

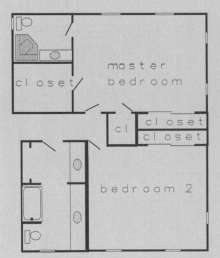

BEFORE

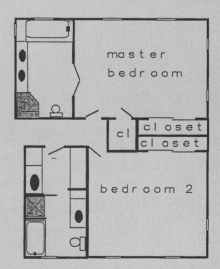

AFTER

THE PROBLEM: A family of five living in a 1950s home wants a larger master bath, plus a children's bath which two or three children can use simultaneously; the changes must not reduce closet space.

THE SOLUTION: Expand the master bath into the walk-in closet, doubling the bath size from 6¹/2' X 8³/4' to 13' X 8³/4', and creating room for a whirlpool tub. Between the master bedroom and the boy's bedroom, remodel three small closets into two large closets; add a new closet on the outside wall of the boy's bedroom. In the children's bath, widen the bathing area about 1' to replace the tub/shower with a 36" square shower and 5' tub; for privacy, provide a pocket door between the bathing area and small vanity.

DESIGN PROBLEM 3
Planning for Two: Rules for the Master Suite

The master suite can be designed for relaxation and pampering. It is an area that can purposefully blur the distinction between bedroom and bath. Let your imagination range free.

1. Aesthetics are especially important in this bath, such as luxury materials (like a marble countertop), entertainment equipment (like a sound system), and custom features (like a platform for a whirlpool). If you select a whirlpool, plan a view; who wants to relax with a view of the toilet?

2. Whether you want to share bathroom space or prefer some privacy, fixtures can be arranged to accommodate either need. Consider these arrangements:

■ **Togetherness in the master bath.** Install a two-sided vanity (side-by-side vanity), whirlpool for two, shower for two (the oversize shower), dressing closet, and clothing storage.

■ **Separate spaces.** Place an additional vanity in the bedroom for grooming; place a whirlpool in the bedroom; add a privacy wall at the toilet compartment; plan a closet or dressing area in the bathroom; locate a laundry in the bathroom. In other words, consider the bedroom and bath as rooms that flow into one another. If you prefer to shower and dress in the bathroom, plan accordingly; if you prefer an area of lower humidity for grooming, locate a vanity, sink, and mirror in the bedroom.

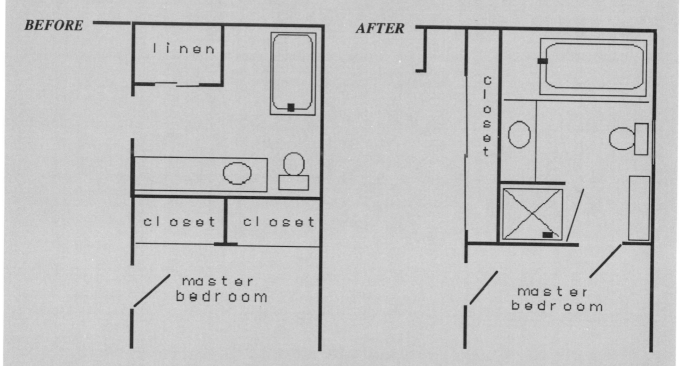

BEFORE

AFTER

THE PROBLEM: Create separate closet/dressing area so early-rising spouse does not wake other spouse; add whirlpool and steam shower to bath.

THE SOLUTION: Replace bedroom closet with 12' long hall closet/dressing area, borrowing about 2' from bath. Although the new bath is 24 square feet smaller than the existing bath — about 7' X 12' compared to 12' X 9' — it accommodates a 6$\frac{1}{2}$' whirlpool that replaces the 3' X 5' tub, a 36" square steam shower, and 42" vanity, as well as a 3' wide linen storage cabinet.

rior wall to the closest above-grade opening; keep the duct run as short as possible to enhance the movement of air through the duct.

Fans are sized by the number of cubic feet in the bath and the cubic feet of air per minute vented. Consider a more powerful fan than needed for actual bath size to handle the extra moisture that is sometimes present in a basement. (See Chapter 16, "Clearing the Air: Ventilation," for details on ventilation systems.)

Heating. The basement bath is a good candidate for *zoned heating*, or heating areas of the home independently. A built-in electrical heating system may be used for zoned heating, which allows heat to be turned on and off and the temperature set in each zone.

For homes with forced-air heat and a basement furnace, planning a duct to heat the bathroom may be a relatively uncomplicated procedure. Careful treatment of insulation as well as proper placement of the vapor barrier will make the bathroom comfortable too. (See Chapter 17, "Bathroom Heating and Cooling," for details on heating.)

Aesthetics. Use all the tricks of the trade for small baths to keep this below-grade space light and bright. (See "Design Problem 1" above.) Particularly effective are mirrors, light colors, and an excellent lighting system. (See Chapter 15, "Good Looks with Lighting.")

Consider glass block if a privacy wall is planned and a glass shower enclosure to visually expand space. Add a touch of freshness with plants.

WORTH REPEATING

1. Planning begins with function, not aesthetics. Locate fixtures first, considering room dimensions, fixture sizes, number of people using the bathroom, clearances, traffic patterns, and existing plumbing hookups.

2. To simplify the task of evaluating a floor plan, enlarge the drawing two or three times, or draw the plan in its actual size with chalk on a driveway, patio, or basement floor.

3. A common design problem is finding room to expand. Borrow space from an adjoining room or closet; expand upward by raising the ceiling; use down-sized fixtures; enlarge space visually with light colors, mirrors, glass shower walls, skylights, or wall-mounted vanity cabinets.

4. Providing privacy and adequate space is another typical problem in the multiuser bath. For privacy, separate the vanity from the bathing area by means of a pocket door; plan a private toilet alcove. Also provide a double vanity, or a single vanity sink and a vanity area for grooming; separate the tub and shower.

5. The plumbing system has two parts, the water supply lines and the drain/waste/vent lines. Codes specify the diameters of the water supply and the DWV pipes for *each* fixture. For example, tubs and showers normally require a $\frac{1}{2}$" supply line; a whirlpool may require a $\frac{3}{4}$" line, depending on its water capacity.

6. Some fixtures may be moved with moderate costs. Examples: Flexible supply lines allow sinks to be relocated in a countertop or a second sink to be added; a toilet may be moved 2" from the stack or rotated 180 degrees; for a separate tub and shower, locate the fixtures next to each other to share plumbing.

7. Additions. A one- or two-story addition is costly, considering new roofing, a foundation or slab, framing, siding, windows, plus new mechanical systems inside and increased property taxes, due to the value added to your home by the addition. Cut costs with a well-planned small addition that can radically enlarge the bathroom, such as pushing out one wall a few feet, making a small bump-out cantilever from the existing wall (such as a walk-in bay), or adding a greenhouse window.

8. Basements. Although the lower level is less desirable living space than it was 30 years ago, adding a bath is especially useful in a walk-out basement or a newer home with a lower level specifically built to be finished in the future. Plusses: when rough-in plumbing or capped water supply lines exist.

5

Design Notebook: Great Bathroom Ideas

Pictures and plans: The master bath, children's bath, family bath, and guest bath.

The floor plans and photographs that follow include prize-winning designs from professionals across the nation. These baths were selected because they use space efficiently and imaginatively. Select your favorite features and adapt them to help solve the problems in your bath.

As you "shop" through the Design Notebook, pay particular attention to the floor plans that accompany the photos. The plans illustrate the bathroom before the remodeling and after the remodeling.

Keep your eyes open for changes in the floor plans. Study the effect of adding space, for example. In most cases, you will see that adding a moderate amount of space enabled two or more people to use the bath at the same time.

Notice the fixtures. Did the positions change, stay the same? Were some fixtures relocated and others kept in the original position? How often is the tub exchanged for a separate tub and shower? Are corner fixtures used? Studying fixture relocations will give you ideas about the flexibility of plumbing arrangements.

The floor plans will also show the advantages of moving walls—opening up, closing, or removing partition walls. And notice details like changing the direction that a door swings to make room for fixtures or cabinetry.

Master Bath for Two

This elegant bath for two with an Oriental feel was once a small, crowded bathroom used by all family members. Putting an 8′ X 8′ addition at one end created room to move in this shared space.

A large whirlpool was added, flanked on three sides by generous windows. For privacy, the owners pull the window shades and enjoy light from two skylights, each 2′ X 2′, in the graceful gable above.

Unusual contemporary-style cabinets individualize the bath. Made of redwood with slab doors, the cabinets are suspended from the wall to visually reduce their volume. The storage system combines cabinets, open shelving, and a glass door unit; handsome door and drawer pulls accent the redwood.

Materials are mixed with a skilled hand. The warm wood contrasts with the glossy black under-mounted sinks, whirlpool tub, and curved glass-block wall. Tall mirrors and light colors of the countertop, flooring, and walls balance the darker tones of the cabinets and fixtures.

Notice the fine points of the design: lights on the dimmer switch; sound system speakers over the whirlpool; Oriental-style lights repeated at the entry and the whirlpool; sculptured, oversize faucets at vanity sinks; strip lighting over mirrors.

A large whirlpool nestles into a well-lighted alcove. The layout allows one person to bathe while the other uses a sink, or for two to use the separate vanity grooming areas at the same time.

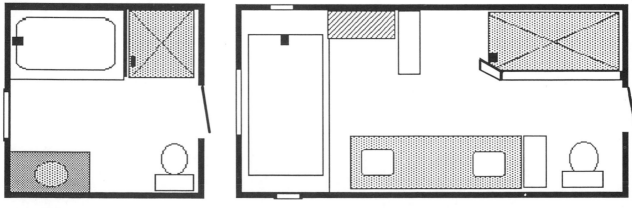

BEFORE   **AFTER**

Master Bath for Two

Locating the tub in the addition at one end of the bathroom allows space for three other centers of activity at the vanity, shower, and toilet. The whirlpool and arched window are the focal points when entering from the hall.

A postage-stamp bathroom was doubled in size by an addition that was part of a larger home expansion project. **The problem:** A long, narrow room was created in which clients required a whirlpool tub, separate shower, double-sink vanity, linen storage, and access from the master bedroom.

The solution: The cathedral ceiling with a Palladian window and skylight creates volume and brings in an abundance of natural light. The double vanity is made from a shallow vanity base with rounded cabinet fronts and doors that give the illusion of a wider room.

Notice the fine points of the design: Double doors from the hall and bedroom do not swing as far into space as a standard door; the shower and closet create privacy area for the toilet; mirror spans entire vanity; small drawers in the vanity front provide extra storage.

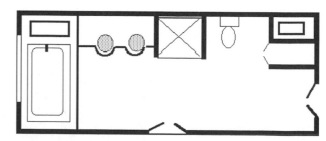

BEFORE

AFTER

Master Bath for Two

Tile, tile, tile! Ceramic mosaic tile on walls, floors, and counter unite this long, narrow bath. On the floor, 1″ X 1″ mosaic tile in three colors; on the counter and wall, 2″ X 2″ tile. On the end wall, the wallcovering pattern echoes the diagonal lines of the floor mosaic.

Subtle in color but lively, the tile mosaic pattern is repeated in the tub surround and apron. Brass fittings gleam against cream-colored tile.

Rambler Addition

A 6′ X 12′ addition to a modest 1950s rambler with two outdated baths created a private vanity/toilet area for each adult, plus a shared shower/whirlpool area. Notice that sink/toilet locations are barely changed; new plumbing for the whirlpool and shower is in the slab foundation.

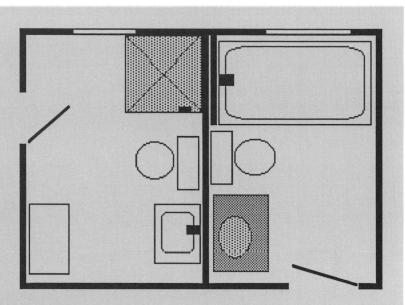

BEFORE

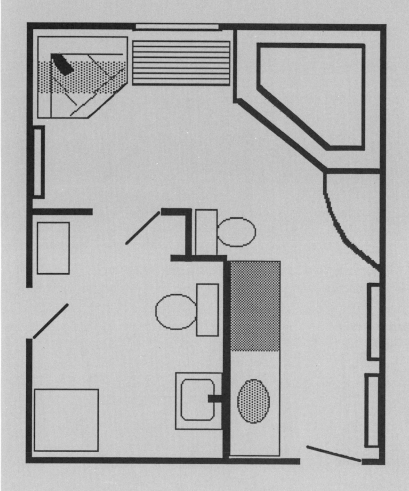

AFTER

Bright Baths for Children

The centrally located tub in a laminate platform is flanked by doors to each grooming area and a glass block wall that lets in light but keeps the area private.

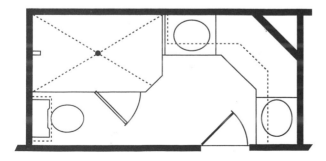

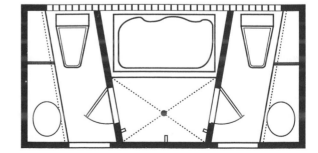

BEFORE   *AFTER*

Laminate cabinets above and below the vanity, plus open shelving, provide plenty of storage for each child.

This bathroom was designed for an eight-year-old boy and a twelve-year-old girl. The designers planned a tub for a common space, then split the room down the middle for privacy. The old bathroom, which the children had shared for years, was torn out, then the space was divided in half with a separate vanity, storage, and toilet for each child, and a central tub and shower.

Decorative laminate covers the cabinetry, counters, and walls. A team of international designers collaborated on this personal room.

Notice the fine points of the design: doubled storage capacity, easy-to-grasp cabinet pulls, recessed lighting over mirror, and nonslip mat at the tub.

Bright Baths for Children

This clever children's bath has a nautical theme and plenty of space for two. At one end of the room is a changing seat and a private toilet area. The changing seat is topped with a low-maintenance, solid-surfacing material to prevent falls while dressing; rounded edges are safer for children.

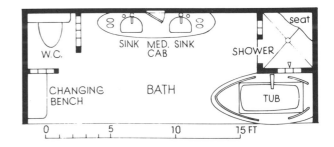

At the other end of the bath is a separate tub and shower. The soft bathtub with a nonslip base helps prevent falls; if a child does fall, the cushioning will help prevent injury. The insulated tub also retains heat. (For more photos, see Chapter 7, "Staying Safe.")

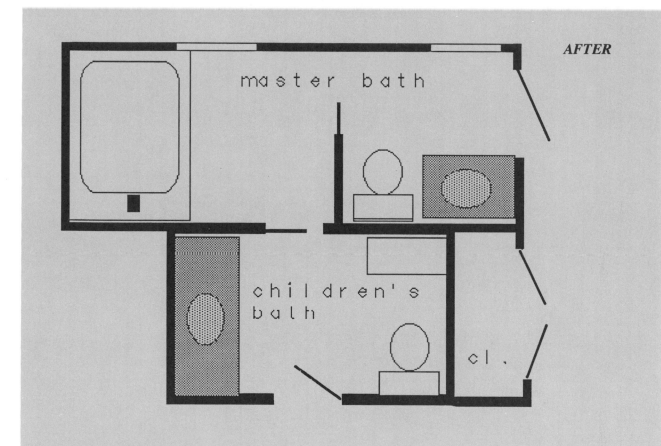

AFTER

master bath

children's bath

cl.

Flexible Family Bath

How do parents and children share a bath? Plan private space/shared space in an addition. When a second child was born, the adults using one tiny bath needed more room and more privacy. A rear porch under the main roof was enclosed and three compartments were created: off the master bath, a vanity/toilet with a window; off the hall, a vanity/toilet for the girls; connecting the two, a tub/shower with dressing space. Close one pocket door and the former porch becomes a complete master bath.

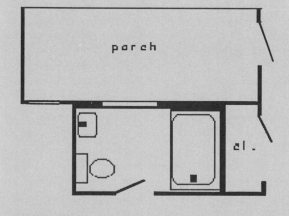

porch

cl.

BEFORE

Baths with a Past

This master retreat has a Victorian theme achieved with cherry wood paneling, cabinets, and molding, as well as Victorian wallcovering, marble, and sparkling brass.

The console sink with a marble top and brass legs is flanked by clever storage in two sets of tall, narrow drawers. Matching brass lamps — with the most contemporary light source, halogen bulbs —

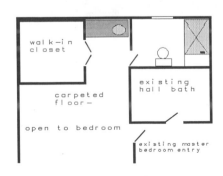

BEFORE

walk-in closet

carpeted floor —

open to bedroom

existing hall bath

existing master bedroom entry

RIGHT Making the most of the space available in an add-on attic bathroom, the shower wall doubles as a partition, giving the toilet almost a room of its own.   CENTER A platform bath with a wide step provides a place to sit and supervise bathing toddlers. Bath and sink are divided by a pastel-edged glass block partition.   BOTTOM Morning traffic jams are minimized when a bathroom has separate sinks. The twin sinks in this bathroom each have brilliant lighting supplied by three vertical rows of lights. Visually enlarging and unifying the room is a band of blue-and-white tiles that recede into a ledge.   LAST COLOR PAGE The blend of Caribbean pastels makes this bathroom almost as refreshing as a tropical vacation. The mix of patterns on the floor and walls around the porcelain sink create a lively and festive effect. Whimsical additions — a goldfish in a bowl and some pink flamingos — add to the room's playful spirit.

FAR LEFT The shower in this dressing room/bathroom is enclosed by curved glass block walls, which inhibit sound, conserve heat, transmit light, and protect privacy.   LEFT Elements of classical Japanese design bring East to West, complete with clouded glass reminiscent of rice paper and Bonsai trees.   BOTTOM Natural materials — wood, marble, glass — create a pleasing blend of earthen colors.   TOP RIGHT This brightly lit dressing room/ bathroom has ample space for clothes, shoes, and toiletries.   CENTER RIGHT The bathroom walls are painted with a faux marbling technique to look like they came from Roman baths of antiquity.   BOTTOM RIGHT Economizing on space, a glass wall is all that separates the shower and bath.

ABOVE *Flowery wallpaper, thick pale carpeting, sheer fabric, and a slipper chair soften a practical space.* LEFT *Creative use of fabric is an easy way to enliven a dull bathroom. A sink skirt, sewn from sheet material that coordinates with the towels, camouflages unsightly plumbing fixtures, while the floor is covered and brightened by a hand-hooked cotton rug.* TOP NEAR RIGHT *Treasures from the sea and seashell palette provide the design scheme for this comfortable bathroom.* TOP CENTER RIGHT *Attic space or an added-on dormer may be the only available space to create a much-needed extra bathroom. Skylights provide more light than ordinary windows.* TOP FAR RIGHT *To visually expand a limited space, this bathroom relies on a blend of similar, unobtrusive patterns in muted colors.* BOTTOM RIGHT *Simple and inexpensive decorating techniques give this bathroom a bright extension-of-the-garden look. The exuberant floral fabric of the curtains and chair cushions balance the finely patterned floral wallpaper, while natural light pours through windows around and above the door opening onto the balcony.*

TOP FAR LEFT Cheerful primary colors are the key to this bathroom's easy-to-achieve face lift. The baseboard and outside of the claw foot bathtub were painted a buttercup yellow. Matching fabric for shower curtains, sink skirt, and coordinating wallpaper border between the double chair rail tie everything neatly together.   BOTTOM FAR LEFT A quilt of decorative mosaic tiles gives this room a distinctive focal point.   BOTTOM NEAR LEFT Horizontal lines visually widen space and this bathroom has two sets. The wall's red, blue, gold, and white prism seems all the more intense when contrasted with the black-and-white horizontal lines of the floor tiles.   TOP Tile in this inventive bath is laid in random blocks of colors like a Mondrian painting. The wooden cabinets, door, and partition have been stained to coordinate.   RIGHT This imaginative window that evokes the cool, shaded rooms of northern Africa, is actually crafted from bricks and covered by etched, clouded glass.

are set in fluted wood columns that accent the console. The tub, flanked by two white columns, and surrounded by marble tile, has an apron with a raised-panel pattern.

Notice the fine points of the design: recessed ambient lighting complements task lighting; brass hand-held showerhead at the tub; the cabinet over the tub with mirrored doors provides needed storage in the tub area. At the console is an adjustable shaving mirror and a handy towel bar beneath the sink.

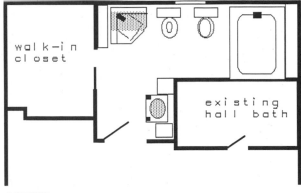

AFTER

A custom-made marble tile shower features a roomy bench, niche for grooming aids, and a hand-held shower. Shower extras include lighting, brass trim on glass panels, and a brass handle.

Baths with a Past

*Love the stories that quilts tell, but wouldn't dream of ruining one in a steamy bath? Put one on the floor
— permanently — with mosaic tile. Mosaic tile, a mix of 1" X 1" and 2" X 2" sizes, matches the platform
tub length. A rustic plant stand and wooden animal accent the contemporary bath.*

Now go forward in time, past the turn of the century, to a simple but rich black-and-white bath, eclectic in style. The black marble-topped console sink on chrome legs, and black-and-white flooring set the tone; a large white soaking tub, sleek rounded mirror, and art prints are contemporary touches. Tile strips on the wall hold the room design together.

This bathroom holds more surprises such as an up-to-date shower stall tucked out of sight and a very contemporary low-profile toilet.

Polished & Private Guest Baths

Nothing's too good for guests, and most families would like to provide a place of privacy, quality, and relaxation for their visitors. Guest baths are often small, so the challenge is to artfully plan the amenities in a tight space.

Now add another problem: Don't move any of the fixtures. In this handsome guest bath that was once just a line-up of three fixtures, the designer removed the tub and replaced it with an angled shower, the focal point of the bath. Enough area remained for grooming areas on each side of the shower.

Notice the fine points of the design: the vanity cabinet anchored to the wall, reducing its volume; floor tiles laid diagonally echo the shower angle; mirror heights match shower height.

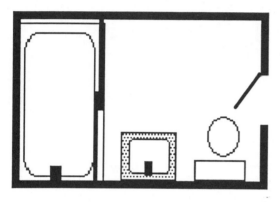

BEFORE

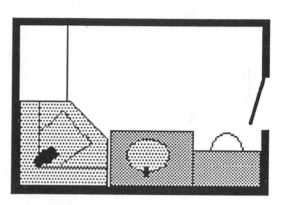

AFTER

The vanity counter extends over the toilet — known as a banjo-top counter — adding needed space to the grooming area. Under the counter is a low-boy toilet. Brushed chrome sink, faucet, and cabinet pulls have a matte finish.

Polished & Private Guest Baths

Excellent lighting is essential at the mirror. Sculptured halogen fixtures on a mirrored strip have the shape of wall sconces but shed plenty of flattering light at the vanity. The frameless mirror and edge detail on the cultured marble vanity top add interest to this simple setting.

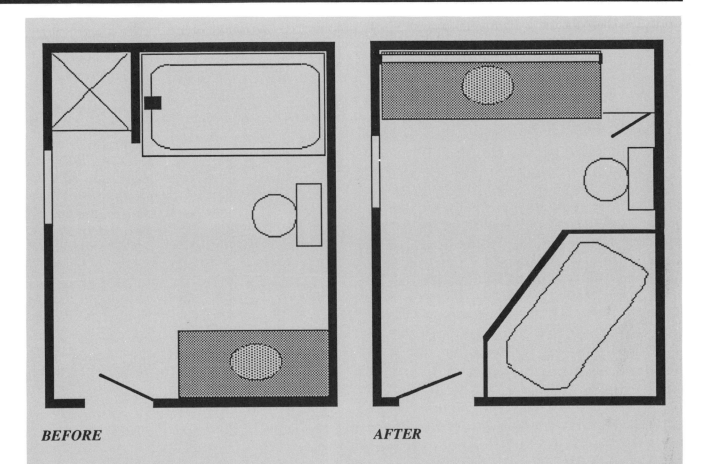

BEFORE   AFTER

Guest Bath
Solution

Here's a tall order for a 7½' X 9½' bath: Serve two lower-level guest bedrooms and the outdoor pool, without adding space. The solution: Switch the tub and vanity locations.

The change yielded a graceful oval cor-ner tub and shower with a glass enclosure, a vanity almost 2' longer than the original, and matching linen storage for pool towels. Hinging the door on the left creates a larger walkway and a view of the lighted vanity mirror at the entry.

Deluxe Master Baths

Nestled into a mirrored alcove is a graceful whirlpool set into a stepped platform. The whirlpool mechanical system is hidden behind a panel in the bath platform step. The TV is angled for viewing from the tub.

A custom-built vanity with an under-mounted sink replaces the old tub. Above and below the mirrored cabinets, low-voltage lighting strips subtly illuminate the grooming area for two.

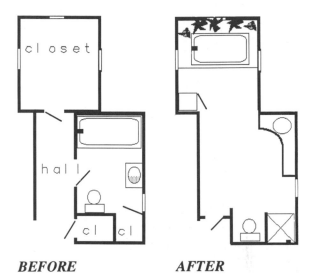

BEFORE   **AFTER**

Coming home carries a double meaning for the couple who remodeled this bathroom. "Home" is the actual house in which the owner grew up. It was important that the original structure was not eradicated during remodeling, but the bath sorely needed updating and reshaping.

Borrowing space from three closets — one large, two small — plus opening a hallway, more than doubled the bathroom. The large closet now houses a sculptured whirlpool flanked by the original windows.

Removing two small closets made space for the steam bath and toilet. The steam unit features a hand-held shower, custom doors, and opulent base trim. The steam generator is in the room to the right of the shower.

Deluxe Master Baths

The curved vanity/tub island is surrounded by closets, toilet, bidet, shower, and laundry in this bath for two.

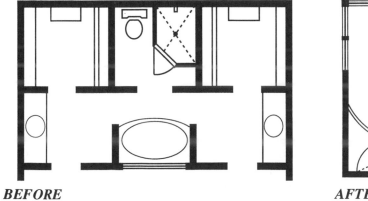

BEFORE

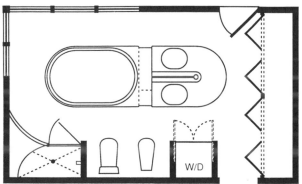

AFTER

Opening up six dark compartments transformed this master bath into one big, beautiful space for a couple who chose to remodel for retirement instead of pulling up roots. They enjoyed the amenities of their old bath, but wanted a softer, more natural room. Other needs included a bidet, separate vanities positioned for conversation, and a laundry.

They got all that, and more, in a laminate bathroom with a handsomely curved double vanity separated from the tub by a privacy wall. Floor-to-ceiling storage cabinets accommodate clothing as well as a laundry. The room's bold lines and curves were created by an international design team.

Clothing closets turn the bathroom into a one-stop area for bathing, grooming, and dressing.

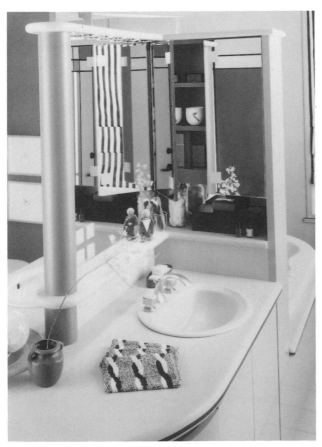

A double vanity with laminate cabinets makes it easy for a couple to talk about their day. Mirrors cover one side of the privacy wall between the vanity and the tub.

This whirlpool tub, set into a deck of solid-surfacing material and laminate, has a view of the garden. A separate shower allows two bathing choices.

Deluxe Master Baths

A lavishly decorated bay houses a whirlpool of cultured marble set off with classical fluted columns and an expanse of casement windows. Companion benches invite relaxing after a soak. For privacy, lower the shades hidden behind flowered valances.

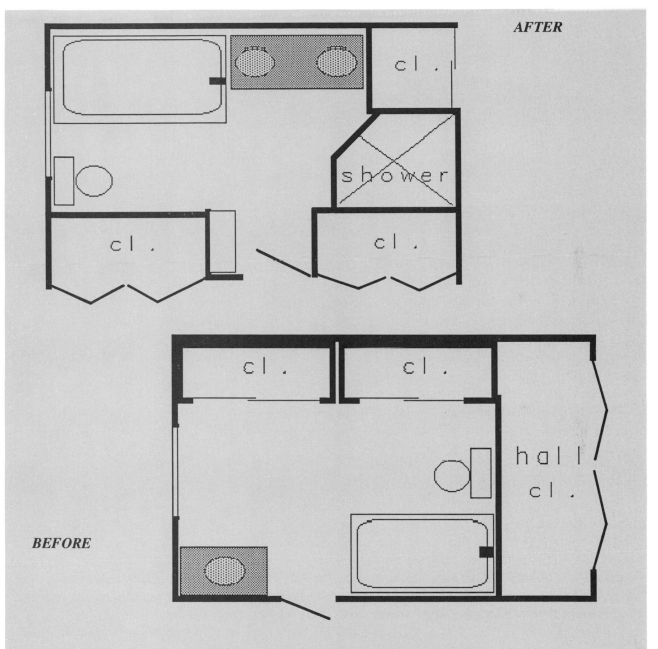

AFTER

BEFORE

Borrow Closet Space

Maximize the bath by rearranging fixtures and borrowing closet space. Substantial plumbing changes were made, but in this ranch home, the plumber had easy access to pipes from the full basement.

A 32" X 60" tub was traded for a 36" X 72" whirlpool for two. Storage is multiplied with a double vanity and linen cabinet; the roomy closets now open directly into the bedroom. The shower door is fitted with a hinge stop so it cannot swing into the vanity.

Bath/Laundry Partners

This elegant white master bath in what was once a dingy attic has a convenient laundry tucked behind sliding doors. A stacked washer/dryer shares closet space with a storage cabinet.

The laundry room has moved up a few notches. Once relegated to the basement, utility room, or garage, the washer and dryer have been elevated to a prime location near the bedroom and bath.

It makes a lot of sense to locate the washer and dryer right by the rooms where people dress. And a supply of hot and cold water is at hand in the bathroom. The only challenge is supplying a gas line or 220-volt service for the gas or electric appliances selected.

Here's a laundry tip. Say goodbye to the laundry chute that jumbles clothes. Instead, supply two sorting baskets, one for darks, one for whites, at the bathroom laundry. Store, sort, wash, and dry in one convenient spot.

Put this bath/laundry near a family room or play area for kids with dirty hands and soiled clothes.

A stacked laundry pair, 27¹/2″ square at the base, fits neatly into a slim closet.

Take out a tub and put in a washer and dryer. That's what the owners of this city loft did. A deluxe spa-shower replaces the tub in an adjacent space.

6

The User-Friendly Bath

*How to make the bath
accessible to everyone.*

Making the bathroom accessible to everyone — the able-bodied, elderly, children, and handicapped individuals — is the purpose of **universal design.** The user-friendly bathroom looks like any other bathroom, but it includes a wealth of adaptations that make everyday living easier for the able-bodied and those with special needs. Whether it is labeled adaptable housing, barrier-free design, or design for independent living, the goal is a bathroom that is easy to use.

Some features of the accessible bath must be built in; others may be added to the existing bath. For example, adequate floor space for turning a wheelchair should be planned in advance, as well as blocking between the wall studs to which grab bars are anchored.

However, other features require little advance planning. A single-lever faucet that is easy to operate, because it requires no gripping or turning, can easily replace an old faucet. Changing cabinet hardware from small round pulls to loop-style handles that require less dexterity to operate can be done anytime. Improving lighting levels for the elderly at the grooming area can be accomplished with some electrical know-how. Strip lights on three sides of the mirror and a lighted makeup mirror on a swinging arm brighten the area for those with low vision.

User-friendly improvements, such as a new faucet or cabinet hardware, can cost relatively little. However, a cushioned bath, with its increased safety and comfort, can cost several thousand dollars. But the most cost-effective improvements don't require special equipment because they work for everyone. A sit-down grooming center is one example; it is comfortable for the able-bodied and a bonus for those with chronic back problems or someone using a walker.

Let's take a look at other improvements that will eliminate barriers from your new bath.

SURFACES

Start accessibility planning with bathroom surfaces. Plan a bathroom with a **light color scheme.** Light-colored walls, floors, ceiling, and counters are easy on the eyes and enhance lighting levels by reflecting light. For the elderly and those with low vision, light colors make seeing the environment easier.

White cabinet interiors make locating supplies easy. All cabinets as well as drawers benefit from a white interior and **white storage accessories**.

The **flooring** surface should be a **nonslip material**, which is safe for everyone and easy on

Planned for an adaptable house, this elegant bath is anything but institutional looking. The whirlpool tub is as high as a wheelchair seat to aid in tub transfer. The offset faucet is more accessible than a faucet at the end of the tub; a nonslip tub bottom and built-in grab bar help prevent falls. The wall-mounted sink has a shroud that covers the plumbing and prevents burns; a narrow counter with a drawer flanks the sink. Other plusses: Grab bars that blend in with trim on tub and cabinets, a 1.6 gallon per flush toilet, tilted mirror, and telephone.

All ages in the family can enjoy this coordinated bath suite. The whirlpool bath, 60" X 38" X 25¹/₂" deep, features a water-tight door that opens for easy entry. A seat for bathing and showering can be folded up to become a backrest for a soaking bath. Faucets are placed within reach of the seat. The console sink has faucets that are moved forward within reach of a wheelchair. The sink overhangs the counter to bring the basin closer to the user. The low-flush toilet is 17¹/₂" high for those with limited mobility. Note the grab bars at the shower and toilet; ceiling lighting in tub and toilet alcoves; privacy screening with curtains at tub and toilet.

wheelchairs and walkers. Choices include **nonslip vinyl** and **slip-resistant ceramic tile.**

Wheelchair Concerns

With the trend toward larger baths, spaces may better accommodate a wheelchair user or a person using a walker. The average wheelchair occupies $7\frac{1}{2}$ square feet of space, compared to $1\frac{1}{2}$ square feet by a person standing on both feet. The chair user needs a 5' turning radius for complete wheelchair maneuverability. If the bath to be remodeled is small, consider borrowing space from an adjacent room or closet.

If doorways can be modified, the ideal is a **36" wide door** which accommodates a wheelchair or walker, instead of the standard 30" door; couple the wider door with a 48" wide hallway. Other ways to expand space include a **space-saving pocket door** that slides into a pocket in the wall. A **special hinge** that allows the door to swing open farther than the standard hinge will more easily accommodate those who use supports for walking. Another choice is a bathroom **door that swings outward** so it does not take up space in the bathroom.

If carpeting is used in the bath or an adjacent area, select a **durable low-pile carpet** which makes wheelchair and walker maneuvering easy.

ACCESSIBLE TUB/SHOWER

The bathtub or whirlpool should have a **seat,** sometimes known as a **transfer seat,** which allows the user to sit on the tub edge or platform, swing the legs over the edge, and slide onto the seat. Many seats are removable or fold out of the way when not needed. Molded fiberglass or acrylic combination tub/shower units also come with built-in seats or a seat that can be removed.

The shower should have **no curb or rim,** which allows complete access for wheelchair users. **Shower doors** for the curbless shower are available that provide seals at the side and floor; an extra-long shower curtain may also be used. For safety, the **shower door must open outward** so it can be opened in case a person falls in the shower. A

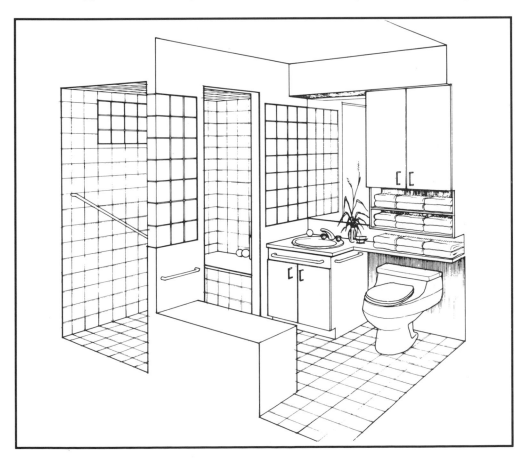

This compact bath for one person, about 7' X 8', has room for all the amenities, including a large shower with seat, dressing seat outside of the shower, lowboy toilet, and plenty of storage. The user will find a grab bar at every turn.

shower seat is just as necessary as a tub seat for safety and comfort; fold-up varieties as well as stools are available.

All shower and tub controls should be easy to operate; use a **single-lever handle**, which operates hot and cold water from one control, because it does not require grasping and twisting. For shower fittings, a **hand-held shower** accommodates family members of all sizes, and enables showering while seated. The **showerhead on a sliding bar** is another way to provide customized showerhead height for everyone. **Dual water controls** in a tub/shower allow the user to control the water while standing or sitting.

Offset tub controls (controls that are set near the outside of the tub) are easier to reach and require

somewhat less bending than those set at one end of the tub. Another control convenience is a **hand-held shower** on a flexible hose that turns a tub into a "shower" without the need for standing; the hand-held shower also simplifies hair washing and cleaning the tub.

For safety, **tub and shower valves that limit water temperatures** to safe levels to avoid scalding and also **regulate water pressure** are a must for safety. **Grab bars** are needed to facilitate entering and exiting the tub/shower and aid in changing from a seated to a standing position. (See Chapter 7, "Staying Safe," for planning grab bar location.) During remodeling, if the tub and shower walls are reinforced with blocking 32" to 38" off the floor, then grab bars can be added, adjusted, or removed

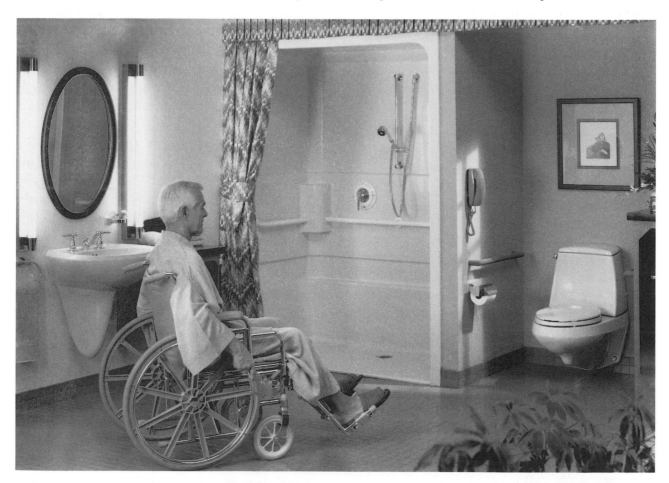

The roll-in shower is the centerpiece of this accessible bath. Measuring 36³/4" X 64³/4", the acrylic shower stall with built-in grab bars and adjustable showerhead has a ¹/2" threshold to make it wheelchair accessible. The wall-hung sink and toilet can be installed at the height most convenient for the user. Tubular lighting at the mirror provides brighter light than incandescent bulbs.

Motion Sensor Lighting

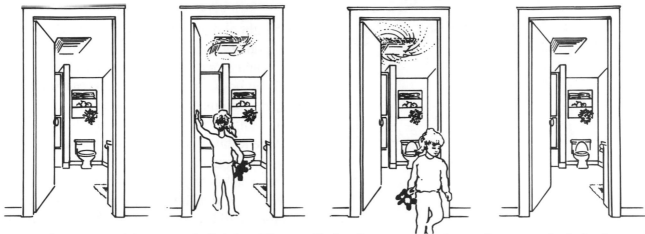

Stay safe at night with automatic lighting. The ventilating fan senses motion and turns on both the fan and the light when a person enters the bathroom. It keeps running until motion ends when the person leaves the room.

at any time. Textured grab bars make gripping safer yet.

Wheelchair Concerns

The wheelchair seat is about $19\frac{1}{2}$" high, but the standard bathtub height is 14" to 16". If the tub is raised to $19\frac{1}{2}$" and a seat or platform at the back of the tub is added, access will be simplified. The tub ledge should be flat, not curved, for security as the user transfers to the bathtub seat. The raised height is also easier on the back of the person who provides bathing assistance. A new tub designed with a door in its side and two interior seats is helpful for those with limited mobility. (See photos in this chapter.)

For a stall shower, the ideal is a **curbless unit** that is large enough to roll into. The NKBA recommends a square shower **60" X 60"**; a minimum is 48" X 48". The wheelchair user then transfers to a **built-in or movable shower seat.** Custom showers can be built in any size desired with ceramic tile, laminate panels, or solid-surface material.

ACCESSIBLE SINK & CABINET

Vanity cabinets were borrowed from the kitchen and for a long time used the kitchen height of 30" to 32 inches. But ergonomic studies of people using a sink

mounted in a vanity cabinet showed that less bending would be required if the vanity cabinet were elevated to 34" to 36 inches. These **"back saver" vanities** are now manufactured.

Pedestal sinks are also available in variable heights and are sold in suites, or sets, with a standard height model and a back saver model. **Wall-hung sinks** also have some flexibility in location. **Automated sinks** can be lowered or elevated to meet special needs. For youngsters, **built-in step-stools** are available with nonslip surfaces for reaching the vanity sink and mirror.

As in the shower and tub, the faucet should be operated by a **single-lever control,** and a **temperature-limiting valve** is a must for safety. Faucet controls may be mounted on the side rather than at the back of the sink to enhance their accessibility.

Stock cabinet lines usually supply a **grooming table** lower in height than a counter, which is a comfortable sit-down place for applying makeup, hair styling, etc. It is essentially a desk, with a set of drawers or a small cabinet on one side and an open space underneath the table or countertop for seating. The grooming counter may be located next to the vanity cabinet or in its own area, with one side braced against the wall. (See Chapter 13, "Bath-

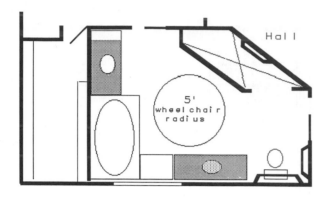

room Storage," for details on cabinet sizes, heights, accessories, and planning guidelines.)

Wheelchair Concerns

The **height of the sink** and the leg-room area under it are primary concerns for wheelchair users. The sink should be designed so the wheelchair can roll under the bowl. If a standard adult wheelchair is used, the recommended area under the sink is 29" to 30" high, 31" wide, and 12" deep.

A **pedestal sink** offers less than ideal accessibility, but it is an improvement over a sink mounted in a cabinet, which has no area underneath for the wheelchair. A **wall-hung sink** with a curved cover or shroud to hide the plumbing and protect the user from hot water pipe burns, is more accessible. Select

This bathroom designed for a wheelchair user and a family member mixes traditional cabinetry with an angled shower of contemporary glass block and ceramic tile. A roll-in shower has no curb and is deep enough so that a shower curtain is not needed. The shower includes water controls and niches for toiletries located at two heights to accommodate both people using the shower.

a wall-hung sink with a **rear drain;** the design of the bowl allows more leg room under the fixture.

Other alternatives include installing a **sink with two legs** wide enough apart to admit a wheelchair. Another option is to install a **sink mounted in a counter** no higher than 32", and no wider than needed to accommodate the sink, with an open space beneath for wheelchair access.

A **mirror** should be mounted so the bottom edge is no higher than 36" from the floor. The **medicine cabinet** may be mounted next to, rather than over, the sink. **Adjustable shelves** are desirable as are pull-out shelves and any accessory that re-

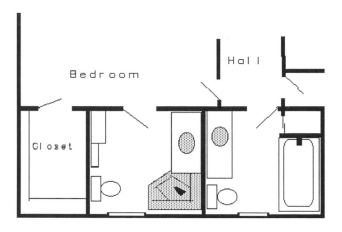

From the pocket entry door, a vanity lowered to wheelchair height with a roll-under sink is accessible; built-in hair dryer and drawers offer convenient storage. Next to the platform tub is a transfer seat. Between the vanity, tub, and shower is enough floor space for a 5′ turning radius, which is above the recommended minimum for a wheelchair.

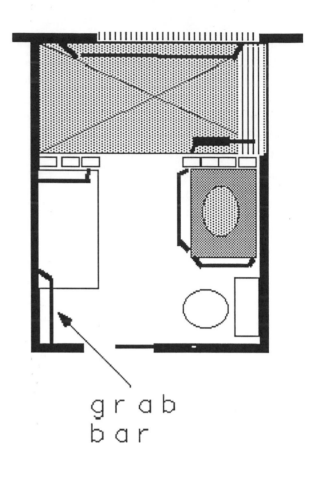

grab
bar

A small bath for a physically challenged child was designed without compromising aesthetics. The 3' X 6' shower with an 18" wide seat was made by removing two adjacent closets. A pocket door replaces the original hinged door, which conserves space inside the bath. Safety features include five grab bars, slip-resistant flooring, and temperature-regulating water controls at the sink and shower to prevent burns.

duces reaching. **Soap dishes and toothbrush holders** should be mounted at a maximum of 42" above the floor.

ACCESSIBLE TOILET

There must be enough wall area **behind the toilet, at the sides,** and **in front for knee clearance** and **walkway** allowance for the area to be comfortable to use. The elongated seat has proven to be somewhat more comfortable than the standard round seat; a contoured rather than a flat seat is preferred.

For floor-mounted toilets, a **removable raised seat** can be added to the toilet seat to raise the toilet height for those with limited mobility. (See Chapter 12, "Fixtures: Sinks and Toilets," for details on toilet space requirements and styles.)

Wheelchair Concerns

The **high-rise toilet,** with the seat 18" high, is elevated 3" above the standard toilet for those with mobility limitations. (And these high-rise toilets are available in both water-saving and low-flush models.) **Grab bars** are recommended at the toilet; supports attached to the toilet are also available.

The toilet may also be **raised on a platform** to match wheelchair seat height, making transfer to the toilet easier. **Wall-hung toilets** are another possibility because there is no base to interfere with a wheelchair.

MORE IDEAS

Small details like cabinet hardware and light switches in the accessible bath tend to have a large impact on convenience and comfort. As mentioned above, cabinet hardware must be easy to grasp for those with dexterity limitations; **bar or loop cabinet pulls** with 1" of clearance from the mounting surface are preferred.

Lighting operated by touch pad controls or controls that can be activated with the fingertips or base of hand are more accessible than conventional switches. Locate switches and electrical outlets no more than 48" from the floor, and preferably 24" to 36" high, depending on the individual's reach.

At the vanity, consider installing a **lighted makeup mirror** for the vision-impaired or a **medicine cabinet with three-way viewing** in which the cabinet doors can be pulled forward. Other options include mounting the mirror away from the wall, closer to the user, or using an **adjustable swing-arm mirror.**

The **threshold** into the bathroom should be smooth. Do not plan **changes in elevation** within the bath because they create a barrier, and falls may occur when stepping from one level to another. If the area is elevated, use a ramp.

Having a bench for the elderly to rest on after having a bath or shower makes good sense. The elderly are often drained of energy after bathing, and a bench is a safe place to dry themselves. From this sitting position they can safely bend to dry legs and feet. Enlarging the bathroom to include a bench for the elderly is a good idea. (See Appendix B for accessible bath resources.)

WORTH REPEATING

1. Light colors on walls, floors, cabinets, and cabinet interiors make it easier and safer to see and move around in the bathroom, especially for the elderly and those with impaired vision.

2. Wheelchair users require expanded space, such as a 5′ turning radius and 36" wide door or pocket door.

3. An accessible bath should have a transfer seat, offset faucet (mounted on tub side rather than end), grab bars, and a nonslip base; a tub raised to 19½" aids transfer from a wheelchair.

4. An accessible shower should have no curb or rim, a shower seat, and a showerhead that adjusts to different heights on a bar, or a hand-held showerhead; for the wheelchair user, a shower 60" X 60" is desirable, 48" X 48" is a minimum.

5. An accessible sink should be high enough to minimize bending, such as the back saver vanity (34" to 36" high) or a tall pedestal sink; a faucet should have single-level or loop handle; wheelchair users need a wall-hung sink or vanity top with leg space beneath (30" X 31" X 12").

6. An accessible vanity should have a grooming table lower in height than a standard vanity, with a seat; cabinets should have white interiors and simple drawer pulls; a lighted makeup mirror helps the vision impaired.

7. An accessible toilet has a comfortable clearance, side-to-side and in front, for knees and a walkway; the elongated seat is comfortable for most people; wheelchair users and those with limited mobility may use a high-rise toilet, with a seat about 18" high, which is 3" higher than a standard toilet seat.

Part Three

ISSUES FOR THE '90s: SAFETY AND CONSERVATION

□ SAFE WATER TEMPERATURES □
□ CHILD SAFETY □ LOW-FLOW SHOWERHEADS □
□ WATER-SAVING TOILETS □

7

Staying Safe

Two hundred thousand bathroom accidents occur each year. Most are preventable. Here's how to reduce bathroom hazards.

Bathrooms are danger zones. About 25 percent of all home accidents occur in the bathroom. The biggest dangers are slippery surfaces and scalding water. Children and adults alike are the unfortunate victims of injuries from falls and burns.

These hazards are the most common cause of bathroom injuries each year:

■ Lack of grab bars at the tub/shower

■ Tub/shower doors made from nonsafety glass that shatters on impact

■ Tub/shower water controls located under the stream of water, which make adjusting water temperature and volume difficult

■ Electrical receptacles and switches located near water and not protected with a ground fault circuit interrupter (GFCI), increasing the risk of shock

■ Protruding objects, such as a storage cabinet located above the toilet

Children are especially vulnerable to burns from scalding water. Every year, almost 5,000 youngsters — most under the age of five — are scalded in the bathtub, reports the National SAFE KIDS Campaign, an educational drive to reduce preventable injury to children.

For the family with several generations living under one roof, it is vital to be aware that older adults are susceptible to bathroom injury too. According to the National Center of Health Statistics, more than half of the sixty-five and older age group have physical problems such as impaired vision, arthritis, chronic back problems, diminished strength, or limited movement that increase the risk of accidents. Every day in the U.S. nearly 500 people turn sixty-five, making bathroom safety an important issue, not only for the multigenerational family, but also for families who have frequent visits by older adults. In fact, 22 percent of all bathroom injuries occur in the sixty-five and over age group.

In spite of these gloomy statistics, bathroom hazards can be minimized and thousands of injuries prevented each year. New products and design standards can transform the bathroom from a danger zone into a safety zone.

PREVENTING BURNS

Did you ever take a warm, comforting shower when, all of a sudden, the water turned red-hot or freezing cold? Or have you watched as an ample stream of water filling the tub dropped to a trickle?

SAFE KIDS
AND BURNS

The National SAFE KIDS Campaign, founded in 1988, is conducting an aggressive effort to educate parents and caregivers about the dangers to children from bathtub scalding.

SAFE KIDS coalitions are working to amend plumbing codes. The amended codes will require devices that control water temperatures for bathing and showering in newly constructed homes. Another goal is to increase the installation of temperature-control devices in bathrooms in existing homes and multifamily dwellings.

SAFE KIDS research shows that bathtub scalds happen when:

■ Children are left unattended in the tub and the child turns on the hot water
■ Children are placed in water that is too hot
■ A child is in the tub and another child turns on the hot water
■ A child falls into a tub of hot water

Hot water can be particularly harmful to children. Children's skin is thinner than adults' skin. In fact, SAFE KIDS has found that children will sustain more severe burns, at lower temperatures, and in less time than adults.

A child exposed to water over 140 degrees for just three seconds can receive a third degree burn — a burn which destroys all skin layers — requiring hospitalization and skin grafts. An adult would have to be exposed to the same temperature for up to five seconds to sustain the same burn.

And it doesn't take 140-degree water to cause burns; water at lower temperatures is dangerous for children too (see adjacent illustration). And when is hot water safe? At 110 degrees. Set the water heater at that level.

A final burn statistic: Of the 5,000 children seen at hospital emergency clinics each year for burns from scalding water, about 17 percent are admitted for burn treatment. The average length of stay in a hospital for a tap scald is seventeen days.

To contact the National SAFE KIDS Campaign refer to Appendix A.

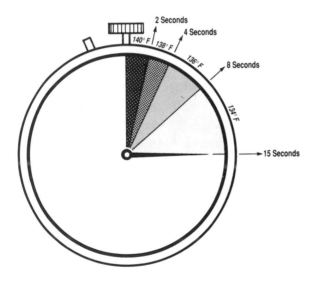

A stopwatch illustrates the amount of time it takes a child to sustain a life-threatening burn when immersed in a tub with water temperatures from 134 to 140 degrees F.

These unwelcome changes in water temperature and pressure are not unusual in home plumbing systems. They result from *pressure changes*, such as flushing a toilet elsewhere in the home.

Living with such an imbalanced system is not only uncomfortable and inconvenient, it is also dangerous because these fluctuations can cause accidents.

Antiscald Faucets

Faucets that balance temperature and pressure are now available for tubs, showers, and sinks. They are sometimes called "antiscald" or "scald-guard" faucets or controls. With one of these burn-preventing controls, it is not necessary to constantly adjust the hot and cold water taps to get the right temperature mix.

These temperature safety controls work in three important ways.

■ *A pressure-balance valve* controls the hot and cold water pressure at the tub, shower, or sink and provides consistent water temperature — usually within two degrees — regardless of changes in water pressure in the home plumbing system.

■ *A temperature-limiting device* allows a homeowner to select water temperatures within a safe range and also puts a cap on the maximum safe-temperature setting. A 110 degree maximum is recommended by the NKBA. In comparison, hot water heaters are often set at 140 degrees, or higher for washing dishes and clothing. This is not necessary, especially with newer dishwashers that heat the water.

■ A *flow-restrictor* with variable settings allows the homeowner to decrease water flow and conserve water.

Not all antiscald systems will have all three features. But to be effective in preventing burns from scalding water, the tub/shower control must accurately regulate temperatures with either a pressure-balance system or a temperature-limiting control.

An antiscald fixture with a single-lever control is recommended for children as well as older adults. However, be aware that the water pressure may be diminished with this type of fixture. This simple control is relatively easy for a child to understand; it is simpler for both children and the elderly to operate than faucet controls that require grasping and twisting.

Codes and Burn Safety

Plumbing equipment manufacturers, bathroom designers, and code boards have been moving toward an endorsement of antiscald safety controls for combatting the problem of bathroom burns. A few years ago, commercial-building plumbing codes started to require the installation of antiscald devices in multifamily dwellings, hotels, health clubs, and recreational facilities.

Next plumbing codes requiring burn-preventing systems for the residential market were passed. Codes in many areas now require pressure-balanced or thermostatically controlled shower valves with a maximum hot water temperature of 120 degrees. In these regions, the plumbing code change affected new construction of all single-family dwellings, beginning in 1992.

Codes regulating antiscald devices are changing. Ask the designer and builder about local plumbing code requirements. Check with a plumbing contractor about diminished water pressure with these products. Or call the building inspector's office and ask about codes yourself. Better yet — even if these codes have not yet gone into effect, choose to install these safety devices. Even better, and less expensive, turn down the temperature at the hot water heater to 110 degrees.

PREVENTING FALLS

After scalding, falls on slippery bathroom surfaces are the second major cause of accidents. The most important ways to prevent injuries from falling are:

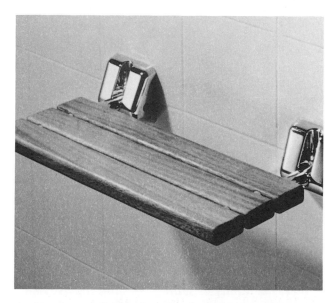

A shower seat helps the elderly shower safely, and is handy for everyone when washing lower legs. When not in use, the seat tilts up out of the way.

Preventing Burns

A single-lever faucet protects against burns from hot water by means of a temperature indicator under the faucet dome.

To set a safe water temperature on this single-lever faucet, use a screwdriver to adjust the temperature indicator to any one of seven settings.

Protect the family by setting the shower valve to a safe temperature. A pressure-balancing unit also protects against temperature shock from sudden pressure changes in hot and cold water.

■ *Install grab bars with a nonslip, textured surface in tub and shower areas;* anchor grab bars to wall studs or to blocking between studs

■ *Select a bathtub with a nonslip interior;* choose a model with a nearly flat bottom surface; curved surfaces inside the tub make it difficult to get a foothold

■ *Install a shower with a nonslip floor*

■ *If tile is selected for the floor covering, consider a nonskid variety*

■ *Eliminate bath rugs in front of the tub and shower,* even if rugs have nonskid backing; substitute nonslip rubber mats

■ *If the tub will be set into a platform, ask for a rim wide enough for a bather to sit on;* from that point, the bather swings the legs into the tub, and this method of entering a platform tub reduces falls

Preventing Falls

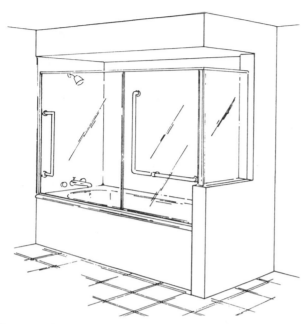

Prevent falls in slippery tubs with a vertical grab bar for entering and exiting and a grab bar on the tub wall for safety when sitting or standing.

A safe whirlpool has only one broad step and a deck wide enough for the bather to sit and swing legs into tub. Note the grab bar opposite the faucet.

Grab Bars

Grab bars, also known as handrails or grab rails, are one key to preventing falls. The purpose of the rail is to help the bather get in and out of the tub or shower safely and to change from a seated to a standing position when bathing or showering.

Towel bars are *not* a substitute for handrails. They are not properly anchored to bear the weight of an adult. A grab rail, on the other hand, is required by the National Accessibility Code to bear a 300-pound load. Anchoring the grab bar to wall studs and/or blocking (reinforcing wood) between studs provides the required support.

Textured grab bars are now available. These bars allow a firmer grip than those with a smooth surface. And they are also available in colors to coordinate with the bathroom decor.

The NKBA offers these guidelines for grab bars and their placement:

■ *Bathtub grab rail* — a horizontal bar on the long wall to help a bather change position from standing to sitting or an angled or vertical bar at the entry to help the bather enter and exit the tub

■ *Shower grab rail* — depending on shower design, a continuous handrail around the interior may be used, or several handrails, one at the entry, one near the shower valves, and an angled handrail by the shower seat

■ *Platform tub/whirlpool* — handrail placed so there is adequate room to enter and exit the tub; some whirlpools have grab bars built inside the tub for aid in standing and sitting

SAFETY AROUND THE BATH

No matter what type of remodeling project is being considered, there are proven ways to make the bathroom safe for the family. Installing antiscald water controls can, and should, be a part of every new bathroom project, from the face lift to the major remodeling. So should single-lever faucet controls and lighting fixtures that brighten the bathroom for low-vision seniors. If windows or tub/shower doors

Safe Bath Project

This double vanity has two sinks, fitted with antiscald faucets. Rounded edges on the solid-surface countertop are safer than corners.

The child-safe nautical bath features antiscald faucets, a soft tub, and grab bars. And there's room for two in the separate tub and shower.

A showerhead slides on a bar to adjust for youngsters and teens. An antiscald pressure-balanced shower valve keeps water temperatures consistent.

A whimsical rowboat has a flexible foam core that acts like a cushion. The 18" high sides keep toddlers out.

are replaced in a minor remodeling project, they should be replaced with safety glass.

On the other hand, some safety precautions, such as installing a bathtub with a nonslip surface, may make sense only during major remodeling. And installing grab bars may require that blocking must be installed before the wall is tiled, for example.

Safety factors are considered in the remaining sections—tubs and showers, cabinets and counters, windows and doors, and electricity.

Tub and Shower

Sunken tubs are attractive, but they do pose a danger because they tend to be difficult to enter and exit. What's more, a guest or child might fall into the tub. It's probably safer to *find a different design*.

BATHROOM SAFETY
CHECKLIST

TUB AND SHOWER

❑ Use pressure-balanced and/or temperature-limiting valves

❑ Limit water temperatures to 110 degrees at the water heater

❑ Position the valve out of water stream

❑ Install grab bars; textured bars preferred

❑ Select nonslip tub and shower base

❑ Install safety glass (shatterproof)

❑ Install doors hinged out

❑ Include shower seat

CABINETS AND COUNTERS

❑ Check door swings

❑ Round counter edges and corners

❑ Maintain an 8" maximum depth for cabinets over toilet

WINDOWS AND DOORS

❑ Place operable windows out of reach for children, within reach for adults

❑ Doors should swing out

FLOORING

❑ Install slip-resistant flooring

❑ Remove carpets or throw rugs

❑ Avoid changes in floor elevation

ELECTRICAL

❑ Install GFCI circuitry

❑ Place timers and switches as far away from water as possible

❑ Install vapor-proof lighting fixture over shower

❑ For supplemental heating, ceiling heaters are preferred

CHILD SAFETY

❑ Position grab bars at proper height

❑ Install easy-to-operate, scald-preventing faucet controls at tub, shower, and sink

❑ Install cabinet locks

❑ Use privacy locks that can be opened from outside the bathroom

❑ Consider installing a night light, intercom

Platform tubs should be designed with no more than one wide step leading to the platform. The NKBA recommends that *a safe step should be about 10" wide* with a riser no higher than about 7 inches. A handrail must be installed for safety.

Shower stalls should be long enough so a person can stand outside the stream of water to adjust the water valve. The stall should be wide enough to allow bending over comfortably to wash the lower legs and feet, or *a shower seat may be installed*, advises the NKBA. The seat should be placed so the water trajectory will not hit the person on the shower seat.

Glass tub/shower enclosures must be made of *safety glass* to prevent shattering. *The enclosure door should swing out* and away from the flow of the water to allow for a safe exit. In the event that a person falls against the door, someone from the outside will be able to reach the victim quickly. Friction or magnetic latches are suggested for use on these doors; *never use a lock on a shower door*.

Cabinets and Counters

Placement of cabinets should be carefully considered so cabinet doors do not swing into narrow walkways. Select cabinetry with door knobs and drawer pulls that cannot catch on clothing; cabinets with concealed magnetic catches or self-closing hinges will eliminate protruding knobs. Ask for drawers with a device that prevents them from being pulled out completely.

Avoid sharp corners on counters; curved edges and radius corners are preferred.

Cabinets over the toilet should be no more than 8" deep, recommends the NKBA. *Cabinets for medicine storage and cleaning supplies* should be locked and/or out of reach of children. *Tamper-resistant magnetic locks* are very effective in preventing children from opening cabinets in which harmful substances are stored.

Windows and Doors

Place operable windows out of the reach of children, but keep them within the reach of adults. Entry *doors should swing out*.

In a bath used by two or more people, no door should interfere with another person's use of the sink or toilet. *Bifold or pocket doors* can eliminate disruptions inside the bath. Make sure that *privacy latches on the entry door can be opened from the outside*, even if the lock is engaged.

Electrical Safety

All electrical circuits must be connected to GFCI (ground fault circuit interrupter) outlets. These safety outlets automatically cut power to any circuit that experiences even a small current flow to ground. For example, a faulty appliance or worn electrical cord plugged into the GFCI and then touched by the user who provides a path to ground may cause a variation in the current flow to ground. The GFCI shuts off the power in a fraction of a second. This protects the user from one type of electrical shock.

Outlets at the vanity should be installed as far away from the water source as possible to avoid the danger of electrical shock should the appliance come in contact with water; check local code for minimum allowances. All switches and timers should be located so they are not easily accessible from the inside of the tub unless nonelectrical controls are employed; switches and timers for the shower should be located at least 3′ from the shower.

The bathroom should have adequate general lighting as well as task lighting and night lighting. A lighting fixture over the shower must be a vapor-proof unit specifically designed for electrical safety in a wet area.

If supplemental heating is needed, select a permanently-installed ceiling or baseboard heater. Avoid portable heaters and wall heaters in the bathroom.

When children are in the home, consider using *timer switches* on ventilating fans and other controls, which allow operating times to be preset by an adult.

8

Using Water Wisely

Two-thirds of your water is used in the bathroom. Cut water bills — and conserve this valuable resource — with water-saving showerheads and toilets.

Conserving water makes sense. In the home, wise water use nets two kinds of savings: lower water bills and reduced water-heating costs. For the environment, water-saving strategies diminish the demand on sewage treatment facilities and stretch water resources in dry and drought-stricken areas.

Starting a home conservation program with water-saving habits in the bathroom will net substantial savings. Here's why: Bathing and showering account for 30 percent of home water consumption; another 35 percent is used for toilet flushing. In fact, flushing the toilet represents the *largest single use of water* in the home each day.

Here's another look at bathroom water consumption. The average household uses 160 to 180 gallons of water per day. About two-thirds of the total — or 110 to 120 gallons per day — are used in the bathroom.

Want to cut that figure in half? Select water-saving products for the remodeling project. Topping the list of water-smart fixtures are *low-flow showerheads* and *low-flush toilets*.

Consider the benefit of the low-flow showerhead. Showering with a conventional showerhead takes 5 to 10 gallons per minute (gpm); however, a low-flow showerhead reduces that rate to 2.5 to 3.0 gpm. Inexpensive, efficient models are available for as little as $10.

The benefit of the water-miser toilet is just as impressive. Low-flush models require only 1.6 (or less) gallons per flush (gpf), compared to 3.5 gpf for the "water-saver" toilet, or a whopping 5 gpf for a conventional toilet. And low-flush toilets cost no more to install than a conventional model.

These efficient bathroom products work so well that water-poor communities in California, Arizona, Florida, and densely-populated urban communities have mandated low-flush toilets for housing developments and/or new residential construction. More states and communities are jumping on the water-saving bandwagon each year as costs for fresh water and sewage treatment rise. In fact, some municipalities have mandated fines for noncompliance.

For a country that flushes away 4.8 billion gallons of water per day, according to the U.S. Department of Housing and Urban Development, the change to low-flow toilets will result in billions of gallons of precious water saved. It's possible to pare down the water and water-heating bills even more with additional water-wise tactics: *efficient water heating* and *water-thrifty habits.*

LOW-FLUSH TOILETS

So how much water is being used in your home each time the toilet is flushed? The answer depends on the age of the home and whether the original bathroom equipment is in place. Prior to the 1950s, toilets used as much as 7 gpf. By 1950, that figure was reduced to 5 gallons. Due to increasing awareness of environmental concerns, another improvement was made in the 1970s with the introduction of the 3.5 gpf toilet. Today the newest model, the 1.6 gpf toilet, uses only 46 percent of the water used by the 3.5 gpf toilet.

At first glance, and in some cases, even on closer inspection, these low-consumption fixtures look like any other toilet. But there are significant differences in the way low-flush models are engineered to accomplish a sanitary flush on only 1.6 gallons of water.

To understand how the water-saving toilet works, it is helpful to look at:

- The flushing mechanism in the *toilet tank*
- The engineering of the *toilet bowl*

Low-Flush Tank Operation

The 1.6 gallon toilet operates with one of two flushing devices enclosed in the toilet tank:

1. Gravity-feed system, the same system found in the 3.5 toilet, which discharges water at the flush valve and refills the tank by means of an inlet valve, or ball cock assembly

2. Pressure-assisted system, which uses air pressure to dispel water from the tank

In the pressure-assisted flush, a valve contains water and air. The air is compressed by the water supply system as the refill water enters the tank. When the toilet is flushed, the compressed air pushes the water out of the tank at a high speed.

Gravity-Feed Bowl Design

Although the gravity-feed system has traditional flushing components in the toilet tank, the bowl has been redesigned to allow the water to move with greater speed so the cleaning action is efficient. Two aspects of the new design are:

1. A toilet bowl with steeper sides

2. An exposed trap, the pipe through which water and waste leave the bowl. (Be aware that the elongated bowl design could affect space planning in very small bathrooms.)

Another change in the low-flush gravity system features holes for water discharge that are drilled all around the toilet rim to efficiently clean the toilet bowl. Conventional models often had outlets in only a few places, and relied on the large volume of water per flush to clean the bowl.

Pressure-Assisted Bowl Design

The pressure-assisted systems vary the most from conventional toilets in the design of the bowl. The new designs are essential to receive water at the high speeds typical of the pressure-assisted system.

Bowls are one of two types:

1. Reverse-trap

2. Siphon jet

The reverse-trap model, the less expensive of the two, has a 2" diameter trap and a $2\frac{1}{2}'$ deep water reservoir. On the other hand, the siphon jet has a larger trap passageway that quiets the flushing action; the interior of the bowl is almost completely covered by water.

DRAWBACKS OF THE 1.6 GPF TOILET

Although these water-miser fixtures offer significant cuts in water costs, some bathroom designers caution homeowners to be prepared for somewhat more noise and more frequent toilet cleaning. With some 1.6 gpf toilets, the surface area of the bowl covered with water is smaller, which usually makes cleaning the bowl tougher. One option is to keep a decorative cleaning brush by the toilet and use it frequently.

In a pressure-assisted system, the noise can be great as the water quickly moves through the system. That noise may disturb other sleepers, especially in a master suite. The noise level may also be unacceptable in a bath that is adjacent to an entertaining area. The solution: Do not place the toilet on a common wall with the bedrooms, and select a quieter model for bathrooms near socializing areas.

LOW-FLOW SHOWERHEADS

Saving water in the shower is simply a matter of *mixing air and water*. A water restrictive device, part of the *aerator* in the showerhead, reduces the water flow from 5 to 10 gpm to between 2.5 and 3.0 gpm.

But the flow can be restricted to such an extent that the volume is not acceptable for showering, especially with some models that reduce the flow to a low 1.7 gpm. Select a 2.5 or 3.0 model with an added pulsating action which makes the water reduction less noticeable.

Another reason to select a model in the 2.5 to 3.0 range is that showerheads delivering below 2 gpm may present a *scald hazard*. In some cases, flushing the toilet while the shower is running sets the stage for scald danger.

Here's what happens: A pressure change in the water supply system occurs when the toilet is flushed. Consequently, in the shower, the cold water is forced back into the cold water supply line and only hot water is available to the shower.

To avoid this hazard, select a showerhead that delivers more than 2 gpm, set the water heater temperature no higher than 110 degrees, and install a temperature-limiting and pressure-balance shower valve. (See Chapter 7, "Staying Safe.")

HEATING WATER EFFICIENTLY

If the water heater in the home is fifteen years or older, it may be time to consider a replacement. The old water heater may not be heating water to the set temperature. For example, think of the times you have waited at the sink, tap running, for hot water, only to receive a tepid flow. That inefficient water heater is also wasting the gas or electricity it runs on.

What is the least expensive way to heat water? A three-letter word spells the answer: *Gas*. The gas water heater, in those areas where gas is available, delivers hot water at a lower cost than the electric heater. That's because, unit for unit, electricity carries a higher energy price than gas, in most areas.

Another important difference between gas and electric heaters is the *recovery rate*, or the time needed to bring cold water up to the temperature set on the heater dial. Electric water heater recovery rates are *slower* than gas heaters. Therefore, a larger tank is necessary for an electric model than a gas water heater; 52 gallons for the former, 40 gallons for the latter.

Water Heaters and Energy Labeling

The familiar Energy Guide labels found on household appliances are also found on water heaters. However, appliances are given an Energy Efficiency Rating (EER); water heaters, whether they are gas or electric, are described with an *Energy Factor* (EF).

The EF is based on the cost of providing 64.3 gallons of hot water per day. The higher the EF, the greater the efficiency of the water heater.

However, an efficient EF for gas is different from an efficient EF for electricity. A good gas rating is 0.64. On the other hand, a respectable EF for an electric heater is 0.95. The different ratings point to the fact that a gas heater always loses some of its heat up the flue, whereas the heat of the electric coils in the electric water heater is transferred to the water.

It is difficult to compare the efficiencies of electric and gas water heaters. However, it is possible to compare the rating of one gas heater to another gas heater or to evaluate the ratings of electric water heaters. Estimates of operating costs based on various energy costs, shown on the Energy Guide label, may assist homeowners in selecting an efficient water heater.

ENHANCING WATER HEATER EFFICIENCY

There are three ways to cut the cost of producing hot water, even with an efficient water heater:

- **Insulate tank and hot water pipes**
- **Install a timer**
- **Select off-peak electric rates**

Even though water heaters have a system of interior insulation, an **exterior insulating blanket**, 2" thick, should be added. This insulation cuts standby losses — the reduction in temperature when hot water is held in the tank, standing by for use.

The hot water pipes also should be covered with flexible insulation to maintain the temperature of hot water in the pipes. Many excellent energy books are available with details on installing water heater blankets and insulating hot water pipes.

The second strategy to reduce water heating costs is to **install a water heater timer**. Just like the electronic timers for furnaces, the timer turns off the water heater during periods of off-peak use and starts it again when demand is high. For example, the timer may be set to turn the heater off overnight, then turn it back on early in the morning, heating the water in time for the morning rush of showering, bathing, and grooming.

A third option to cut water heating costs is to **select off-peak service** for gas or electricity rates from the local utility. A homeowner who selects this service plans the majority of household water use during off-peak hours, or during the hours when the demand for water is typically low. These are usually late evening hours. Thus, a homeowner may use the whirlpool during these off-peak periods. However, **all** utility use must be planned for off-peak hours, which may not meet family needs or schedules. If off-peak service is selected, use a timer to control the water heater during periods of high water demand.

Evaluate your family's water needs and water use patterns carefully before signing up for such a service. The local utility will often provide guidelines for figuring the potential savings for the homeowner on this type of plan.

HIGH-DEMAND FIXTURES

Not all bathroom fixtures use water as efficiently as the low-flush toilet or the low-flow showerhead. For example, the whirlpool, a wonderful bathroom addition for relaxation and health, requires a hefty 50 to 120 gallons of water. Jet spray showers, with multiple showerheads, require much more water than the 3.0 gpm produced by the low-flow showerhead.

Introducing these fixtures to the bathroom de-sign requires an examination of water heating capacity. If two heaters are necessary, hot water costs will, of course, rise. However, the NKBA recommends several tactics for keeping heated water use moderate:

■ Consider a **quick-recovery water heater**, which is designed to reheat a tank of water faster than a regular heater, for use with high-demand fixtures

■ Adjust use patterns so only one water heater is needed

■ Size the water heater to provide enough hot water to fill two-thirds of the capacity of a whirlpool; the balance is cold water

But if household water needs are only marginally met and a whirlpool is selected for the remodeling project, the NKBA recommends:

■ Increasing the size of the heater

■ Installing two water heaters side by side

■ Installing a hot water heater just for the whirlpool (unless a model with a built-in heater is selected)

■ Installing an in-line heater, which maintains the water temperature in the tub, eliminating the need for hot water refills

POINT-OF-USE HEATERS

Another option in heating water is the tankless, or point-of-use, water heater. This product heats water on the spot by means of a gas burner or an electric element. The water is heated as long as the demand continues.

The purpose of the tankless water heater is to completely eliminate standby losses, because the water is heated only when it is needed and where it is needed.

However, the largest tankless heater provides about 3 gpm, which is enough for a low-flow showerhead, but not enough for more demanding uses. The point-of-use heater may be a good choice for a vacation home or in a half-bathroom, remote from plumbing supply lines.

The hazard of scalding also is a consideration with the tankless heater. The heater is regulated to raise the water a set number of degrees. However, the incoming water temperature may not be constant. If the incoming water is warm, and the tankless heater automatically raises the temperature, scalding could result. Therefore, it is important to select a thermostatically controlled tankless heater to avoid the danger of scalding.

MORE WAYS TO SAVE WATER

Cut water bills even further with efficient use of water in the home. Cultivate these four important water-saving habits:

1. Install flow restrictors on faucets. Consumption is reduced dramatically, from 1 to 2 gpm.

2. Repair leaky faucets and toilets. A dripping faucet can waste from 15 to 20 gallons of water per day. One drop per second from a leaky hot water faucet can add up to more than 3,000 gallons of wasted hot water a year, according to the American Gas Association. Many toilets "silently" leak, unbeknown to the consumer. Do the trick of putting food coloring in the bowl. See if the tank becomes colored.

3. Take showers rather than baths. It takes about 30 gallons of water to fill the average tub. A shower, with a flow of 3 gallons of water per minute, uses 15 gallons in five minutes. Assuming you use half hot and half cold water for bathing, you would save about 5 gallons of hot water every time a

WATER USE HABITS

FIXTURE	TYPICAL USE	WATER-SAVING USE
Shower	20-40 gallons (5 gpm)	2-3 gpm, five minute shower with low-flow showerhead
Tub Bath	20 gallons (when full, adult user displaces about 15 gallons)	12-15 gallons (half full or less)
Sink		
Brushing teeth	2 gallons (tap running)	1 pint (wet brush, turn off water, rinse briefly)
Washing hands/face	2 gallons (tap running)	1 gallon (fill sink, rinse briefly)
Shaving	3-5 gallons (tap running)	1 gallon (fill sink, rinse briefly)
Toilet flush	5-7 gallons	3.0 gallons (water-saver toilet)
		1.6 gallons or less (low-flush toilet)

shower is substituted for a bath, according to the Water Works Association. And substituting one shower for one bath each day nets an annual savings of 2,000 gallons of hot water. To time a shower, install a battery-operated, waterproof timer, available at many home center stores.

However, if a flow-restrictor is *not* in use, the shower produces from 5 to 10 gallons per minute. And if the shower is longer than five minutes, the gallons add up quickly. In this case, a half-full bathtub (15 gallons) would require less water than a shower.

4. Do not run water continuously when shaving, washing, or brushing teeth. Up to 5 gallons of water per minute go straight down the drain when faucets are left running. Turn on the faucet only when needed, and run the water at a moderate volume.

WORTH REPEATING

WATER-SAVERS' CHECKLIST:

Toilet
- Select a low-flush toilet
- Do not use the toilet for flushing waste paper

Showerhead
- Install a low-flow showerhead
- Install a timer in the shower
- Take showers, using a low-flow showerhead, instead of taking baths

Faucet
- Install flow restrictors on faucets
- Repair leaky faucets and toilets immediately
- Never let the water run continuously when washing, shaving, or brushing teeth

Water Heater
- If installing a new water heater, check the Energy Guide label
- Compare energy costs of electric and gas hot water heaters
- Insulate the water heater
- Insulate hot water pipes
- Lower water heater temperature to 110 degrees
- Add a timer to turn off water heater when not needed
- Consider reduced time-of-day electric rates

Part Four

THE CHANGE BEGINS

□ FINAL PLAN □ FINANCING □ CONTRACTS □
□ CONSTRUCTION PROCESS □ CODES □
□ HANDLING PROBLEMS □

9

Understanding Paperwork: From Bids to Loans

Increase your level of knowledge concerning construction specifications, bids, contracts, and financing agreements.

It has been said that a remodeling project has three parts: design, installation, and *paperwork*. There is some truth to that statement. A room make-over does produce many important documents, from the design contract to building permits.

But sorting out the important papers doesn't have to be tough. In actuality, the flow of documents needed to get construction underway follows a logical process. Here are its basic parts:

■ The designer prepares a detailed *plan*, which contains the information necessary for the *specifications*, a complete listing of fixtures and materials for the remodeling.

■ The *specifications* and *plans* are sent to several contractors, who each draw up a *bid*, which is a detailed quote of labor and material costs for executing the *plan*.

■ The homeowner compares *bids*, selects a contractor, and negotiates a *construction contract*, spelling out the remodeling work in detail.

■ The lender studies the *plan*, *specifications*, and *construction contract* before drawing up a *fi-*

nancing contract with the homeowner.

■ The municipal building department reviews the *plans and specifications* to verify the structural integrity of the project and to check compliance with codes before building permits are issued.

SPECIFICATIONS

Whether the design professional is a contractor, interior designer, a bath design specialist on the staff of a bath dealer, or a designer at a design/build firm, one of the primary services of the designer is to prepare plans and specifications.

Think of plans and specifications as communication tools in the remodeling process. They contain the details that tell the remodeling pros *exactly* what you want. Professionally prepared plans communicate — by means of before and after floor plans, detail drawings, elevations, and electrical drawings — exactly what products and materials will be used and what work will be done. And, equally important, detailed plans and specifications are the basis for comparing contractors' bids.

When the homeowner acts as the designer, he or she submits to the contractor or design/build firm a rough floor plan, along with any fixture and material choices. (The following section, "Writing Specifications," explains how to describe the fixtures and the materials selected.) In this case, the builder is usually responsible for drawing the final plans and writing the specifications list, in consultation with the homeowner.

WRITING SPECIFICATIONS

The look of specifications sheets will vary from designer to designer, but most will contain the following elements:

1. Listing of products by manufacturer, type of product, model number, size, quantity, color, plus any other descriptive information. For example, a sink may be specified "American Standard Elegance bowl, #431, rose" rather than "American Standard bowl."

2. Products specified for each area of the job, including fixtures and fittings, cabinetry, plumbing, electrical, flooring, wallcovering, trim, etc. For example, electrical specifications may include all switches, dimmers, ground fault circuit interrupters, tub/shower lighting, recessed lighting, and vanity cabinet lighting. This information is taken from the Electrical Plan.

3. Reference to the actual plans on which the specifications are made. Wording such as: "Specifications per attached plans, prepared by (designer's name and firm)."

4. For each item, indicate whether the bath specialist or homeowner is responsible for supply, installation, and/or hookup. For example, a homeowner who is an antique buff may supply a period pedestal sink for the job. Another example: The designer completing the specifications (spec) list may perform none, or all, of the installation tasks. Or, the designer may hire plumbing and electrical contractors to complete the necessary hookups. (If the design firm will act as the general contractor for the project, a separate installment agreement should be provided and reviewed with the client.)

5. Notation of existing equipment that will be reused, if any.

6. All categories on the spec form must be completed, or a designation such as "not applicable" should be inserted to ensure that no product areas have been overlooked inadvertently.

7. A provision that any materials and equipment not listed will be provided at an additional cost.

THE BIDDING PROCESS

The homeowner needs to obtain bids from contractors. A bid is a *quote* of labor and material costs. The better the specifications list given to all bidders, the better chance each contractor has to prepare a bid that truly reflects installation costs.

The purpose of the bidding process is to select the most qualified contractor who can deliver the project at a reasonable cost. To begin the bidding process, prepare copies of plans and specifications and submit them to the contractors you have selected. (See Chapter 3, "Working with the Pros," for a discussion of choosing a contractor.)

It is advisable to obtain at least three bids for adequate comparison of project costs. And, because it takes a substantial number of hours to complete a construction estimate, allow several weeks for the bidding process to be completed.

It is essential that all contractors bid on the same specifications. This procedure allows a basis to compare the cost estimates.

Comparing Bids

All of the bids will include a cost estimate for labor, materials, and a margin for overhead and profit, which may range from 15 to 25 percent of the total project. But who's the best for your project? Here are some guidelines to help you select the winning bid.

■ **Evaluate the presentation of the bid.** The construction cost estimate should be clear, concise, and detailed as to materials and labor supplied.

■ **Verify that all bidders have quoted prices on the exact materials listed on the specifications sheet.** It is not uncommon for a contractor to offer suggestions on different ways of executing the project, but the actual bid should be made on the specifications and plans submitted.

Making the comparisons involves plenty of detail work, but it's worth the effort if you discover, for example, that one contractor substituted a lower grade of vinyl floorcovering or switched midrange mirror lighting to top-of-the line designer quality fixtures.

■ **The lowest bid may not be the best bid.** Quality of work does not show on the contractor's estimate. Neither does the ability to supervise construction or the experience of the crew.

Evaluating those qualities is best done during an interview with the contractor and an inspection of several recently completed remodeling projects. If the company looks good on paper, passes the tests of professionalism in the showroom, and gets high marks for the quality of work during the project inspection, you've got a winner.

■ **Discuss bids with contractors to understand variations in price.** Sometimes a low bid is made because items have been omitted from the specifications list. On the other hand, a higher price may be worth paying, if materials of a better grade

are used or the work to be completed is more extensive. There should be no question of material grade or the extent of the work bid if the spec sheets and plans are complete and comprehensive. A contractor who is unwilling to discuss quote differences may not be your best bet.

A WORD ABOUT WARRANTIES

As you evaluate the bids, ask each contractor if the firm is enrolled in the Home Owners Warranty Corporation (HOW). The HOW program provides up to ten years of warranty/insurance on the remodeling work provided by its remodeler members.

Under the HOW program, the remodeler provides the homeowner with a limited written warranty for one year against faulty work and materials. An additional provision is offered for a two-year limited warranty against defects in major systems — wiring, plumbing, heating, cooling, and mechanical systems — as well as major structural defects identified in the HOW plan.

In addition to the two-year warranty, the remodeler carries another three years of insurance to cover the cost of repairs to specific major structural

---

SAMPLE SPECIFICATION
SHEET 1

CABINETS: Shop-built cabinets with a white Kortron interior. Birch exterior with a stain to match the existing door and trim. Cabinets to include: 84" high linen cabinet with deep drawer behind door at bottom; vanity bases with three drawer unit on left, tilt-out sink front and sliding shelves to right; vanity unit to finish out at 34" from floor with top and toe space to be 6" high by 6" deep. Cabinet door and drawer style to be as per Wood-Mode square raised panel Hallmark style. Also including cabinet over stool. Round solid brass knobs included.

MEDICINE CABINETS: Three upper cabinets as per plan with white Kortron interiors, European hinges, beveled glass doors with 1" bevel, beveled spacer strips between to allow doors to open, birch overlay ends and bottom trim, birch top trim to match top trim of linen cabinet and cabinet over stool.

COUNTERTOP AND DECK: Vanity countertop will be ½" thick Avonite with built up ogee style front edge made in curved shape with curved outside corners with inlaid brass near front edge. Color to be #210 Almond Parchment. Also included is Avonite tub deck, curved steps both with built up ogee edge and brass inlay near the front edge. There are ½" thick jamb pieces for 4 sides of 2 windows and small triangle at the vanity.

defects on the remodeled portions of the home. An additional three to eight years of structural defect insurance protection is available.

The HOW program also offers a dispute settlement service for remodelers and homeowners if disagreements about the warranty coverage occur. Remember that a contractor offering the HOW program should also be a state licensed contractor.

The homeowner pays to enroll in the HOW program. The premium depends on the size of the project. If your bath project falls into the $9,000 to $15,000 range, expect to pay a few hundred dollars. For current costs, check with the contractor or HOW. (See Appendix A.)

Your remodeling project may be protected by other warranties. Some states require remodelers to warrant their work for up to twelve years. If so, be sure that the warranty is included in the contract.

Many of the products in the remodeling will carry a manufacturer's warranty. Instruct the contractor to turn over all warranty papers to you.

11 SIGNS OF A FAIR CONTRACT

The contract spells out the responsibilities of the contractor and the homeowner; it is also designed to protect both parties. Verbal agreements can be very difficult to enforce. Get it in writing. Here's how.

1. State a bathroom construction starting date and completion date. Shipping delays and other unforeseen events are inevitable. But to ensure that the job moves along smoothly, consider a penalty clause that requires the contractor to pay an agreed upon amount for other delays. Many contractors, however, may actually decline the job if such a clause appears. Some delays are inevitable and the homeowner should expect them. On the flip side, consider a bonus for early completion, providing that quality work is evident throughout the project. In most cases, keying payments to stages of work completed is the best impetus to keeping the job on schedule.

2. Understand the terms of payment. Such terms as the total price, payments, payment sched-

ule, and cancellation penalty, if any, should spelled out clearly. On most home improvement jobs, a significant down payment is required. Some states (California, for example) limit the down payment to 10 percent. In any case, this payment is negotiable. Progressive payments should be made during the project. Payment should follow the amount of work completed. By the time 50 percent of the work is completed, 50 percent of the money should be paid out. A final payment is made upon completion.

And, speaking of money matters, homeowner financing should be obtained before putting contractors through the bidding process.

3. Specify that final contractor payment is dependent on receiving a release of lien from all subcontractors and suppliers. You pay the contractor, but if the contractor doesn't pay his/her subcontractors and/or suppliers, they have the legal right to bring a lien (construction lien, mechanic's lien) against your home and sue you for payments due; you can potentially pay *twice*. A lien release from a subcontractor or supplier states that payment has been received and the claim against your property is released. Protect yourself in two ways: Consider obtaining legal advice — lien laws vary from state to state — and pay the contractor through an escrow account according to the payment schedule and as releases of lien are received.

4. Put in a cancellation clause. Homeowners have three days in which to change their mind and cancel the contract. The contractor or contractor's representative must inform you about cancellation rights orally and in writing, and provide the forms to sue for cancellation. The cancellation clause is mandatory in some states; check with the state Attorney General's Office or consumer information department.

5. Specify all materials in detail. Specifications are vital, and that goes for specifications in the contract too. For example, the contract should state, "Install Andersen oak casement window #543, size X35, on east wall, as specified in plan." Also spell out any materials or labor to be provided by the homeowner.

6. Obtain warranties in writing and read them carefully. A *full warranty* will provide for repair or replacement of the product, or a refund of your money. A *limited warranty* will put some type of limit on repairs, replacements, or refunds. Who provides the warranty, and its terms and conditions, should be written in clear language.

7. Specify compliance with codes. State that the contractor will comply with all building, plumbing, and electrical codes. The contractor will obtain necessary permits, pay permit fees, and arrange for building inspections as required by local regulations.

8. Include a change order policy. A change order is a written directive during construction to alter the original plans. A change order is signed by both the homeowner and the contractor. The smaller and fewer the change orders, the less you pay. These orders usually are billed separately from the contract. Designate the individuals who will evaluate and approve change orders. Specify the method of payment for change orders too.

9. Establish a procedure for handling unforeseen construction expenses. And unforeseen expenses do come up in remodeling. Who knows what may be inside a wall — plumbing in need of replacement, subgrade framing, or some other costly surprise. Include a clause about handling these extras.

Include a clause such as the following about handling extra charges: If unforeseen expenses arise due to site conditions, or any other conditions, the contractor will notify the homeowner, detailing the work and estimated costs; work will proceed when the homeowner gives approval. The new work and estimated costs will be described by the contractor in writing.

10. Outline other contractor responsibilities at the job site. Keeping the work site clean is important to most homeowners, as is job site cleanup when work is completed. Debris removal usually is assigned to the contractor. Include special

---

SAMPLE SPECIFICATION SHEET 2

(partial listing of materials)

TILE for counters, shower, wall:
SYA 501 lilac tile

102 sq. ft. field tile @ $6.29	$641.58
56 lin. ft. bullnose tile @ $2.29	128.24
6 corners @ $.78	4.68
35 lbs. mauve joint filler	31.57

TILE for shower base:
American Olean A77 Heather 1" X 1"

12 sq. ft. @ $4.68	56.16
8 lin. ft. S-812 cap @ $3.10	24.80
Mauve joint filler from above	

FIXTURES, His bathroom:

K2221 Portrait pedestal sink	401.00
Delta 3523PB lavatory faucet, 8"	210.00
K3490 Portrait Lite toilet with seat	335.00

FIXTURES, Her bathroom:

K2166 Fleur self-rimming lavatory	337.00
Grohe 21.184 brass faucet	286.00
K3408 Cabarnet with seat	670.00

requests such as saving lumber or old appliances, storage areas for remodeling materials, and any other instructions regarding the home and its inhabitants.

11. Establish a means of solving disputes. Several alternatives to spending time and money in the courtroom are available. Notable among them are mediation and arbitration programs sponsored by the Better Business Bureau and the American Arbitration Association. (See Appendix A.) Specify in the construction contract that parties will work with these agencies, or others, to settle problems that arise.

OBTAINING FINANCING

Financing home improvement usually is a simpler matter than qualifying for a mortgage or refinancing a mortgage loan. This is especially true if the loan is based on the collateral you have in your home.

Home equity loans often have a lower rate than *home improvement loans*. But both provide cheaper money than unsecured personal loans or credit card debt, for example.

A home equity loan allows the homeowners to borrow against the cash they have put into mortgage payments. Two types of home equity loans are the *lump-sum payment* and the home equity *line of credit* in which the homeowner may borrow funds as needed up to the credit limit.

Home improvement loans, like the home equity loans, may be secured by the homeowner. A lump-sum payment is made when the loan is approved. But unlike the line of credit home equity loan, regular payments to amortize the home improvement loan are made over a predetermined number of months or years.

The lender will establish a current market value for the home, then figure the loan limit on a maximum percentage of the home's value — usually 80 percent. Within that limit, the amount available for the remodeling project depends on homeowner credit history, income, debt, and assets.

Shopping for the best rates on a loan is always a way to cut financing costs. It is the best way to compare:

- The maximum amount of the loan
- The interest rates
- The terms
- Tax issues

The contractor may assist with financing; quality firms may develop relationships with banks. Contractors are also familiar with the many financing options available. Checking out the contractor's financing does save footwork, but the homeowner should still compare what the contractor offers to other loan sources in the marketplace.

WORTH REPEATING

1. Plans are the cornerstone of the remodeling project. From the plans, a specifications list of materials and equipment is drawn. Contractors base the project bid on the specifications list.

2. The specifications list describes exactly what you want in your new bath. Fixtures and materials are described in exact detail. The product type, manufacturer, model, color, and size must be specified for each item in the remodeling.

3. All contractor bids must be based on the same plans and specifications. The purpose of the bidding process is to enable the homeowner to select the most desirable quote. Comparing bids is impossible unless all contractors bid from the same plans and specs.

4. The lowest bid may not be the best bid. To compare bids, first determine that the bid is made on the actual specifications and plans. Check the quality of workmanship and experience of the contractor. Discuss the bid with the contractor to understand variations in price; if a contractor refuses to discuss the bid, find another contractor.

5. Identify warranties offered by the contractor. Some remodelers supply a warranty program; others may be members of the HOW program. Check the provisions of the warranty.

6. Contracts: Put it in writing. Verbal agreements don't count. All provisions regarding labor and materials should be specified in detail in the construction contract.

7. The construction contract should include these provisions: start and completion date, payment schedule, three-day cancellation right, materials and equipment specifications, warranties, procedures for code compliance, and a policy regarding change orders. Additional provisions should include how to handle unexpected expenses, contractor responsibilities, and a means of conflict resolution.

8. Qualifying for and processing a home improvement or home equity remodeling loan is simpler than obtaining a mortgage loan for credit-worthy homeowners. The contractor may offer financing options too.

10

Construction: Roles and Responsibilities

How to talk to the contractor.
Understanding codes and permits.

By the time construction begins, the homeowner has put plenty of hours into the new bathroom. For the effort, the homeowner has gained an exciting bathroom remodeling plan created by a trusted designer. The construction bids have come in, the installation contract has been scrutinized and signed, and the bank has approved the loan and put money on the line. Now the homeowner's job is to communicate with the remodeling contractor.

WHO'S IN CHARGE

During construction, the homeowner, or a professional hired by the homeowner, has the right to:

■ Inspect construction regularly

■ Receive construction progress reports from the job supervisor

■ Ask the supervisor questions, and seek solutions as problems occur

The bathroom designer may be hired to inspect the work, confer with the building contractor, and convey the client's questions and concerns. An additional fee is negotiated for this service. (See

Chapter 2, "Money Matters.")

One advantage of this arrangement is that the designer has a thorough knowledge of the bathroom plan and is versed in construction practices. Having the designer on board to troubleshoot may be attractive to a homeowner attempting remodeling for the first time.

Whether the bathroom designer or the homeowner acts as the contact person, communication is simplified if *one* person takes on the responsibilities of this role. Likewise, avoid trying to resolve problems with installers or subcontractors. Instead, go to the boss. The workers get their orders from the construction supervisor; getting new instructions from a homeowner may be confusing, cause delays, and cost money.

TALKING ABOUT DELAYS

Even the most well-organized remodeling job will have its share of construction delays. What's important is that the contractor and homeowner communicate about the source of the delay and establish a plan that will get the work rolling again.

The two most common construction holdups relate to receiving materials and scheduling labor. No matter who supplies materials for the project — the design firm or the builder — shipping problems may stall material deliveries. Receiving damaged goods or incomplete deliveries means more delays and waiting for replacements.

With the number of professionals involved in a bathroom remodeling, scheduling the work is a job for the skilled manager. For example, if the drywall is not installed before the electrician arrives to make the electrical hookups, he or she may leave to work on another job.

One strategy for handling delays is to add a clause to the contract that stipulates:

■ The definition of a delay; a period of two days
■ The reason for the delay

Act on the delay clause immediately. A delay can mean extra days or weeks of inconvenience for you. It may also prevent other professionals from doing their work. For example, if an electrician cannot make the deadline, the drywaller coming the next day cannot drywall. Talk to the contractor about the reason for the delay. Ask the designer to talk to the contractor with you; the designer may be able to offer a solution to the problem.

Agree on a plan to end the delay, and a time frame within which the problem will be solved. Follow up immediately after each step of the plan is completed. If delays continue, you may consult a mediator or arbitrator to solve the problem. (See "How to Handle Problems," page 111.)

Some designers advise their clients to prepare a "second best" list of selected fixtures and materials to substitute for first-round choices. If delivery on any materials or fixtures will be delayed, use the second-best list to select an alternative so the remodeling can continue. Take advantage of guidance from the design professional and make these choices during the project planning stage.

TALKING ABOUT CHANGES

Be ready to talk to the contractor about minor changes in the remodeling plan, because some changes may be necessary.

Perhaps an element of the plan isn't appealing once you see it, no matter how carefully the design was planned on paper. Or, in spite of taking careful measurements, an unforeseen framing adjustment must be made to install the vanity or storage cabinets. Or maybe the contractor suggests an alteration that will save time and money without substantially changing the bathroom design.

Whatever the change, get it in writing. A *change order* should be completed for each alteration that occurs during the course of construction. The order should:

■ Refer to the original contract specification
■ State clearly the nature of the change
■ Specify differences in costs, if any
■ Contain signatures of contractor and homeowner

Let's say the job specifications include a ventilation fan with lighting and oak trim, but when the fan arrives, the trim stands out against the white ceiling. So a fan with white trim that costs a bit less is ordered. The change order for this material might be written: "Substitute ABC Company dual-light fan #345 with white trim for dual-light fan #345 oak trim. Credit homeowner $20.00."

The completed change order becomes an amendment to the contract. Verify that changes have been made — and made correctly — during inspection of the remodeling work.

WHAT THE CONTRACTOR DOES

The responsibilities of the contractor have been spelled out in a carefully written contract. When construction begins, the words of the contract — "specifications," "permits," and "codes" for example — turn into reality.

Generally speaking, the job of the contractor is:

■ To coordinate the work and schedule workers efficiently so delays are minimized
■ To ensure that the work is performed according to specifications
■ To ensure that work is in compliance with codes and zoning regulations and to obtain permits and arrange inspections

WHAT ARE CODES?

Building codes set *minimum* standards for construction. They are written, in a general sense, to ensure the safety of the home.

Codes cover electrical, plumbing, mechanical, and structural systems. They regulate energy efficient construction practices, as well as fire safety. But remember that codes are not a **guarantee** of quality workmanship.

A bathroom design may include specifications *above* the minimum standards. For example, a code related to windows specifies that the window area equals at least one-tenth of the floor area. In an 8′ X 10′ bath, that means 8 square feet of window. But let's say a whirlpool will be installed under a bay window that frames a garden view. That bay window will be well above the 8 square foot minimum.

MODEL CODES

Today, *three model codes* are used in the U.S. to guide the construction process. These codes are written by nonprofit groups made up of professionals in the building industry, who also train building inspectors and conduct research on building practices. (See Appendix A.)

■ The model codes are amended every three years to reflect approved practices.

■ Each state, city, or county has the right to adopt one of the model codes. The code is enforced through building inspections.

5 WAYS TO SURVIVE A REMODELING PROJECT

Remodeling is more than planning and paperwork, contracts and financing. It's about people, the people who live with the project, and their needs. Before the project begins, think about family needs and prepare for the inevitable disruption of remodeling.

1. Expect to clean out the old bathroom. Don't be caught unprepared when the first workers arrive and find the bathroom full of toiletries, combs, brushes, and towels. The homeowner usually has the job of removing all personal items from the bathroom, or hiring someone to do it.

Pack up the room as if it were moving day. Empty cupboards, cabinets, and shelving. Remove window coverings, shower curtains, linens, and decorative items.

2. Expect to prepare an alternate bathroom. Having a second bath will help ease the family through the remodeling process. Establish a schedule for family use, especially during the morning rush period. Equip the alternate bathroom at least one day in advance of the remodeling. And because that bathroom is going to get more traffic than usual, expect a clutter of toiletries, towels, clothing, and extras to accumulate.

3. Expect periods when the toilet, shower, tub, or sink is not available. The contractor may arrange for portable toilet facilities to be brought to the work site. Or ask a neighbor for permission to share their bathroom. Go to a health club; take a weekend getaway.

4. Expect to be without some portion of the electric and water service occasionally. The utilities that are taken for granted each day become important when they are not available. Ask the contractor to indicate, as far as possible, if and when these services will be lost. Have water on hand, get away for a few hours, or consider dining out.

5. Expect that the job will be messy and sometimes noisy. Remove or cover valuables. Establish a route for tradespeople to enter and exit the home, and for the removal of rubbish. Move breakables out of this path, and protect the flooring with sturdy runners. Ask the contractor to protect adjacent areas by securing tarps or plastic to doorways. And plan to live with the disorganization and dust until the job is over.

■ Local governments may amend the model code to include preferred construction methods.

The complexity of the code system makes it critical that the professional builder keep up with changes. Codes are changing, for example, in relation to requirements for low-flush toilets in homes.

THE RESIDENTIAL CODE

The creation of the One- and Two-Family Dwelling Code by the Council of American Building Officials (CABO) has simplified the code system. CABO was formed by the three model code groups to publish the residential code.

■ This code applies to residential, rather than commercial *and* residential construction, described in the model codes.

■ Many of the residential code provisions are adopted from other codes, such as the National Electrical Code and the National Plumbing Code.

■ In most areas, the contractor has the choice to work under the guidelines of the CABO code or the model code adopted by the community.

■ The One- and Two-Family Dwelling Code is said to be the easiest code to understand.

INSPECTING THE BATHROOM

What does a building inspector look for in bathroom remodeling? The items on this list probably will be inspected in most remodeling projects.

ROUGH INSPECTION
Rough Framing:
- ❑ Nail plates to strengthen framing joints
- ❑ Floor joists
- ❑ Blocking (structural reinforcement in framing) for installing accessories such as towel bars
- ❑ Blocking for installing grab bars
- ❑ Blocking for installing electrical equipment — ventilating fan, light fixtures, junction boxes

Insulation:
- ❑ Insulation at exterior walls
- ❑ Insulation between door and window frames

Rough Plumbing — Upgraded, moved, or installed as specified in plan:
- ❑ Supply lines
- ❑ Drains
- ❑ Vents

Rough Electric — Upgraded, moved, or installed as specified in plan:
- ❑ GFCI outlets
- ❑ Wall fixtures
- ❑ Ceiling fixtures

Rough Mechanical — Upgraded, moved, or installed as specified in plan:
- ❑ Duct work
- ❑ Heating, ventilating, and air conditioning

Other:
- ❑ Tempered glass
- ❑ Exits
- ❑ Window area
- ❑ Drywall nailing

FINAL INSPECTION
- ❑ Finish plumbing installed
- ❑ Finish electric installed
- ❑ Finish mechanical completed
- ❑ Shower door installed, each piece of door imprinted with "tempered glass"

So how do you know which code is used in your locality? By your contractor? Ask the building inspection department, and ask the contractor.

PERMITS AND CODES

A *building permit* is required when structural changes are made or when the living area of a home is changed from a storage space to a "livable" space, such as a basement conversion.

Separate permits may be issued for each part of the project; structural, electrical, plumbing, and mechanical work are covered under building permits. The contractor obtains the necessary permits and pays permit fees. It is important that the contractor perform this service because the person who obtains the permit is considered liable if the work fails to pass inspection.

Along with the building permit comes a timetable for *inspections* by the local building inspector. The contractor is responsible for arranging these inspections. Inspections of rough-in carpentry, plumbing, and electrical work must be made before the drywall goes on; inspectors also inspect the finished work.

If the work fails to meet any portion of the building inspection, the contractor is required to correct the work and call for another inspection. For specific questions about code requirements, call the local building department.

FINISHING THE JOB

At the end of the remodeling job, the *final payment* is made and the *completion certificate* is signed by contractor and the client. But agreeing on what "completion" means is not always easy.

Often a few jobs are left hanging, like the order for a new vanity cabinet light fixture to replace the one that was defective. Or the toilet tissue holder that got chipped during construction.

One way to arrive at a completion date is to stipulate in the contract that the final payment will be made within a few weeks after construction. This "waiting period" allows the homeowner to live with

the project and find any deficiencies.

Make your own final inspection of the project with the design professional on hand, if desired. Note any jobs which are incomplete. During the "waiting period," the contractor has the responsibility to complete the work in order to receive final payment.

Sign the completion certificate only when all the work is done. The bank will also require the completion certificate to release the final payment to the contractor.

HOW TO HANDLE PROBLEMS

Problems do arise in remodeling, even with the best of intentions. That's why homeowners are advised to include a clause in the remodeling contract that requires the contractor and homeowner to work out disputes with a neutral third party.

One settlement option is *alternative dispute resolution*, the process of settling disagreements out of court. Trade associations such as the NAHB and NARI® offer such services to their members; so does the Council of Better Business Bureau and the American Arbitration Association, among others.

Three ways to resolve disputes are *conciliation*, *mediation*, and *arbitration*.

■ In *conciliation*, a third party presents the views of the customer to the business owner, and vice versa. The conciliator also passes along offers made by either side to solve the problem.

■ In *mediation*, a trained mediator clarifies and rephrases problems, then helps both sides talk things out. His or her job is to help people reach a solution, not decide who is right or wrong.

■ In *arbitration*, a trained (nonbiased) arbitrator listens to the views of each side, then makes a decision about resolving the dispute. In binding arbitration, the conflicting parties are required to abide by the arbitrator's decision; in nonbinding arbitration, the decision is a "suggestion," which may or may not be followed by either party.

For more information on specific programs, see "Dispute Resolution," Appendix A.

WORTH REPEATING

1. The homeowner has the right to receive regular reports from the contractor on construction progress.

2. The homeowner has the right to appoint a job inspector, such as the design professional.

3. A contract must be amended with a written change order when a change in contract specifications is made. The change order describes the new work in detail and the cost or credit, if any.

4. The methods for handling delays and disputes — discussion with the contractor, conciliation, arbitration, or mediation — can be stipulated in the contract.

5. Building codes set minimum standards for construction practices; they do not guarantee the quality of work.

6. Code compliance is determined when the work is inspected and approved by a municipal building inspector.

7. Sign a completion certificate only after the job has been inspected and the contractor has been allowed a reasonable period to correct problems.

Part Five

PRACTICAL PRODUCTS

□ TUBS □ SHOWERS □ TOILETS □ SINKS □
□ FAUCETS □ CABINETS □ COUNTERS □
□ TILE □ WALLCOVERINGS □

11

Fixtures:
Tubs and Showers

*About one-third of the
remodeling budget goes
for fixtures.*

The tub/shower combination, found in many homes of the '50s and '60s, gradually is being replaced by a separate tub and a shower. The tub is often a whirlpool. The shower is either a manufactured stall or a custom shower built on site.

The shower in the old tub/shower duo is less functional than a separate shower because it has:

■ Relatively high tub sides, compared to the low curb on a shower stall

■ Curved tub sides and bottom, which make standing more difficult

■ A width too narrow for showering

■ Faucets placed so it is necessary to step into the stream of water when adjusting water temperature and pressure

An older tub has drawbacks too:

■ Slippery tub surface

■ Absence of grab bars

■ Tub not contoured for comfort

Separately, each fixture can better do the job for which it was intended. For example, tubs now have slip-resistant bottoms, built in grab bars, and some have contoured head and arm rests for comfort. And jetted tubs (whirlpools), with contoured seats and soothing hydromassage action, do an even better job of providing a relaxing soak. Showers, like tubs, now include safety features, and they are often sized larger than the 32" X 32" mandated by building codes.

But installing a separate tub and shower presents the challenge of fitting four fixtures (tub, shower, sink and toilet) into a space where three (tub/shower, sink, and toilet) sufficed. Space-saving fixtures like corner tubs and showers help solve this problem, as well as "borrowing" space from bedrooms, hallways, closets, and adjacent rooms. (See Chapter 4, "Problem-Solving Floor Plans.") Costs are a consideration too. They include the cost of plumbing changes, removing a heavy tub, and structural changes such as reinforcing the floor to support the weight of a whirlpool.

In some cases, space constraints and budget limits may dictate the use of a combination tub/shower unit. The good news is that tub/shower surrounds molded from acrylic or fiberglass often have grab bars, nonslip bases, and contoured tubs.

Safety is an important factor. If you are considering a whirlpool, steam shower, or sauna for your remodeling, remember that these features stimulate the cardiovascular system. Individuals with heart disease or circulatory problems, high blood pressure, diabetes, or epilepsy, and the elderly should consult a doctor before using them. Steam showers and saunas usually are not recommended for children under twelve; whirlpool time should be limited to a few minutes, under supervision.

MATERIALS

Bathtubs, whirlpools, and showers are manufactured from four materials:

- Cast iron
- Enameled steel
- Cast polymers such as cultured marble and cultured onyx
- Plastics such as acrylic and fiberglass

Cast iron is formed by heating iron to its liquid state and then molding it. The molten iron cools to a solid state; the tub is smoothed, then a powdered glaze is applied and the tub is fired. This process has been used for over 100 years to manufacture bathtubs.

Enameled steel is formed in a cold state. A sheet of steel is pressed into a form. Parts of the fixture then may be cut or formed by a method called stamping; some enameled steel fixtures require welding. When the shape is completed, a coat of enamel is sprayed onto the fixture, and it is fired.

Although cast iron and enameled steel tubs may look alike, they are quite different. The enameled steel is a lighter weight, less expensive cousin of cast iron. The enamel coating on cast iron is thicker than that on enameled steel, so it is not likely to chip; the finish resists scratches and stains. Moreover, if an object is dropped on an enameled steel tub, it will move slightly, but the enamel coating will not move with it. Consequently, the enamel may chip.

Both enameled steel and cast iron are good heat conductors, so water will cool more rapidly in both of them than in a tub of plastic. Because cast iron tubs are cool to the touch, they may be uncomf... able for a few moments when the bather rests against the back of the tub above the water line. Enameled steel tubs tend to be noisy.

Cast iron is heavy, so heavy in fact that tubs are usually limited to 36" X 72" and 42" X 60", according to the NKBA. Getting a cast iron tub up a long flight of stairs or maneuvering it into a tight spot will be more difficult and cost more than moving an enameled steel tub.

Cast polymer, such as cultured marble or cultured onyx, is formed by a molding process. The mold is sprayed with a gel coat and cured; a mixture of ground marble and resin is added. For a marbleized pattern, a second color is swirled into the mold, then cured.

The gel coat is often sprayed by hand, so there are variations in the thickness of the coat. If the gel coat is too thick or too thin, crazing or cracking will eventually appear, especially in the drain area. The quality of cast polymer fixtures tends to vary because they are made by many small manufacturers around the country. Select a product that has been certified by the Cultured Marble Institute and the National Association of Home Builders Research Center. (See Appendix A.)

Plastics, including **fiberglass-reinforced acrylic** and **acrylic**, are good insulators so tub water does not cool as quickly as it does in an enameled steel or cast iron fixture. They are also warm to the touch, lightweight, and can be molded in a tremendous variety of shapes.

Acrylics are harder than fiberglass. Their colors are brighter, and the color goes all the way through the surface. Acrylics are repairable and are more expensive than fiberglass. Although fiberglass is economical, it is subject to scratching and fading. Care must be taken to clean fixtures according to the manufacturer's instructions.

A versatile addition to the tub is a **hand-held shower,** which is convenient for washing hair, rinsing the body, and cleaning the tub. In the shower itself, the **hand-held shower,** or the showerhead that slides vertically on a bar, is ideal for the family with people of different heights. They are also useful at the shower bench, especially for the elderly who may prefer to shower seated.

Body sprays are located in a series of two or three showerheads along opposite walls for a water massage from the shoulders to the knees. These multiple-head systems require careful planning to provide an adequate supply of water (delivered at an adequate pressure) to each head. **A body mist** consists of several jets on a bar to gently wash the body without getting the hair wet.

TUB BASICS

Bathtubs and whirlpools are classified as recessed, platform, corner, or free-standing.

The recessed tub has one finished side, or apron, and fits between two end walls and a back wall. The walls are finished on site, usually with tile or solid-surface material. Tub sizes range from 30" to 34" wide, 14" to 20" deep and 60" to 72" long. Bathtubs have been improved to include: (1) contoured interiors, built-in head and arm rests, and

10 TIPS ON FITTINGS

Fittings for the tub, whirlpool, and shower include the tub spout, valve (on/off control), showerhead, and waste (drain).

1. Water supply lines should be sized so the tub can be filled before the water gets cold. A typical ½" water supply line brings in 20 to 22 gallons per minute (gpm), which is adequate to fill a 30" X 60" tub; a ¾" supply line brings in 30 to 35 gpm, which is more suitable for a whirlpool.

2. Spout size should match the supply line diameter. For example, if a ¾" supply line is used for a two-person whirlpool, a ¾" faucet must be used or the water will not be delivered quickly enough.

3. Understand diverters. Diverters are used in a plumbing system to switch the water supply from one outlet to another, such as from tub to shower in a combination unit or from one showerhead to another in a multiple-head shower.

4. Consider fitting construction. A brass body is best; it is strong, durable, and resists corrosion. Zinc is stronger and more durable than plastic, but must be plated to withstand water. Plastics, the least expensive, are not as strong or as durable, unless they are "plating grade." Fittings with washers to control water flow will eventually require washer replacement; those with the faucet's working parts in a plastic or ceramic cartridge will last longer, and the cartridge is easy to replace.

5. Consider fitting finish. Polished chrome is very hard, bright, and durable. Solid brass or plated brass will maintain its looks longer with a protective coating of epoxy rather than lacquer. Enamels and epoxies are desirable for their range of color and ease of maintenance. Gold-plated brass, polished or satin finish, will not tarnish but must never be cleaned with abrasives; gold wash or gold flash plating is thinner than gold plate and may wear quickly.

6. For platform tubs, check that the spout and valves will fit on the platform. The spout and valves should be located so they are not in the bather's way as he or she enters the tub.

7. Pressure-balanced and temperature-limiting valves for the tub and shower are a must to prevent scalding and falls due to temperature shock. (See Chapter 7, "Staying Safe.")

8. Water-conserving showerheads that restrict the flow of water are highly recommended. (See Chapter 8, "Using Water Wisely.")

9. Showerhead spray characteristics. Spray may be adjusted from fine to coarse, from gentle to pulsating action. Avoid sprays that release water only around the rim. Spray controls on the side, rather in the center, of the head are easier to operate.

10. Plan access to water shutoff and supply lines through an access panel for future servicing.

grab bars; and (2) a flange that prevents water seepage between the wet wall and tub. The designations "left" and "right" refer to the end on which the drain is located.

A few inches make a big difference in comfort in a tub. If you are removing an old 30" X 60" tub, replace it with a wider, deeper model that offers more soaking comfort and fits in the same recess as the standard tub. Or replace it with a 60" long whirlpool.

The **platform tub** has a lip on all sides but no apron. It is designed to be dropped into a platform built on site, usually of tile or solid-surface material over wood framing. If a platform tub is also used as a shower, the surround may match the platform. If it is used as a bath only, the wall around the tub needs to be protected with 4" to 12" of material, similar to a backsplash at a sink.

The **corner tub** is an excellent alternative for stretching space. Several configurations are widely used, including the angled tub, in which three sides are finished, and the sculpted tub in a variety of smooth curves. These tubs may require from 4' to 5' on the back wall and extend into the room 5' to 6' from the back corner.

The **free-standing tub** literally stands on its own, like an old Victorian clawfoot tub; some are available as jetted tubs. The free-standing type requires no recess, platform, or corner access. For varieties, consult a designer or showroom. These tubs do not make good showers; their high, steep sides make entering, exiting, and standing difficult.

Tub Refinishing

Refinishing the tub and tub enclosure rather than replacing them cuts the cost of remodeling. Not only do you save the cost of a new fixture, but also the cost of replacing any plumbing fixtures, walls, backerboard, and flooring material which may be damaged when the old tub is removed. Consider refinishing for a face lift or minor remodeling in which the location of the tub is adequate.

One resurfacing process is to spray a polyurethane or enamel paint onto the surface after it has been cleaned and prepared. However, there is a risk that the paint may chip, flake, or peel. A more permanent solution is to bond a simulated porcelain product to the tub after it has been cleaned and etched; the simulated porcelain is chemically cured. Expect the resurfacing job to put the bathtub out of commission for about two to four days.

Resurfacing methods and products vary from company to company, so the quality of the job is really dependent on the company selected. Determine how long the company has been in business and the qualifications of the installer who will do your job. Ask for a detailed explanation of the resurfacing process, costs, warranties, and references to customers. Of course, ask to see some completed tubs done in nearby homes. Whatever finishing method is used, consider it to be delicate, and clean it according to the resurfacer's instructions.

WHIRLPOOLS

Bubbling waters of the whirlpool (or hydromassage) increase blood circulation on the skin surface which relaxes joints and muscles. Tubs are 5' to 7' long, 30" to 60" wide, and 16" to 30" deep. (The 30" deep tubs are a special type called steeping or soaking tubs.)

Whirlpools are contoured for comfort, and include lumbar, head, and arm supports. A jetted tub contoured for two people, sitting side by side, is comfortable at 42" wide; two people sitting opposite each other need a tub 36" wide. Try a whirlpool on for size, the same way you would test fine furniture.

Recessed, platform, and corner units are available. Enameled cast iron and acrylic are the premium materials for whirlpools. Always check the whirlpool warranty, what it covers, and how long the company offering it has been in business.

Features to consider in a whirlpool purchase are **water capacity, hot water supply, number and kind of jets, pump, and switch.**

Whirlpool Water Capacity

Whirlpool capacity varies from 50 to 140 gallons of water. Because of the increased capacity, it may be necessary to change both the branch line and spout

Tub Styles

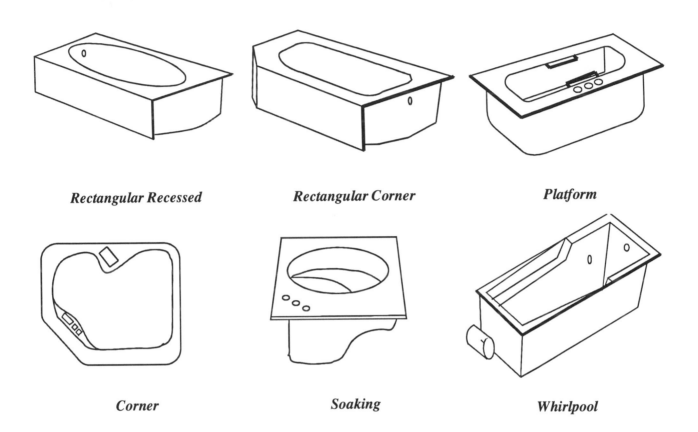

Rectangular Recessed   **Rectangular Corner**   **Platform**

Corner   **Soaking**   **Whirlpool**

from the standard $\frac{1}{2}$" to $\frac{3}{4}$" so the tub fills before the water becomes cold. The tub's floor may also need extra structural support because of the increased weight of both the tub and the water. The weight of the filled tub and the pounds per square foot that the floor is designed to carry are compared to determine if extra support is necessary. The ability to assess the load that the floor can bear must be delegated to a plumbing contractor, designer, or architect.

To provide an adequate **hot water supply**, size the water heater for two-thirds the capacity of the bathtub (the balance is cold water), suggests the NKBA. If the current heater is not large enough, purchase a larger water heater, install two water heaters side by side, or provide a heater that serves the whirlpool only. To maintain water temperatures for a long soak, consider installing an in-line heater, which requires a 240-volt circuit.

Whirlpool Jets

A rule of thumb about jets: Expect smaller whirlpools (those close to the size of a standard tub) to have at least four jets; larger models, six to eight jets. Two widely used systems are: (1) *few jets with large outlets* that produce a swirling action throughout the tub; and (2) *many jets with small outlets* (called pinpoint jets) that deliver water to specific points.

The large jets have supply lines that deliver a *high volume of water at a low pressure* to create the swirling action; water supply lines are larger than those for pinpoint jets. This system tends to be the noisier because of the volume of water pushed through piping. A desirable feature is an air control, which mixes air and water so bathers can vary the massage action.

Pinpoint jets with small outlets that deliver water to specific points are serviced by *smaller*

Showers and Tub/Showers

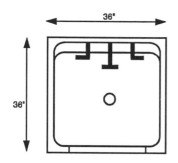

Square Shower Surround

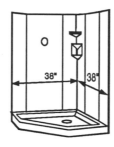

Corner Shower Surround

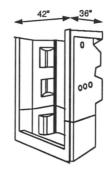

Rectangular Shower Surround

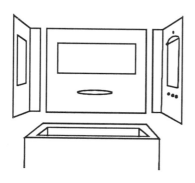

3-Piece Tub/Shower Surround

1-Piece Tub/Shower Surround

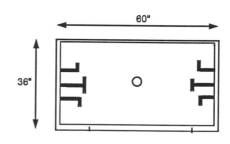

Rectangular Custom-Built Two-Person Shower

water supply lines that deliver a low volume of water at a high pressure; jets should be directionally adjustable to increase bathing comfort.

Be cautious about drilling jets on site. The manufacturer's warranty is voided if the tub is jetted after it leaves the factory. Unless you are dealing with a skilled craftsperson experienced in fabricating jets, it may be less risky to have a preplumbed tub that is covered by a factory warranty. Also check that the whirlpool pump assembly is UL listed and approved by the International Association of Plumbing and Mechanical Officials (IAPMO).

Brass has proven to be a good jet material because it functions well with prolonged exposure to water. Do not confuse the jet which is barely visible with the decorative mounting plate around the jet. The plate usually matches the tub fitting so

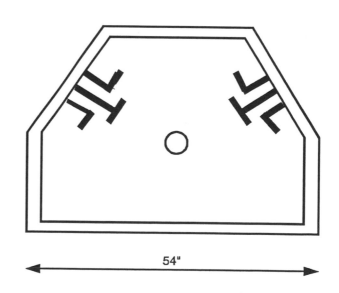

Angled Custom-Built Two-Person Shower

Tub and Shower Fittings

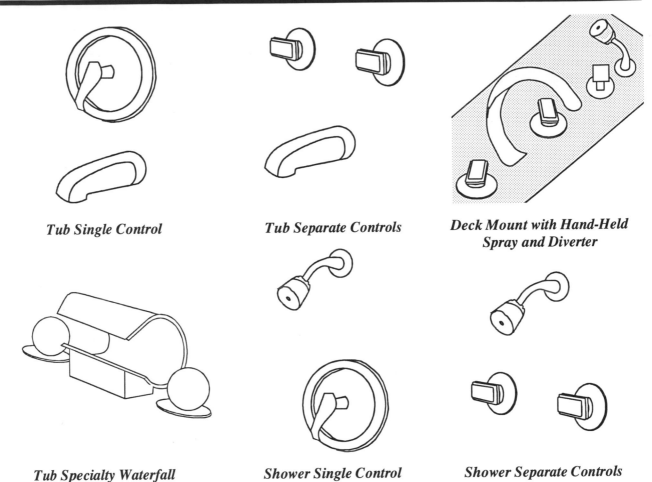

Tub Single Control

Tub Separate Controls

Deck Mount with Hand-Held Spray and Diverter

Tub Specialty Waterfall

Shower Single Control

Shower Separate Controls

the plate may be made from brass, chrome, acrylic or other materials.

Whirlpool Pumps

Pumps are usually $\frac{1}{2}$ to $1\frac{1}{2}$ horsepower; a pump less than 1 hp operates on a standard 120-volt circuit, but those over 1 hp require a 240-volt circuit. Another measure of the pump power is to consider the gallons of water per minute (gpm) pushed through the jets. It is usually 5 to 7 gpm. Some pumps have two-speed or variable-speed controls, which allow the water action to change from gentle to vigorous.

The whirlpool pump must be accessible for servicing. The factory-installed pump fits within the tub unit itself. Some manufacturers offer a remote-location pump which may be placed up to 5' from

the tub and concealed in a vanity cabinet or closet, for example.

Switches and Timers

Air switches and electric timers are available to start the tub. An air switch is nonelectric so it may be located safely and conveniently on the whirlpool itself. The bather can operate the air switch without leaving the tub.

An electric timer, on the other hand, must be located 5' away from the tub, according to codes, so it is necessary to leave the tub to reactivate it.

SHOWERS

Select a prefabricated shower with walls and doors or a site-built unit, which is more expensive. The advances in shower design include:

Shower Sprays

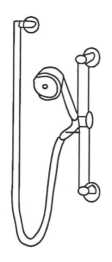

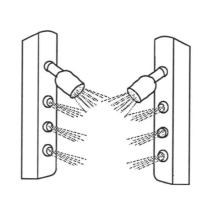

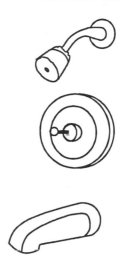

Adjustable Shower Spray on Slide Bar

Adjustable Shower Body Spray

Tub/Shower Single Control with Diverter

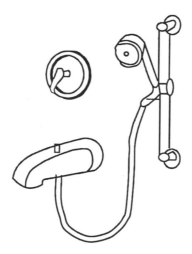

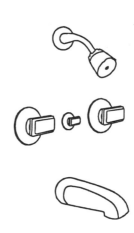

Tub/Shower Single Control Pressure-Balanced, Temperature-Limiting with Spout Diverter

Tub/Shower Single Control with Adjustable Spray on Slide Bar

Tub/Shower Separate Controls with Diverter

■ **Showers of every size** are available in square, rectangular, and angled shapes, which are space-savers

■ **Adequate sizing** based on ergonomic studies of how the shower is actually used

■ **Improved safety devices** — grab bars, shower seats, shower valve located outside of the water stream, slip-resistant base

■ **Improved comfort** — the use of shower lights, post-shower ceiling heaters, and ventilating fans located as close as possible to the shower

■ **Frameless shower doors** that visually expand space

First, determine the size of the shower, taking into account the height of those who will use it and accessibility requirements. The shower must be big enough so the user can step out of the shower stream to adjust the water temperature and pressure. Ergonomic studies show that a shower at least 36" X 42" is better for washing hair, bending to wash legs, etc.

...man the 32" X 32" prescribed by code Determine whether two people use the shower or one. For two, large showers with two showering heads are available. Think about whether you prefer a deep shower that requires no shower curtain. Determine the amount of floor space necessary for a safe shower door — one that swings outward.

For information on sizing the shower for the elderly or the physically challenged, see Chapter 6, "The User-Friendly Bath."

Second, take a look at materials. Economical manufactured units of acrylic or fiberglass come in many shapes and sizes to fit most remodeling jobs. For a custom-made shower of safety glass, expect to pay about three times more than normal.

Third, look at the shower interior. The showerhead spray should be directed to the body, not the head. Consider making the showerhead adjustable. Heads on sliding bars offer variable height adjustments to suit the entire family. Another alternative is a personal shower on a hose for rinsing hair and body. Decide whether or not you want multiple sprays for a shower hydromassage. Include a bench for safely washing feet and legs and to accommodate the elderly or handicapped. Provide grab bars for entering and exiting, as well as changing from a seated position to standing. Add a shelf for soap and hair care items, which is safely recessed into the wall rather than protruding into the shower.

Other shower details. The shower **pan**, or base, is selected according to size, shape, and drain location. The **drain** location must be compatible with the existing drain, or the plumber must rough-in a new one. Like a recessed tub, the shower pan has a flange on three sides which prevents water from entering between the shower stall and the wall. The front of the pan has a ledge, called a **curb** or threshold. The lower the curb, the more accessible the unit.

TUB/SHOWER COMBINATION

The tub/shower and surround may be manufactured or finished on site. Options include:

■ Install wet wall and end wall finish on site, the most expensive method, with such materials as ceramic tile, solid surface material, or laminate panels

■ Install a one-piece tub/shower and surround, usually fiberglass or acrylic

■ Install four wall panels in the same material as the tub/shower

The one-piece unit is seamless so it is resistant to leaking, and it is very easy to clean. However, the unit is bulky; be sure that there are adequate clearances in the home to carry it to the remodeling site.

The tub/shower with a three-piece wall system is not as leak-proof as the one-piece models, but it is easier to carry to the remodeling site.

STEAM HEAT, DRY HEAT

Consumers have a smorgasbord of fixture styles and colors from which to choose, as well as a variety of bathing styles: the soothing bath, steeping bath, swirling whirlpool. Add two more bathing choices to the list: the **steam shower,** a smaller version of the steam rooms found in health clubs, and the dry heat of the **sauna.**

Steam Shower

The steam shower offers a way to relax in less space than a whirlpool. A steam shower is a steam bath contained in a shower enclosure. It consists of three parts: a shower enclosure with walls extending to the ceiling, a steam generator, and a seat. The steam generator boils water by means of an electric heating element, producing steam. The steam is piped to the shower where it enters through one or more steam heads or valves. The steam generator is located outside of the shower.

Steam generators that are smaller, lighter, and less costly are making the home steam shower a reality. And they are efficient too. A steam bath fifteen minutes long consumes about $1\frac{1}{2}$ quarts of water and 1.8 kilowatts of electricity, according to the NKBA. The initial cost is high; generators start at about $1,200. Size the generator according to the number of cubic feet in the shower enclosure.

To prepare an area for the steam bath, installing a vapor barrier on the ceiling and wall studs is recommended to prevent steam from getting through tiny cracks and rotting the framing; tile or stone, which withstand heat and humidity, may then be installed following the "mud" method, or by installing over fiberglass-reinforced cement backerboard. (See Chapter 14, "On the Surface: Walls, Floors, and Counters.") Some, but not all, solid-surface materials work well in steam showers too. A tight-fitting floor-to-ceiling door is a requirement.

Walls also must be insulated for the steam generator to develop the 115 to 130 degree temperature necessary for a steam bath. The ceiling and bend should have a slight slope for run-off as the steam condenses. The base of all shower fittings (showerheads, valves, etc.) must be carefully sealed with silicone to prevent steam from escaping.

The generator requires a 220-volt circuit and should be professionally plumbed and wired. A generator may be located a few feet from the steam shower and concealed, so it does not interfere with the design of the bathroom. Expect to clean the shower more frequently than a standard shower to slow the growth of bacteria, mold, and mildew in the warm, moist environment.

SAUNAS

The sauna's soothing dry heat can be enjoyed after any kind of physical activity or after a day of work. Water may be splashed on the sauna stove rocks for a burst of humidity at the end of the sauna bath. Follow the sauna with a bracing cool shower.

Saunas, traditionally made of aspen, are often made with redwood today because they can withstand temperature extremes. Redwood is used for sauna walls, ceiling, and floor because it acts as an insulator and remains warm to the touch even when the sauna temperature reaches the recommended high of 190 degrees.

A one-person sauna can fit into a 3' X 3' space; add about 7 square feet for each additional person. A traditional family-size unit is about 6' X 6' with upper and lower benches, each measuring 20" wide by 6' long, large enough for laying down.

Saunas are designed and built to retain heat. For example, the low ceiling (usually 6½' to 7' high), helps keep the heat in. The wall, ceiling, and floor are also insulated, usually with 3½" fiberglass batts. A narrow door, usually 20" to 24" wide, without a lock, should swing out to help conserve heat.

The sauna stove may be gas or electric. The stove size, measured in kilowatts for electric models and BTUs (British Thermal Units) for gas unit, depends on the number of cubic feet in the sauna. Smaller heaters may operate off a standard 120-volt circuit; family-size saunas will require a 240-volt line. Sauna designs should include a protective fence or other device around the heater to avoid burns. A temperature control is usually located on the sauna exterior; the temperature is set before entering the sauna.

The sauna room also needs an air intake, an outlet for cross ventilation, and a pleasingly soft lighting system that is also controlled from outside the sauna. Because saunas need both air intakes and vents, they may not be suitable for apartments in which gaining access to exterior walls is difficult or impossible.

Costs range from about $1,500 for the smallest units up to $6,000 for the family unit made of top-grade redwood with a large heater.

Prefabricated sauna kits are available with a heat unit, ventilation, and lighting system appropriately sized for the sauna.

WORTH REPEATING

1. Tub and shower are being separated because the tub is not ideal for showering. Tub/shower combinations present problems, such as relatively high rim compared to the shower curb, curved sides that make standing difficult, and narrow tub width.

2. Safety features that should be included in tubs and showers are grab bars, nonslip bottoms, shower seat, and shower controls located outside the stream of water from the showerhead.

3. Fixtures are changing shape to reflect the way they are used, thanks to ergonomic studies. Tubs are contoured to the human body and include lumbar supports and head and arm rests. Shower stalls are larger than the 32" X 32" units prescribed by code; 36" X 42" is a better fit for the body for showering tasks.

4. Cast iron is the premium tub material for durability and color retention, but enameled steel is lighter and less expensive.

5. Whirlpool jets may produce a directed, pinpoint action, or an all-over swirling water motion. A control to mix air with the water will vary the water action.

6. Larger whirlpools may require an in-line heater to maintain temperatures for long soaks, extra floor support, a 240-volt circuit for a pump over 1 hp, and a separate water heater.

7. "Try on" a whirlpool the same way you would test fine furniture to make sure it fits the people who use it.

8. Consult the sidebar on "10 Tips on Fittings" for guidelines on spouts, shower valves, showerheads, diverters, and plumbing.

12

Fixtures:
Sinks and Toilets

Sinks and toilets, the two most frequently used fixtures, must be extremely durable. Invest in the best fixtures money can buy.

The choices in sinks and toilets have multiplied in the past decade. The beauty of materials, colors, and styling have elevated the utilitarian sink and toilet to a featured place in the overall design of the bath. Water conservation and safety are built in too.

Among the changes:

■ **Water-saving toilets,** requiring 3.5 gallons per flush (gpf), are being replaced with even more efficient water-miser toilets that use a mere 1.6 or less gpf. (See Chapter 8, "Using Water Wisely," for details.)

■ **Faucets are temperature-adjusted to avoid scalding.** (See Chapter 7, "Staying Safe," for details.)

■ **Quality fittings,** identified by a corrosion-resistant brass body, durable ceramic cartridge regulating water flow, and finish of brass, chrome, or epoxy.

■ **Space-saving fixtures** include the pedestal sink, the wall-mounted sink with a decorative shroud to cover plumbing, and the corner toilet.

■ **The integral vanity sink,** or sink formed in one sheet with the countertop, of elegant solid-surface material or cultured marble.

■ **Introduction of the "back saver" sink,** elevated from 34" to 36", which ergonomic studies show is a more comfortable height for bending over the sink.

■ **Two sinks in one counter:** Extensive use of the double vanity for the two-person bathroom.

■ **Toilet placed in a compartment** for privacy, or separating toilet from bath with a privacy wall, to enhance use of bathroom by two people at the same time; or toilet placed so it is shared by two bathrooms, conserving space and reducing fixture expense.

■ **Decorated fixtures** — flowers, stripes, etc. — which require a second glazing and, therefore, cost more.

■ **Popularity of the bathroom suite,** a set of fixtures matched in styling and color.

MATERIALS

Vitreous china, a ceramic material, is the primary choice for sinks and toilets because it can be molded

Countertop Sinks

Integral, single bowl

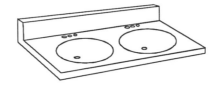

Integral, double bowl

Undermounted

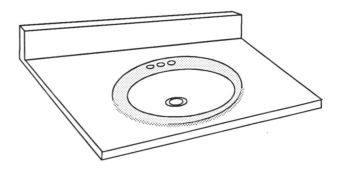

Self-rimming

easily. It is also sanitary, meaning that it is highly resistant to moisture absorption. Compared to other ceramics, such as wall tile with absorption rates as high as 10 percent, vitreous china has an absorption rate of .5 percent.

Vitreous means glass-like, the result of glazing at very high temperatures. A "slip" (a mixture of flint, feldspar, and water mixed with different clays) is poured into a plaster of Paris mold with two sections that form the inside and outside curve of the product. The slip is cured, inspected, and glazed in a kiln for twenty-four hours, then reinspected.

Sinks and toilets with a design, striping, or decal are fired once again. The decoration process and additional firing explain why these fixtures are more expensive than simple colored fixtures.

Some flaws can be repaired; others cannot. If an imperfection in the tank of a one-piece toilet cannot be repaired, for example, the entire piece must be destroyed, which accounts for the fact that these units cost more than other toilet styles.

Vanity sinks and pedestal sinks are also manufactured in **enameled steel, enameled cast iron,** and **cultured marble** or **cast polymer.** (For a discussion of these materials, see Chapter 11, "Fixtures: Tubs and Showers.") Specialty materials include **solid-surface sinks** cast in one piece with the countertop, **stainless steel, plated brass,** and even **gold-plated sinks.**

SINKS

A rule of thumb: Sinks should be as large and as deep as possible for face, hand, and hair washing, recommends the NKBA.

The **free-standing pedestal sink** saves space in the small bath because no cabinet base is needed for support. However, the pedestal sink offers no storage, so team it with a ledge or shelf, vanity wall cabinet, or tall storage unit.

The pedestal sink has two parts, the base and the sink, which may be joined with hardware provided by the manufacturer or by bolting the sink to blocking between wall studs. The back of the base is usually open, or partially open, to accommodate plumbing. The rough-in plumbing must be precisely placed so connections will fit within the narrow base, unlike the vanity cabinet which allows more room for plumbing. The width and shape of the deck (the area behind the bowl), the backsplash (if any), and the number of holes drilled determine which faucets will fit the sink.

Bathroom sinks may vary from 22" to a generous 38" wide in a multitude of styles and colors; one

Pedestal Sinks

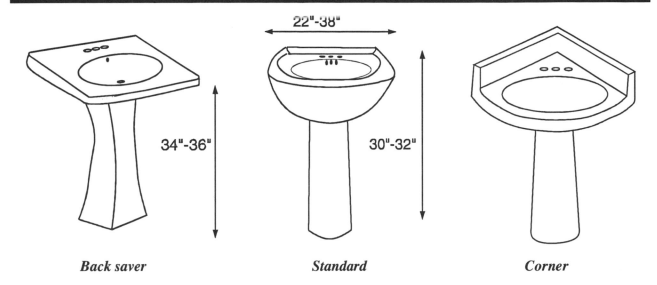

Back saver   *Standard*   *Corner*

of the smallest is the corner pedestal sink with one faucet hole. The standard height is 30" to 32"; 34" to 36" is the **back saver model**. Create your own back saver model. Raise the unit to the exact height needed by installing a platform finished with the flooring material. Pedestal sinks are the most expensive types.

Wall-hung sinks, available in square, round, or corner models, are an improvement because unattractive plumbing can be concealed behind a curved plate called a shroud or trap cover. Like the pedestal models, the wall-hung sink conserves floor space. Blocking must be installed before the wall is finished; the sink is attached to the blocking by means of a bracket. This style accommodates wheelchair users. Wall-hung sinks are easy to install and are the least expensive sink.

The **console sink** resembles a sink in a "table" with an integral bowl and counter supported on two or four decorative legs. The console visually expands space, like the pedestal and wall-mounted sinks, because no cabinet is needed. It also offers

Wall-Hung Sink

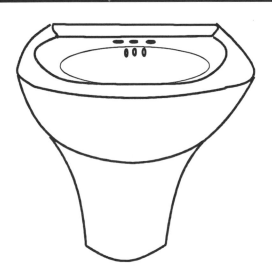

Console Sink

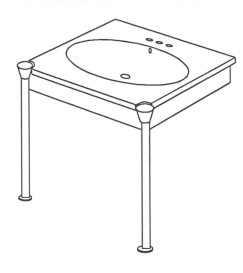

12 TIPS ON FITTINGS

1. For safety, a temperature-limiting device is recommended for sink faucets to avoid scalding.

2. For accessibility, a single-lever control is recommended because it is simpler to operate than dual-controls that require a twisting motion.

3. The sink fittings include the control lever(s), spout, and pop-up drain. To select a faucet, first consider the **type of faucet control** — single control, single-hole center set, or spread fit.

4. The single control combines faucet and control in one unit, with the control located above the spout or to one side. The control is turned left or right, pulled up or down, or pushed front to back, usually through 15 degrees of motion. As soon as the control is activated and the faucet valve is open, the water flow should start; some controls do not start water flow until the lever has been moved 7 degrees, which decreases the user's control of water flow.

5. The single-hole faucet combines a single-lever control, or separate hot and cold handles, on a base. This type may have an *escutcheon*, a plate at the base, to cover any extra holes predrilled in the sink.

6. The center-set has hot/cold controls and faucet mounted on a single base; it requires three predrilled holes. The 4" size is common, and is economical, but handles are close to the faucet so it may be hard to operate and clean for some people.

7. The spread-fit (or widespread fit) faucet has no escutcheon plate or base, with flexible spacing, 8" to 12 inches. The hot and cold controls and spout are mounted separately. This is a decorative style, easy to operate and clean.

8. Select a faucet that fits the sink drilling. The number of holes predrilled in the sink and the distances between them — 4", 6", or 8", and up to 12" for spread-fit styles — will determine which faucets fit the sink.

9. For a sink with no drillings, the faucet is installed in the countertop. Space must be allowed at the back or on the side of the counter for the fitting.

10. Select construction, finish, and attachments, such as a spray or drinking fountain. See Chapter 11, "Fixtures: Tubs and Showers," for a review of construction materials (brass, zinc, and plastic) and finishes (solid brass, plated brass, chrome, enamel, epoxy and gold-plated brass).

11. Washer vs. washerless. The washer faucet, called a "compression" faucet, in which a washer raising or lowering at the water inlet valve provides the on/off water action, is prone to leaking as the washer becomes worn. **Washerless types** control water flow by means of a cartridge containing the "works," a ball, or a disc. The cartridge and disc systems are longer-wearing, especially in ceramic, which is more expensive than the less durable plastic cartridge or disc.

12. For a coordinated look, match fittings throughout the bath; coordinate with accessories such as towel racks and toilet paper holder.

---

more usable space around the sink, but supplemental storage should be provided. The console is primarily a decorative bathroom element and complements period designs.

COUNTERTOP SINKS

Sinks combined with a vanity countertop include the **integral sink**, the **self-rimming**, and the **undermounted sink**.

The **integral sink** is made from one piece of material, usually solid-surface material or cultured marble. It is easy to clean because there are no seams around the bowl; no seams also means no leaks. (See Chapter 13, "Bathroom Storage.") These two materials (solid-surface or cultured marble) offer the flexibility of custom design. Holes are predrilled for fittings. Single and double bowl designs are available.

Toilets

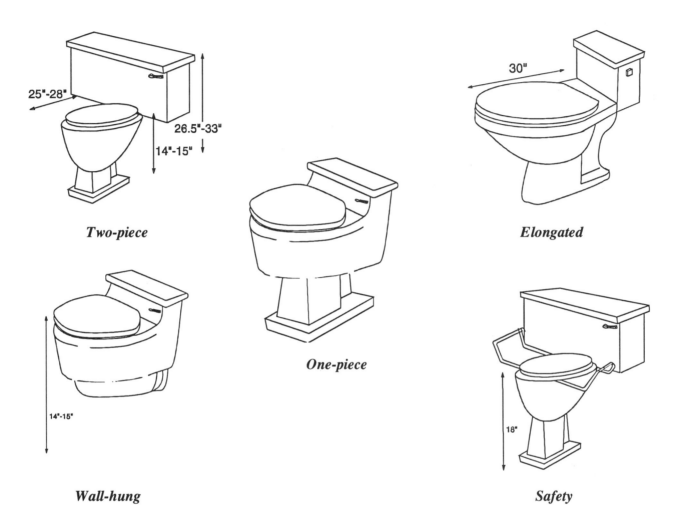

Two-piece

Elongated

One-piece

Wall-hung

Safety

The integral sink has a few disadvantages. The integral bowl tends to be shallow; therefore, a standard height faucet, rather than a high-rise model, is best for preventing water from splashing out of the bowl. And, if the sink is damaged, the entire counter must be replaced.

The most frequently chosen sink is the **self-rimming sink**. It is mounted above the countertop. The self-rimming sink is set into a cut-out in the countertop made with a template; the bowl rim overlaps the cut-out. Sealant is placed between the rim and counter to prevent water leaks. Some bath specialists recommend using the sink itself instead of a template to get an exact cut-out. Many, but not all self-rimming sinks, are drilled for faucets; for those without drillings, care must be taken to select a vanity cabinet that will accommodate both sink and faucet.

The self-rimming types replace the need for metal trim, usually stainless steel, that was formerly used to seal the sink perimeter. Now the rim is a decorative element that is absent in the integral and undermounted types; cleaning where the rim meets the countertop is a bit more difficult than cleaning an integral sink. The self-rimming sink has the greatest variety of styling and color of any type sink, including an oversized fixture with a pull-out, hand-held spray for washing hair.

The **undermounted sink** is a rimless sink. It is installed from below the counter and held in place with metal clips. The countertop extends over the narrow lip of the sink. The NKBA suggests that the rim be glazed in case any part is exposed by the counter cut-out. Cleaning the undermounted sink is easier than the self-rimming, but the design interest is limited to the shape of the cut-out; there is no edge detail. Therefore, a material with an interesting pattern and texture, such as stone, solid-surface material, or cultured marble, is recommended for an undermounted installation.

Placement

Federal minimum standards were published several decades ago to guide space planners:

■ Walkway in front of the bathroom sink: 21 inches

■ Clearance between the center of the sink and the side wall: 12" (leaving 2" of counter between sink rim and wall)

■ For double bowl clearance, the distance from centerline to centerline: 30 inches

But the standards did not take into account the way in which people use these areas and the dimensions of the human body. The NKBA developed the following measures to better fit the human body and contemporary bathroom use patterns:

■ Walkway: 30" recommended; 36" liberal allowance, if used by one person; 42" if used by two people at the same time

■ Side wall clearance: 18" recommended (6" of counter between sink rim and wall); 24" liberal allowance (12" of counter), which gives usable storage space beneath the counter

■ Double bowl clearance: 36" recommended; 48" liberal allowance, for two people using the space at the same time

TOILETS

Features to consider when selecting a toilet are **amount of water used per flush, type of flushing action, quietness, ease of floor cleaning, price,** and **styling.**

For a complete discussion of water-saving toilets, see Chapter 8, "Using Water Wisely." For a quick review, keep these points about water use and flushing action in mind:

■ The **washdown** toilet, requiring 5 to 8 gallons of water per flush, is the least efficient and is now

Bidets

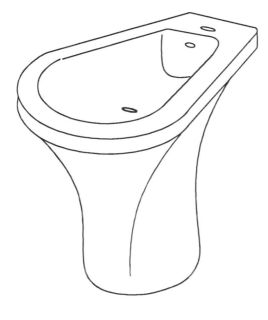

Center-fit

Spread-fit

prohibited by some codes. They are the least expensive, and the noisiest.

■ The quieter **reverse trap** toilet has a smaller water area and trap (passageway through which wastes are removed) than the washdown or siphon jet toilet. It is a step up in price from the washdown models.

■ A **siphon jet** toilet has a larger water surface, a larger trap and is less likely to clog. A siphon jet is quieter than a washdown or reverse trap, and costs more than either.

■ The **siphon action** toilet is the most expensive, most efficient, and quietest. It is available as a one-piece toilet, and its bowl has the largest water surface.

Water-saver toilets usually have smaller tanks and shallower traps than conventional models; the 3.5 gallon-per-flush (gpf) models are now outdone by the super-efficient 1.6 gpf types. These efficient models are available in one- and two-piece styles, as well as floor-mounted and wall-hung units. Their flushing action is either *reverse trap* or *siphon vortex*.

Installation

Toilets are **one-** or **two-piece,** mounted on the floor or wall. If there is not already a wall-hung toilet in the bath, the wall framing must be modified to provide a base of support for the new wall-hung toilet. The flooring must also be altered.

One important measure to consider when replacing a floor-standing toilet is the *rough-in dimension*, or the distance from the center of the drain outlet to the finished wall, which today is usually 12 inches. Older homes may have toilets with a 10" or 14" rough-in dimension; unfortunately, the selection of contemporary toilets with this rough-in dimension is limited. The alternative is to use a flange which will allow the toilet to be offset up to 2"; a contemporary 12" rough-in toilet can then be installed.

Other plumbing changes may be necessary, depending on the toilet selected. A low-profile toilet, for example, requires a $\frac{1}{2}$" diameter rigid supply line, rather than the $\frac{3}{8}$" lines typically used with a two-piece toilet. The height of the supply lines is different too for a one-piece toilet.

Toilet Styling

One-piece toilets have a low profile, usually 19" to 26" high. The tank is noticeably reduced in height. Both floor- and wall-mount versions are available with reverse trap, siphon jet, or siphon action flushing. Their contemporary design, efficient use of water, and easy installation make one-piece toilets popular. They are somewhat easier to clean and sanitize than two-piece models, but more expensive.

Two-piece toilets have a separate tank and toilet bowl and can be mounted on the floor or wall. The *close-coupled* models bring the tank and bowl together more closely so they resemble one-piece units; the tank is bolted to the bowl and supported by it. *Corner toilets* have a triangular tank that fits neatly into small spaces.

A two-piece **safety or high-rise toilet** has a seat 18" above the floor, compared to 14" or 15" for a conventional bowl. Teamed with grab bars or side rails, the high-rise toilet provides comfortable seating for the elderly and the handicapped.

Bowl shape varies with **round** and **elongated** configurations available. The fixture with a round bowl has an overall depth from 25" to 28 inches. The elongated bowl adds another 2" to the overall depth and is more comfortable for both men and women; it is more expensive than the round bowl. The NKBA recommends that the elongated bowl be specified for bathroom projects. A **contoured seat** distributes the weight more evenly than a flat seat, so it is more comfortable.

THE BIDET

The **bidet,** an idea imported from Europe, has been described as a sit-down wash basin that is used for cleansing the pelvic area. This personal hygiene fixture is designed for use by all family members. The bidet area must be stocked with soap and towels within easy reach.

The user straddles the bidet, facing the hot and cold water controls, which deliver water in a *hori-*

zontal stream* much like faucets at a sink, or in a *vertical spray* in the center of the bowl. The elongated shape is also recommended for the bidet. Manufacturers design fittings for the bidet fixture; fittings from other manufacturers may or may not work.

The bidet is placed next to, or opposite, the toilet. Because the bidet and toilet are located together, the bidet is designed to match the toilet in rim height and overall shape.

Placement

The recommended allowances for placing toilets and bidets are again derived from the NKBA. Toilets may be located next to a privacy wall or another fixture, or in their own compartment. Codes require a minimum of 30" of *wall space* behind the toilet when it is located between two walls or objects; the allowance recommended by the NKBA is 36", or 45" for a luxury bath. For *knee clearance*, 16" from the front of the bowl to a door should be

allowed. The *walkway* in front of the toilet should be at least 30" wide; a more liberal allowance is 36" if one person uses the bathroom, 42" for two people.

For a toilet located in a *compartment with a door,* the building codes provide a minimum width of 30", but a 36" space is more desirable. To determine the depth, measure the toilet length — from 24" to 30" — and the door swing. The NKBA recommends a 60" deep area for a 30" deep fixture and a door 2'-6" wide.

Bidets, when located next to a toilet, should have a minimum of 30" of wall space behind them, measuring from the edge of the toilet on one side to the wall or fixture on the other side. The NKBA recommends 36"; a more liberal allowance for large bathrooms is 42 inches. Be sure to check local codes to determine whether bidets are allowable.

When the bidet is opposite the toilet, the minimum clearance is 21" from the front edge of each fixture; 30" is recommended and 36" is a liberal clearance.

WORTH REPEATING

1. Vitreous china, a pottery product molded and fired in a kiln, is the material most resistant to water absorption and, therefore, sanitary for use as a sink or toilet; decorated vitreous china is fired twice so it is more expensive than a plain fixture.

2. Select a water-saver toilet, 3.5 gallons per flush, or a water-miser toilet, 1.6 gpf.

3. Toilets are one or two piece, mounted on the floor or wall; low-profile one-piece units are 19" to 26" high overall; **high-rise safety toilets** for the elderly or handicapped have an 18" seat height.

4. The siphon action type of flushing is the most efficient, the quietest, and the most expensive style of all.

5. Sinks should be as large and as deep as possible for face and hand washing and teeth brushing, and to avoid the problem of running water splashing back at the user.

6. Sink types include the free-standing pedestal sink with plumbing in the base, the wall-hung sink with the plumbing covered by a decorative shroud, the console sink, and the counter sink with one of

three bowl types: integral, undermounted or self-rimming.

7. A quality faucet has a brass body, an inner cartridge made of durable ceramic that controls water flow, and a finish of solid brass, plated brass, or chrome; epoxy and enamel are desirable for their color variety and ease of cleaning.

8. A single-lever faucet is recommended for ease of use by all family members; also select a faucet with a **temperature-control device** that sets a maximum temperature to eliminate the hazard of scalding.

9. To select a faucet, first pick the type of control — single lever or one of the two-control models, center set and spread set — then make sure that the faucet fits the holes drilled in the sink.

10. Follow recommended clearances for locating sinks and toilets in the planning stage, including the space from the sink to wall, between double sinks, width of toilet compartment, clearance for knees at toilet, and walkway in front of sink and toilet.

13

Bathroom Storage

*In the bathroom, every inch counts.
Here's how to buy quality cabinets
that stretch bathroom storage.*

Bathroom cabinets and storage accessories play a larger role in bathroom design than ever before. The range of storage products has expanded well beyond the basic vanity and medicine cabinet.

Developments that have placed storage items in the spotlight include:

- **Adding tall storage cabinets,** 84" to 96" high, similar to kitchen pantry cabinets
- **Larger vanities** (in length) for larger baths
- **Back saver vanity**, 36" high instead of the standard 32"; designed to make bending over the sink for washing and brushing teeth easier on the back
- **Cabinet accessories designed exclusively for bathroom use,** such as tilt-out hampers, pull-out towel racks
- **Vanities sized for two people to share**
- **Combining specialized storage with the vanity,** such as drawer units, open shelving, vanity table for seated grooming
- **Adding floor-to-ceiling storage walls**
- **Moving linen storage** from the hall closet into the bathroom
- **Adding drawers and cabinets for apparel** in baths that double as dressing rooms

- **Adding closet storage systems** in baths with complete closets
- **Extending bathroom cabinetry into the bedroom** for use as clothing storage, nightstand, desk, wall unit, entertainment center

CABINET TYPES

There are many options in cabinet styling, price, and quality, but understanding two key cabinet characteristics will help you to sort out the choices:

- **Stock** cabinetry versus **custom**
- **Frame** construction versus **frameless**

Stock and Custom Cabinets

Stock cabinets are mass manufactured in standard sizes and shapes; base cabinets are made in modules of 3" increments, starting at 9" wide and ending at 48"; they are usually $28\frac{1}{2}$" to $29\frac{1}{2}$" high. Cabinet styles are limited to those listed in the manufacturer's catalog. The quality of stock cabinetry varies widely; many attractive, durable lines are available with a range of storage options.

Custom cabinetry is made-to-order after a bathroom has been designed. Generally, these units are made in 3" increments like stock cabinets, but special sizes can be made to fit the site. Custom work is done by both custom manufacturers and local craftspeople.

Which is better? Stock cabinets are desirable for their price, which may be 40 to 50 percent less than custom cabinets of a comparable style and material. And stock cabinets may be delivered more quickly than made-to-order storage.

On the other hand, custom storage offers more options in woods, finishes, shapes, and accessories than stock cabinets. Another plus is that the local craftsperson can thoroughly understand the remodeling project by visiting the site, taking measurements, and discussing the design face-to-face with designer and client. That's a good way to get a unique look for the bath.

However, be careful; just because a cabinet is custom-made, its quality is not necessarily guaranteed. Shop as carefully for a custom cabinet maker as you do for a designer or contractor.

There is a middle road: **semi-custom cabinetry,** which may be produced by both stock and custom manufacturers. These cabinets are mass-produced, but selected pieces in the line can be made in different sizes. More accessories are available, although not as many as there are for custom cabinets. Prices fall between custom and stock cabinets.

FRAME AND FRAMELESS CABINETS

Frame cabinets are constructed by traditional methods. A narrow frame is fitted to the top and sides of the cabinet box — also known as the case — and sometimes in the center of the box where doors meet. The doors are mounted to the frame by means of an exterior hinge. The width of the frame that shows after doors are in place is called the *reveal.*

Traditional-style wood stock cabinets with raised-panel doors form a complete storage system, including a three-door vanity cabinet, tilt-out hamper (left of vanity), stacking linen storage, and apron desk with drawers for a second grooming area. Above the counter, shallow open shelving keeps towels at hand.

The advantage of frame construction is that the frame makes the cabinet more stable. On the other hand, the vertical rails of the frame on each side and sometimes in the middle of the cabinet slightly diminish storage space and make the cabinet interior less accessible.

Frameless cabinets, which came to the U.S. from Europe, may be thought of as a simple box. Doors are attached by means of a hinge mounted inside the box and on the back of the door. The doors completely overlay the cabinet box and fit flush with each other and the drawer fronts. Some frameless doors can open as wide as 180 degrees.

Because this style requires a tight fit between doors and drawers, the hinges are adjustable to correct any misalignment. To compensate for the lack of a frame, these cabinets are made with a heavy-duty particleboard core for strength.

Accessible storage is a plus in frameless cabinets; doors open wide, and there are no face frames in the way of storage accessories like roll-out bins or shelves. On the other hand, there's little room for error in installation; cabinets must be precisely aligned to look their best.

There's a middle road in this category too. Combine: (1) the frame cabinet, and (2) the flush-fit doors of the frameless cabinet; attach the hinges on the inner door face. The result is a hybrid cabinet with the strength of the frame cabinet and the sleek, unbroken front of the frameless style.

LOOKING FOR QUALITY

Some hallmarks of a quality cabinet are easy to see, such as perfectly aligned doors, smoothly gliding drawers, or evenly applied finish. But other indications of fine cabinetry are hidden: the strength of cabinet joints, the density of the case material, and the strength of shelves and drawer bottoms.

Evaluate these cabinet characteristics to spot a quality cabinet:

■ **Cabinet materials:** Wood and laminate, core materials, drawer sides and bottoms, shelves, interior finish, hinges, drawer glides, drawer and door hardware

■ **Cabinet construction methods**: Type and location of joints

■ **Strength and performance:** Ability of cabinet to withstand loads; smooth operation of doors and drawers

CABINET MATERIALS

About 70 percent of the cabinets manufactured in the U.S. are finished with wood, according to the NKBA. Of those, 75 percent are oak; cherry and maple figure in the total too.

Most of the remaining 30 percent are surfaced with laminate or melamine. **High-pressure laminate** — laminate bonded to a substrate such as particleboard under high pressure — is preferred to **low-pressure melamine**, which is less expensive, but more susceptible to damage on impact.

Remember that a wood cabinet is rarely made entirely of solid wood. In fact, solid wood is subject to shrinking and warping. So a "wood" cabinet may have *parts* of solid wood, such as doors, drawer fronts, and frame. The cabinet box, shelves, and drawer bottoms and sides can be made from a wood veneer or a wood-patterned laminate, and a core of pressed wood, such as plywood, particleboard, or fiberboard.

All three **core materials** help strengthen the cabinet and overcome the tendency of wood to shrink and swell. The core material is very important in frameless cabinets because there is no frame to stabilize and strengthen the cabinet box.

Plywood is made of thin wood sheets laminated in alternating directions. It is stronger and more stable than solid wood. *Hardwood plywood*, made from deciduous trees, is usually a better quality core than *softwood plywood*, which is made from evergreens. Wood veneer door and drawer fronts often have a core of plywood.

Hardwood plywood is graded by the Hardwood Plywood Manufacturers Association; it should carry a grade of A on one side, which means that face veneers are smooth and the edges are tightly matched. The other side should be rated no less than a sound grade of 2, which allows for some discoloration, knots that will not pop out, and face veneer unmatched for grain or color.

Particleboard is made of wood chips, shavings, and fibers bonded with resin under pressure. Small, fine particles are on the surface; larger wood chips are found in the core. Compared to plywood, particleboard is heavier but not as strong.

For laminate cabinets, a substrate of industrial-grade particleboard (also known as 45-pound commercial grade) is preferred, because it can support the laminate. If a lesser quality particleboard is used, screws and/or staples may eventually loosen and cabinet components may separate.

Medium-density fiberboard (MDF), the preferred fiberboard for cabinets, is made of very fine wood fibers that are glued and bonded under high pressure. Its density gives it better screw-holding power than particleboard, an asset in cabinet construction. MDF has the advantage of a smooth surface and a tight, clean edge that can be shaped and painted. MDF is less expensive than plywood but more costly than particleboard.

Frame Cabinet Construction

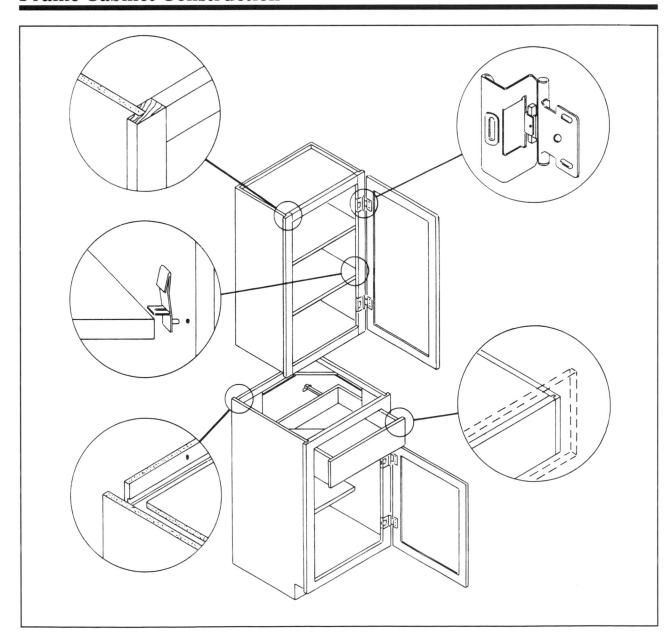

Expect a top-of-the-line wood cabinet to have solid wood doors, drawer fronts, exposed sides, and frame (unless it is a frameless cabinet). The trend is toward interiors of melamine or laminate for a clean, light look and easy maintenance. Check the back of wood doors and drawer sides; are they wood, wood veneer, or pressed wood?

A step down in price is the wood veneer cabinet. Look for an easy-care laminate interior and shelves; a pressed-wood interior should cost less than a melamine or laminate interior.

Top-of-the-line quality laminate cabinets are made of high-pressure laminate over a core of industrial grade particleboard, with a melamine or laminate interior. All edges must be banded — usually with vinyl or laminate. Edge banding must be uniform in width and securely adhered to the edge.

Frameless Cabinet Construction

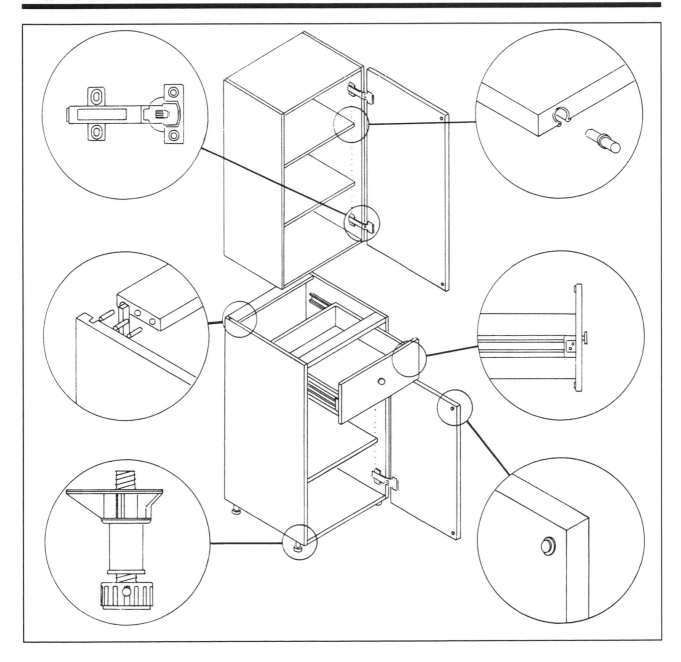

TESTING QUALITY

The Kitchen Cabinet Manufacturers Association (KCMA), a national organization of cabinet manufacturers and their suppliers, sponsors a voluntary cabinet testing program that may help you select a quality cabinet for the bath. A 60-item assessment determines whether cabinets meet or exceed performance standards and construction requirements of the American National Standards Institute. Cabinets that pass the test — and a retest annually — carry a blue and white certified cabinet label.

Although not all cabinets are submitted for testing, products of the top ten U.S. cabinet makers (by business volume) are tested, according to the KCMA, as well as dozens of other manufacturers. (See KCMA, Appendix A.)

One of the advantages of KCMA testing is that it covers quality you cannot see. Structural tests for hinges, doors, drawers, shelves, and the cabinet box simulate normal use over the life of the cabinet. Five of the thirteen tests are:

■ **Shelves and cabinet bottoms** are loaded at fifteen pounds per square foot for seven days. **Checkpoint:** No visible sign of joint separation or failure of any part of the cabinet or the mounting system.

■ **Wall cabinets** are loaded to ensure that the cabinet will accept a five hundred pound load. **Checkpoint:** No visible sign of failure in the cabinet or mounting system.

■ **Cabinet doors and hinges,** in open and closed positions, are struck with a ten-pound sandbag to test the ability of the cabinet to withstand impacts. **Checkpoint:** The door must operate as it did before the test and show no damage or sign of separation or failure.

■ **Drawers** are loaded at fifteen pounds per square foot and operated through twenty-five thousand cycles. **Check point:** Drawer is operable with no failure in any part of drawer or glide, and drawer bottoms must be square.

■ **Cabinet finish** is subjected to substances typically found in the kitchen and bath, such as vinegar, lemon, orange, catsup, coffee, olive oil,

and 100-proof alcohol for twenty-four hours. **Checkpoint:** No discoloration, stain, or whitening that will not come out with ordinary polishing, and no indication of blistering, checks, or other film failure.

Cabinets must meet the following twelve general construction requirements, among others, to earn the KCMA certification seal (from the annual *Directory of Certified Cabinet Manufacturers*). These requirements should also be met by any bathroom cabinet you choose.

1. All cabinets must be fully enclosed with backs, bottoms, sides, and tops on wall cabinets; and backs, bottoms, and sides on base cabinets.

2. All cabinets designed to rest on the floor must have a toe space at least 2" deep and 3" high.

3. All utility cabinets must meet the same construction requirements as the base and wall cabinets.

4. Doors must be properly aligned, have means of closure, and close without excessive binding or looseness.

5. All construction materials must ensure rigidity. **Face frames,** when used, must provide rigid construction. **For frameless cabinets,** the ends, tops/bottoms, and back shall be thick

DRAWER TEST: Loaded at 15 pounds per square foot and operated for 25,000 cycles (one open/close is a cycle), the drawer must remain operable.

enough to provide rigid construction.

6. Corner or lineal bracing must be provided at points where necessary to ensure rigidity and proper joining of components.

7. All wood parts must be dried to a moisture content of 10 percent or less at the time of fabrication.

8. All materials must be suitable for use in the kitchen and bath environment where they may be exposed to grease, solvents, water, detergent, steam, etc.

9. All exposed plywood and composition board edges must be filled and sanded, edge-banded, or otherwise finished.

10. All exterior exposed parts of cabinets must have nails and staples set and holes filled.

11. All exposed construction joints must be fitted in an expert manner.

12. Interior exposed surfaces should have at least one coat of clear finish.

DOOR TEST: When loaded with a 65-lb. weight and operated for 10 cycles, door and hinges must show no visible signs of damage.

STRUCTURAL TEST: Loaded with 500 lbs., wall cabinets and mountings will not fail. A door test: In 25,000 cycles, the door latch must hold the door closed.

TOXINS IN CABINET MATERIALS

Some particleboard, plywood, and flakeboard products used in the construction of cabinets may contain the toxic chemical formaldehyde. The cabinet base is the area in which wood products with formaldehyde are most often found.

In a moist room such as the bathroom, the formaldehyde may be released as a gas from the cabinet. This release of formaldehyde is most likely to occur during the first heating season after installation, when the heat dries the wood.

Formaldehyde may cause health problems for people with a chemical sensitivity. In fact, some people suffer not only from formaldehyde in plywood or particleboard, but from the cumulative effect of chemicals found in such common household items as carpeting, foam-filled cushions, and insulation. These individuals require homes that are chemically free.

Currently there are no government guidelines on "safe" levels for formaldehyde in the home — or any of the seven thousand chemicals in building materials and home products that cause problems, according to the NKBA. But the area of chemically healthy homes and indoor air quality issues is developing rapidly. Ask your designer, contractor, or

Contemporary-style laminate stock cabinets, wall-mounted over the vanity, plus handsome wooden shelving, and six drawer/door units multiply storage at the double vanity. At the right, an idea borrowed from the kitchen: Install a tall, pantry-style cabinet with adjustable shelving.

cabinet salesperson about formaldehyde in cabinetry, or consult the reference librarian for current literature on chemically-free homes.

JOINERY

Frameless cabinets are usually manufactured with **dowel joints,** in which two cabinet parts are joined by glue and two or three dowels that extend about $3/4$" into predrilled holes in each cabinet part. Dowel joints are very strong and are also found in high-quality frame cabinets.

Other desirable joints, such as mortise and tenon, dovetail, tongue and groove, and rabbeted joints are strong because an *extension* of one cabinet part fits into an *indentation* in the other part. Dovetail and dowel joints are excellent for drawers.

On the other hand, joints in which wood is placed side by side (butt joints) or overlapped (lap joints) tend to be weaker, because the parts do not

fit into one another. Lap joints may be found in low-cost cabinets.

All joints should be glued. The cabinet case should be glued, and stapled or nailed. The staples or brads hold the joint together while the glue cures. Nails will hold the case together better over the life of the cabinet.

FINISHES

The stain applied to a wood cabinet enhances the grain and should have a uniform appearance. Selecting the stain is a matter of personal preference, but the trend is toward light-colored stains.

To protect the stained wood, a finish is applied, often of polyurethane, shellac, or varnish products; three relatively expensive high gloss finishes are lacquer, polyester, and enamel. Some manufacturers also develop finishing products of a unique chemical composition.

10 WAYS TO CUT CABINET COSTS

1. Reface, don't replace. If existing cabinets are sound and the bathroom layout is workable, refacing the cabinet frame and other visible surfaces with thin plywood and veneer, and replacing door and drawer fronts save as much as 50 percent. Build in quality. Select wood veneer for cabinets, and top-quality drawer and door fronts. Or add some color with laminate refacing.

2. Add to existing cabinets. For a minor remodeling or face lift, add a tall narrow cabinet, for example, to expand storage. Check the cost of a custom-made cabinet or shelving that matches the existing vanity.

3. Shop for cabinets. See if you can beat the price of cabinets offered by your kitchen retailer or contractor, but remember that many cabinet lines are distributed only through dealers and contractors. Be sure the contract specifies that the owner provides the cabinets.

4. Select and install interior storage accessories. Wood storage accessories are the most expensive. Instead, shop for epoxy-coated wire storage or heavy-duty plastic accessories such as roll-out baskets, roll-out shelves; put a tall plastic container on a slide-out base and use it for a hamper. Check that accessories will fit cabinets ordered.

5. Consider a vanity wall cabinet. This old standby provides a wealth of shallow storage for those small items that clutter the vanity counter. Select an updated version, recessed between wall studs, with double or triple doors faced with mirrors, adjustable shelving, and electrical outlets.

6. Large vs. small. Combining several small vanity components — a sink base, drawer unit, and shelf unit, for example — usually costs more than using a few large components that fit into the same space.

7. Buy a simple door. As a rule, the more ornate the door, the higher the cabinet price.

8. Look for adjustable shelving. Adjustable shelving usually costs more than stationary shelving, but it allows customized interior storage space so that every cubic inch is used.

9. Stretch the double vanity. Locating sinks at each end of the vanity makes good use of the cabinet space in the middle. Remember to allow enough elbowroom between sinks and walls.

10. Use the walls. The freer the floor space, the greater the design flexibility. So use wall storage that costs less per lineal foot than a vanity cabinet; coordinate style and material with the vanity cabinet. Examples: Shelving between wall studs, especially in the wall adjacent to the vanity; an 8" deep toilet-topper shelving unit; kitchen wall cabinets; a mirrored vanity cabinet is not limited to the wall space above the vanity.

Applying the finish may be a labor-intensive process with as many as twelve steps for custom cabinet finishing. The longer the production time, the greater the cost.

Make sure that the finish is evenly applied and that it covers all outer surfaces and edges. Beyond these criteria, it is difficult to visually judge the finish quality. However, one guideline is to consider a cabinet which has been certified through the KCMA program. The certification program tests the ability of the finish to withstand extreme temperatures and resist damage from prolonged exposure to soap and water.

In a laminate cabinet, high pressure laminate is harder and thicker than low pressure laminate. So high pressure laminate has a more durable finish. It also resists dents and nicks better than low pressure laminate.

HARDWARE

The most important job of **hinges** is to properly align doors with the cabinet box and to provide strength for opening and closing over the life of the cabinet. Frame cabinets may have surface-mounted or concealed hinges. Self-closing hinges are desirable for convenience; hinges that wrap around the frame prevent the door from opening too widely and are also self-closing.

Concealed hinges are available for face frame cabinets but their construction is different than those for frameless cabinets. They do not offer more support than hinges on the face frame; it is a matter of aesthetics to leave hinges concealed or install decorative hinges.

Unfortunately, many hinges on frame cabinets are not as easily adjustable as they are on frameless units. If a door is not properly aligned, then the entire hinge may have to be moved, and the screw holes filled.

The concealed, adjustable hinge of the frameless cabinet is heavy-duty hardware that is designed to support twenty pounds per hinge. Some doors may be adjusted up, down, and sideways by simply turning screws that position the hinge arm.

Drawer glides operate very smoothly on nylon wheels or ball bearings made of polymer or steel. In frame cabinets, the glide may be mounted on the side, bottom, or at the corners; frameless cabinets typically have side-mounted glides. The glide should allow the drawer to open smoothly without tilting downward or sticking.

A full-extension glide opens the drawer completely without it falling out of the cabinet and allows complete access to the drawer contents; three-quarter glides are also available. When the drawer closes, bumpers should cushion the impact of the drawer against the cabinet.

Door and drawer pulls are available in a tremendous variety of shapes and sizes and in wood, brass, plastic, porcelain, metal, and chrome to match faucets, counter, or tile. U-shaped handles are easy to grasp. For safety, pulls should have no sharp corners.

The concealed pull, a groove under the drawer front, is fairly easy to grasp and has no protruding elements. Another version is the continuous pull, which is a grooved band, usually wood, situated across the drawer or door front.

Adjustable shelving is more desirable than fixed and adds to the cost of cabinets. The strength of the shelving brackets, the thickness and strength of the shelf, and a durable coating are marks of quality in cabinet interiors.

Adjustable shelving may be supported by metal clips snapped into metal channels on the cabinet wall or plastic clips inserted into holes drilled at regular intervals. The channel system allows somewhat more flexibility, because there are more mounting slots. However, the drilled system gives a cleaner look to cabinet interiors.

SIZES

Bathroom cabinets are not as deep as kitchen cabinets, 21" compared to 24 inches. The standard height has been 30", like the kitchen cabinet. But for brushing teeth or washing at a 30" high vanity, the sink is actually *below* 30" and may require considerable bending to reach. To correct this problem, manufacturers now offer vanities 32" to 36" high, called the back saver vanity, as part of their standard bathroom cabinet line.

Base cabinets may incorporate drawers, shelves, or both. Ask if a second shelf is available for flexible storage. Over-the-toilet cabinets, or toilet toppers, are usually 8" deep, so there is no danger of striking the head against the cabinet when rising from the toilet.

Wall cabinets manufactured on 3" modules vary from 9" up to 48"; measure 12" or 24" deep. Tall cabinets are 84", 90", and 96" high, 12" or 24" deep; narrow widths from 12" to 30" usually fit the bathroom best. The most accessible storage space is from 22" to 56" above the floor. Put the most frequently used items in this space; lesser used items, above and below.

For a stock cabinet line, consult the manufacturer's catalog for a complete listing of cabinet sizes. Each catalog should also have illustrations of cabinet configurations.

PLANNING STORAGE

Planning storage in the bathroom is as important as planning it in the kitchen. Here are some principles from home management specialists:

■ **Store all supplies at the point of use.** For example, provide washcloths and hand towels at the vanity, bath towels at the tub/shower.

■ **Store items so they are visible at a glance.** Many small items are stored in the bathroom. Several shallow compartmentalized drawers are more useful than a large deep drawer. Other useful storage includes roll-out shelves and bins in the cabinets, shallow shelf storage, and door shelving systems.

■ **Store frequently used items within easy reach.** Store frequently used items on shelves that are between 22" and 56" high. Store less frequently used items above or below. Where shallow storage is not available, store the most frequently used items in front of those less frequently used.

■ **Items that are used together should be stored together.** Shaving equipment is an example. Store together razor, blades, electric razor, shaving lotions, after shave, skin conditioner.

To start planning the storage system, **consider the type of bath planned.** For example, a child's bath requires storage for toys, plenty of towels, a large hamper, a step stool, and so on. The teen's bath has different requirements than a large master suite shared by two which is, perhaps, used as a dressing room.

Next list all the items stored. Hair grooming, face care, cosmetics and makeup, shaving needs, hand and foot care, personal hygiene, perfumes, towels, soap, paper goods, cleaning supplies, medical needs, and so on. Plan storage for items that are very small — lipsticks, dental floss — and those that are large — bath sheets, multipacks of toilet paper.

Note problems with the current storage system. What items lack storage? Is there enough room for grooming appliances, such as hair dryers? Do traffic jams occur at any one storage area? How easy are cabinet interiors to clean?

Identify special needs. The elderly may have

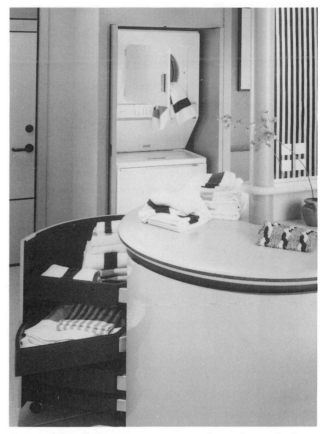

Several small compartments, such as these shallow swing-out drawers below the laminate vanity, often make better use of space than large storage units. Linen storage is conveniently located close to the vanity and the washer/dryer.

a limited range for reaching and bending, as well as declining eyesight, so plan easy-to-open cabinets with white interiors that are within their reach. Children may need a pull-out step at the sink; provide locks on doors and drawers for safety. The athletic family may want a ventilated hamper for wet garments or extra towel storage. The working couple may need complete closet facilities.

Estimate the maximum floor area allotted for storage. How can wall storage — especially storage placed between wall studs — supplement the total? That 15" space between wall studs can accommodate a towel ladder, tall cabinets, or shelving. (In cold climates, storage between studs on an outside wall is not usually recommended because it creates uninsulated space.)

WORTH REPEATING

1. Cabinet quality is determined by both the cabinet finish — wood or laminate — and the core materials under the finish. For wood cabinets, plywood and medium-density fiberboard (MDF) are durable; industrial-grade particleboard is desirable under laminate.

2. Joints are another important hallmark of quality and durability. Frameless cabinet components are usually joined with dowels that fit into drilled holes, a strong joining method; on wood cabinets joints, such as mortise and tenon, tongue and groove, and rabbeted joints are strong because the joint pieces fit into one another. Dovetail and dowel joints are excellent for drawers.

3. Cabinets that are certified by the Kitchen Cabinet Manufacturers Association have passed tests that show the strength of the cabinet components over its expected life.

4. Expand storage capacity and free floor space with wall cabinets and shelving built between studs.

5. To use every cubic inch of storage inside cabinets, select storage accessories that fit the items stored, such as multicompartment dividers for cosmetics and pull-out trays for storing linens in deep cabinets.

14

On the Surface: Walls, Floors, and Counters

Choose coverings for bathroom walls, floors, and counters that are water-resistant, durable, and beautiful.

Walls, floors, and vanity counters in the bathroom have a tough job. They must withstand constant heat, humidity, and water, and at the same time, be easy to clean.

That's a tall order. But serviceable, water-resistant materials such as ceramic tile, marble, laminate, and vinyl flooring, among others, can withstand the bathroom environment and come out looking good.

WHAT'S UNDERNEATH

Finishing walls and floors requires a stable, level, clean, and dry surface. If the existing walls and floors meet those requirements, and the existing finish material is securely bonded to the substrate, it may be possible to install the new finish material directly over the old. For example, **resilient vinyl tile** or **sheet flooring** can be installed directly over old vinyl, according to major manufacturers, provided that the old flooring is properly adhered and is not cracked or otherwise damaged. However,

cushioned or embossed vinyl must be removed or covered over with an underlayment of plywood. Degloss or roughen a vinyl floor before installing **ceramic tile;** if the floor surface is uneven, trowel on latex floor filler to level it.

For walls, the American Tile Council recommends removing any loose or damaged wallcovering, paint, or plaster before applying the new tile.

Yet some remodeling jobs call for *replacing* old walls and flooring, especially if the finish material does not adhere to the base, or if there is water damage, excessive soiling, wear, or a springy surface that needs stabilizing. Floors may need strengthening to support the weight of a material such as ceramic tile.

Removing the finish material reveals the condition of the base; it too may need replacing. For example, the plywood subfloor underneath old vinyl flooring may have suffered water damage; the damaged areas, or the entire subfloor, must be replaced. Another example: During demolition, when an old fixture is removed, the wall behind it may be damaged; the wall must be repaired.

Be prepared for these hidden surprises; set aside money in the budget — as much as 10 percent of the contract — and time in the installation schedule to install new subsurface materials if needed. Also indicate in the construction contract that repairing any damaged subsurface materials will require extra time and money.

Mix-and-match tiles coordinated for consumers by the manufacturer create a custom look for a moderate cost. This black-and-white bath combines 6″ white tile for floors (matte glaze) and walls (gloss), 1³/8″ accent squares, and 6″ long strips. The simple lines of laminate cabinets blend with geometric tile design.

UNDER THE FLOOR

In many homes beneath the bathroom flooring is a two-layer sandwich including the:

■ **Structural subfloor:** Panels of plywood or flakeboard, ½" to ¾" thick, glued and nailed to joists to make a rigid base for the floor; called structural subfloor because it is part of the floor support system.

■ **Nonstructural subfloor:** Plywood panels are used under a vinyl floor; for ceramic tile, a concrete panel called backerboard is recommended, or a mortar base. The purpose of the nonstructural subfloor, or underlayment, is to provide a stable surface for the floor.

UNDER THE WALL

Under the tile, paint, or wallcovering on the bathroom wall are:

■ **Drywall:** a panel, usually 4X8 and ½" thick, with a plaster-like core and a thick paper coating, nailed and glued to the 2X4 wall studs.

■ **Backerboard:** a water-resistant grade of drywall especially for use around tubs, usually installed as 4X8 panels, ½" thick, or, concrete board.

■ **Plaster:** applied wet in at least two coats to a base called a lath; widely used for home construction until the 1950s.

In a major remodeling, it is likely that original drywall and/or backerboard will be removed completely, and new panels installed to accommodate changes in the placement of fixtures or cabinets, or changes in the position of walls. If tile is removed from walls, the drywall, backerboard, or plaster underneath probably will be damaged so as not to be usable; replace it before installing a new wall finish.

In a minor remodeling or face lift in which all walls will not be replaced, defects in drywall or plaster may be repaired if they are not too extensive. Because plaster is quite a durable material and has good sound-insulating qualities, the NKBA advises that it should be saved, if possible. Nailing drywall over old plaster is another option; however, the room dimensions will be decreased by the thickness of the drywall panels.

A complete shell of 12" marble tile (on walls, floors, and ceiling) expands this 5' X 10' bath and adds a touch of elegance. Marble tile also covers the platform of the sculpted whirlpool tub.

AT THE VANITY

Preparing the vanity counter to receive a new surface is somewhat simpler than resurfacing walls and floors because structural support is not as critical. On the other hand, it is just as important for the counter substrate to be dry, level, and clean.

In a major remodeling in which the old cabinet and counter are removed, the new cabinets must be square and level. The area just above the cabinets will act as a base for the backsplash. It must be sound, dry, clean, and level.

In a minor remodeling or face lift in which only the vanity counter will be replaced, it is necessary to remove the entire counter and supports before installing the new surface material.

SURFACE MATERIALS FOR WALLS, FLOORS, AND VANITY COUNTERS

TYPE	USES	PRICE	PROS	CONS
MARBLE/GRANITE				
Marble: A soft, porous stone created from limestone recrystal-lized under the earth's pressure and heat **Granite:** Igneous rock with coarse grain; resistant to moisture absorption	Floor/wall tile; shower/tub surround; counter	Luxury-price; five times as much as a plastic laminate counter	Durable; granite is denser, easy to maintain; thermal finished type has matte finish suitable for flooring	Variations in patterns; marble is soft and porous so may stain/scratch if not sealed; marble is somewhat slippery so slip-resistant finish is desirable
LAMINATE				
Plastic: Layer of thin plastic sheet, colored paper, and kraft paper bonded under high pressure; may be bonded to a particleboard backing. **Color-through:** All layers bonded contain color **Laminate board or composite panel:** Formed under low pressure; lighter than high pressure types; for vertical applications	Counters (plastic, color-through); walls (laminate board)	Moderate; for counters, plastic is $10-$50 per linear foot, color-through is $30-$75 per linear foot	Range of colors, patterns; easy to clean; blends well with other materials; on color-through, nicks and scratches are less visible and no black seams occur where edges meet	Plastic cannot be repaired; laminate-covered wallboard limited in colors
SOLID-SURFACE				
A **cast plastic resin,** either polyester or acrylic, blended with additives and formed in color-through sheets $\frac{1}{2}''$ and $\frac{3}{4}''$ thick; opaque; colors or marble-like pattern	Walls, especially tub/shower surround; counters	High, $100-$150 and up per linear foot, although less than marble or stone	Nonporous, stain resistant, repairable; seamless look	High cost, installers require special training so installation costs are higher than laminates
WALLCOVERING				
Solid vinyl backed with fabric recommended	Walls, excluding wet areas	Low, $5-$35 per roll (25 to 30 square feet)	Low cost, washable, can be stripped; very wide selection of colors/patterns; repairable	Proper surface preparation, adhesive use, and installation essential for adherence; least permanent product

TYPE	USES	PRICE	PROS	CONS
PAINT				
High-quality **alkyd** or **oil-base** advisable	Walls	Low; $15-$20 per gallon (500 square feet coverage)	Easy application, wide color selection, washable, repairable; semigloss resists soil and marking from steam and water splashes	May peel or crack if wall is not prepared and sealed properly; requires mineral spirits for cleanup
RESILIENT VINYL				
Tile or **sheet**, with wear layer	Floor	Low, $9-$30 per square yard	Resists moisture, easy to clean, rapid installation, wide pattern selection	Cushioned vinyl provides comfort but is susceptible to denting; thick vinyl wear layer loses gloss more quickly than thinner urethane wear layer

TOXINS IN SURFACING MATERIALS

Just as formaldehyde may be present in some particleboard, plywood, and flakeboard used in cabinet construction (see Chapter 13, "Bathroom Storage"), it also may be present in subflooring and in the substrate of laminate counters. For individuals with a chemical sensitivity, these building products may cause health hazards. Ask your designer, contractor, or retail salesperson about the formaldehyde content of subflooring and laminate counters.

CERAMIC TILE

The bathroom is probably the only room in the home in which one material — ceramic tile — works equally well for both floors and walls. Because tile is resistant to moisture, scratches, and stains, and is easy to clean, it is a natural for vanity counters too.

The cost is moderate — $2 to $30 per square foot, and up to $40 for imported and custom-made tiles. However, the labor costs for installation boost the price. For example, an installer may charge per tile, by the square foot, or by the linear foot. Understand which method is being quoted. Remember too that installation time and price are reduced with pregrouted panels and sheets of mosaic tile.

Changes in tile products have made custom looks available for a moderate cost:

■ **There are coordinating colors** for tile and tubs/sinks/toilets.

■ **Coordinating colors/patterns** for wall and floor tiles are available.

■ **Accent tiles** coordinated with tiles of different sizes, shapes, colors, and patterns, which simplify the process of creating dynamic patterns, are available.

■ **Tile murals,** in which several tiles are combined to create a scene or still life, are widely available as stock items rather than custom-ordered and/or handpainted.

■ **Trim pieces** for counter or tub edges, baseboard, etc., that match tile colors and patterns are available.

■ **Larger tiles** are available. Domestic tiles measure up to 12" X 12", breaking the rule that small rooms need a small tile pattern; large and small tiles are combined in unique patterns. Also, 18" X 18" and 21" X 21" tiles are available from Italian tile sources.

■ **Edge tiles** for counters are available in an increasing array of styles, colors, and patterns.

■ **Grout** (the material that fills the tile joints) and tile in matching or accent colors.

CERAMIC TILE BASICS

Composition. Tile is made of clay, shale, or porcelain that is formed and fired in a kiln at very high temperatures for hardening. The higher the temperature and the more times the material is fired, the harder and less porous the tile.

Next, the tile may be left unglazed, or glazed with a coating of minerals and stain, then returned to the kiln for one more firing. The glaze forms a glass-like surface on the tile.

Differences in raw materials and firing make some tiles more durable for heavy-use areas such as floors. The harder the material, the more suitable for floors. The firing method affects the moisture ab-

sorption rate and makes some tiles more appropriate for use in a high-moisture area such as a bathroom. *Always check the manufacturer's recommendations for tile use.*

Tile types. The Tile Council of America describes four categories:

■ **Glazed wall tile**, thinner and less strong than floor tile because it takes less wear.

■ **Quarry tile**, made of shale, clay, or earth; deep red, tan or dark/neutral color; a wide range of quality in this type; usually unglazed but may be glazed; unglazed may benefit from sealing to resist staining and moisture; for use on floors.

■ **Paver**, made of clay or porcelain, usually with a textured surface and rounded or irregular edges; available in glazed or unglazed; dense, hard, easy to maintain; for use on floors.

■ **Mosaic,** glazed or unglazed; the smallest tile, not to exceed 6 inches square, is available in squares, hexagons, rectangles; for use on floors, walls, counters, curved surfaces.

Tile Finish. Glazed tiles have a surface which may be matte, high-gloss, or textured. **Unglazed tiles** show their natural colors throughout the body of the tile, rather than on the surface, like glazed tile.

Natural stone tiles for floor, whirlpool platform, and shower combine with a solid-surface counter. Notice the tile shapes on the curved surfaces, the bottom row of wall tile, and the shower curb.

Note that unglazed tile must be sealed to prolong its appearance and enhance water resistance.

The glaze or finish often determines the use of the tile:

■ **Unglazed** and sealed quarry, pavers, and ceramic mosaic tiles are recommended for floors with **heavy traffic.**

■ **Slip-resistant tiles** must be used for floors for safety; although glazed tiles are often slippery when wet, glazed tile treated to be slip-resistant may be used for the floor.

■ **High-gloss glazed tiles** may dull somewhat with use; these tiles are appropriate for areas with little wear such as walls.

■ **Dark-colored glazed tile** show wear more quickly than light colors; consider light colors for floors and counters.

■ **Matte-finish glazed tiles** do not show wear as readily as high-gloss tile. (Yet both are equally hard.) A matte glaze may be selected for floor and counter.

Porosity. Tile with a low porosity is desirable for the bathroom, especially floors and counters, because it is hard and resistant to staining. According to standards developed by the American National Standards Institute, the lowest porosity tile is **impervious,** which absorbs less than 0.5 percent water; **vitreous** tile absorbs 0.5 to 3 percent; **semivitreous** absorbs between 3 and 7 percent; and **nonvitreous** absorbs more than 7 percent. Impervious and vitreous tile are desirable for bathroom applications. Be sure the tile you choose is suitable for use on the intended surface — floor, wall, or counter.

Sizes and shapes. The most popular tile shapes are squares, rectangles, hexagons, and octagons. Accent pieces in narrow strips and small diamonds, for example, are also becoming more popular. Tiles range in size from the ceramic mosaic, which is 6 inches square or less, to the wall and floor tile, which is 12 inches square.

Grout. Grout is the material that fills the spaces between the tiles. Apply sealers to grout lines in areas of heavy wear, such as counters. Sealers also preserve grout colors.

Silicone rubber grout has elasticity and moisture resistance, which makes it popular for bathroom floors and walls. **Sanded grout,** in which sand is added for strength, is used in joints up to $\frac{3}{8}$" wide, usually for floors and mosaics. Stain and mildew resistance are also important in bathroom grout. Match or contrast grout color to tile. **Epoxy** is used where superior strength is needed, such as vertical joints in backsplashes. It is the most expensive grout.

Panels/Sheets. Pregrouted panels are available for tub and shower walls. Although the choice of colors and patterns is limited, the pregrouted panels cut installation costs significantly. **Ceramic mosaics,** mounted on sheets for easy installation, are available. Grout is spread into the joints after the sheet is put into place.

INSTALLING TILE

There are three basic methods for installing bathroom tile:

1. Mastic. Tile is applied directly to the subfloor, cement backerboard (for wet applications), or vanity top deck (plywood or lumber) with a troweled-on adhesive, either organic-based or cement-based; used for walls and floors. Mastic may be used over wood, plywood, paneling, brick, or concrete. The advantage of mastic is that it increases the wall thickness and changes the floor height the least of the three methods.

2. Mud-set or mortar bed. Mortar, or mud, is troweled over a wire mesh or lath until the bed is $\frac{3}{4}$" thick. Tile is then installed on the bed; used for floors and counters. This method is a good option when floors are heavily worn. It provides a water-resistant base, structural stability, and permanence. The floor will be raised by the combined height of the bed and tile, so a threshold transition between new and old floors must be planned.

3. Thin-set over backerboard. Water-resistant backerboard takes the place of the wire mesh/mortar bed; the board is only one-half the weight of the mortar bed. A thin coat of adhesive is troweled on the board, and the tile is set in place; used for walls and counters.

If tile is being applied over an existing wall, the Tile Council of America advises removing loose and damaged plaster, wallcovering, and paint. Thoroughly clean painted surfaces; high-gloss paints should be deglossed with a strong solution of TSP or paint deglosser.

COUNTER MATERIALS

Plastic laminates are often the first choice for vanity counters because they come in such a wide array of colors, patterns, and textures and are moderate in price. Laminates reproduce the look of marble, granite, and wood. A new texture is designed to resist water spots. Seams are invisible with color-through laminates.

While laminates are durable and easy to maintain, they are not totally impervious to stains (although finishes are being introduced that increase the stain-resistance of laminates). Solid-color laminates (color-through laminates) take some of the worry out of cuts or scratches because the color goes all the way through the laminate instead of just the top surface.

The base under the laminate is usually particleboard or plywood, ¾" thick. First the top is test-fit to the cabinets, then cut-outs for sinks are made. Next the counter is secured with screws and glued to the cabinet.

Solid-surface material offers the elegance of marble or granite, the flexibility of custom forming, and the practicality of stain and scratch removal. First introduced more than 20 years ago, solid-surface materials are sold under various names. Check with your local building supply center or home center.

Most varieties are available in ½" to ¾" sheets, usually 24" to 30" wide and up to 12' long. Handsome rounded edge treatments may be selected; different patterns and colors may be joined in one countertop. Stains can be eliminated with a mildly abrasive scrubber.

One of the material's advantages is that a single or double bowl may be formed as part of the counter, called an **integral bowl,** or as a separate sink mounted under the counter surface (**under-**

A Roman-style tub and surround of cultured marble demonstrate the extent to which the material can be shaped. The unit is molded in separate pieces — walls, tub, platform, and apron.

mounted bowl). The integral bowl has no seam whatsoever into which water can leak. The undermounted bowl requires no sealing rim.

Marble and granite, the most expensive counter materials, are cut from natural stone that is quarried in the U.S. and also imported from all over the world. Because marble grain and coloration vary from slab to slab, the designer may go directly to the stone yard to select a piece for the bathroom counter. Granite graining varies less than marble so it may be selected from a smaller sample.

Granite is sold in slabs ¾" and 1½" thick; marble, ¾" or 1¼" thick. Granite slabs may measure up to 4½' wide by 9' long, more than large enough for almost any vanity counter. Some designers suggest the ¾" thickness of granite or marble to reduce costs; others prefer the thicker slab for strength.

Costs may be reduced by selecting two smaller pieces of marble for a counter rather than one large slab. Another alternative for counters and backsplashes is the use of marble tile, which comes in many sizes.

Granite is more stain resistant than marble because it is less porous; it does not scratch. However, granite is more brittle than marble, so care must be taken during shipping and installation. Cut-outs for sinks or faucets must be 3" or more from the edge.

The markings and colors of marble — red, green, white, yellow, and black — are caused by minerals. Veins result from discoloration by water; they are like small fractures and may break under pressure.

Generally speaking, the more colorful and decorative the marble, the weaker it is, and, ironically, the more expensive. The Marble Institute of America has developed a four-step scale to rate marble strength. A and B marble is stronger, easier to maintain, and produces less cutting waste than C and D marble.

Granite and marble require specialized installation by trained craftspeople. The fabricator or importer of the material usually provides skilled installers.

WORTH REPEATING

1. Ceramic tile is the most durable, water-resistant material for bathroom walls and floors.

2. The glaze and **composition of the tile body** dictate the appropriateness of a tile for walls or floors; check the manufacturer's recommended use before buying.

3. A slip-resistant finish is required on ceramic floor tile for safety.

4. Cut tile installation costs by selecting pregrouted ceramic tile panels or mosaic tile on sheets.

5. Walls and floors must be dry, level, and stable before new finish is applied; if not, remove old covering and repair or replace subfloor and/or drywall.

6. Install ceramic tile with mastic or mortar for permanence.

7. Moisture-resistant cement backerboard must be used for wet-area walls.

8. Refer to the chart titled "Surface Materials for Walls, Floors, and Vanity Counters," on pages 148 to 149, for detailed information on these finishing materials: marble, granite, laminate, solid-surface materials, wallcovering, paint, and resilient vinyl.

Part Six

BATHROOM SYSTEMS

☐ WATER HEATING ☐
☐ BATHROOM HEATING/COOLING ☐ LIGHTING ☐
☐ VENTILATION ☐

15

Good Looks with Lighting

*How to get the most out
of natural and artificial
lighting, day and night.*

Although most bathrooms are relatively small, the lighting requires careful planning to meet specific needs. A well-lit mirror for shaving and applying makeup is an essential, for example; tub/shower lighting is both practical and safe. The elderly require brighter lighting levels. And night lights help keep the bathroom safe for everyone, particularly the young.

Bathroom lighting is not only practical, but also decorative. Imagine a skylight brightening a colorful tile bath with daylight. Or a well-placed greenhouse window becoming the focal point of a bathroom. Install a dimmer switch on lighting in the tub area, and lower the lights for a relaxing after-work soak.

Energy efficiency is also a concern when selecting both windows and lighting fixtures. Learning to compare energy costs of bulbs, fixtures, and windows saves money in the long run.

TYPES OF BULBS

Incandescent bulbs are the least expensive and most widely available bulbs for home use. They render color without distortion or muting, and they have a life span of 750 to 1,000 hours, depending on the wattage.

Fluorescent tubes have a higher initial cost than incandescents, but they have a longer life — from 9,000 to 20,000 hours, depending on the type. Fluorescents in the past had poor color rendition, but today they are available in several "shades" of white. For the bathroom, select **warm white** fluorescents which blend well with incandescent light. Their screw-in base fits incandescent fixtures.

Light output from both incandescents and fluorescents is measured in **lumens**, not watts. Fluorescent light is more energy efficient than incandescent light, because it provides more lumens (light output) per watt (electric power used). According to the American Lighting Association (ALA):

■ Fluorescents produce 40 to 100 lumens per watt while incandescents produce 12 to 21 lumens per watt

■ Fluorescents consume three to five times less energy than incandescents

For example, a 60-watt incandescent bulb could be replaced with a 22-watt circular fluorescent lamp to produce the same number of lumens. The fluorescent saves 38 watts per hour over the life of the tube, which is about 9,000 hours. With energy costs at $.08 per kilowatt hour, you'd save about $27 in energy costs.

Standard Bulb Types

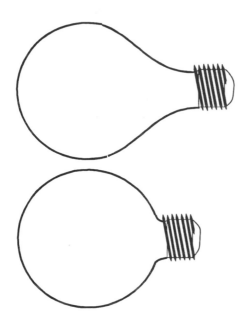

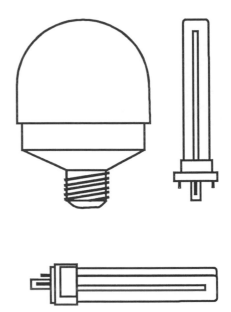

INCANDESCENTS: Standard (above); incandescent globe (below).

FLUORESCENTS: Screw-in (top left); compact twin (top right); compact quad (bottom).

The New Generation

Both incandescents and fluorescents have undergone changes in efficiency and styling. **Tungsten-halogen incandescent lighting** and **compact fluorescents** are being used more widely in the home.

Halogen bulbs, which have a capsule filled with halogen gas rather than argon and nitrogen like the standard incandescent, provide a whiter light than incandescents. Because of this excellent **color rendering**, halogen is a natural for lighting at the vanity mirror.

Halogen bulbs get good marks for energy efficiency too. They supply more lumens per watt than standard incandescents and have a longer life span, according to the American Lighting Association (ALA). For example, a 150-watt incandescent has an average life span of 750 hours; a 150-watt halogen has an average life span of 1,500 to 2,000 hours.

Another halogen benefit: Tungsten-halogen bulbs between 40 and 75 watts are available. They provide *25 percent more lumens* than a comparable standard incandescent.

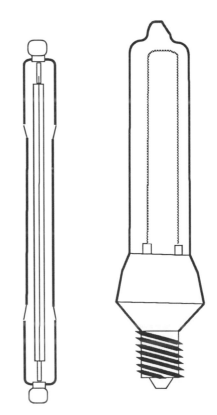

HALOGEN: Double-ended (left); single-ended (right).

The halogen bulb is also very compact — about the diameter of a pencil and half as long. Its small size allows lighting designers to create smaller fixtures, especially accent lighting, in a much greater variety of designs.

The minilights used in accent lighting are **low-voltage halogens.** They operate on 12 volts and require a transformer to step-down the standard 120-volt household current. Flexible strips of these minilights can be placed under wall cabinets, in the cabinet toekick area, or on steps in a whirlpool tub platform, creating a thin glittering ribbon of light. These low-voltage lights are helpful to the elderly especially at places like the steps to a platform tub to highlight the change in elevation.

Compact fluorescents are designed to *replace* incandescent lighting from 40 to 75 watts. Some compacts contain lamp, ballast, and socket all in one unit. They screw into standard light fixtures, just like incandescents; others require an adapter base to fit the fixture.

Compact fluorescents produce a warm, pleasant light and save energy because they use less power to produce the same amount of light. A 13-watt compact twin fluorescent, for example, can replace a 60-watt incandescent. Over the life of the compact — about 10,000 hours — the yearly savings based on $.08 kilowatts per hour is $43, reports the American Lighting Association.

BATHROOM LIGHTING PLAN

There are three ways to light a room:

1. Ambient lighting. Source(s) of overall illumination in a room, such as a bathroom ceiling light fixture combined with a ventilating fan

2. Task lighting. Lighting for a specific activity, such as shop lights over a workbench or a reading lamp

3. Accent lighting. Decorative lighting, such as recessed ceiling lights that accentuate a fireplace of handsome brick or a lighted china cabinet

In the bathroom, **ambient lighting** (where the light fills the room) at one time was limited to an incandescent fixture mounted in the ceiling or on the wall. However, relying on a single ceiling fixture

to light a bathroom just doesn't work. It produces a harsh glare, which tires the eyes; the absence of lights at the mirror creates shadows on the face. When fluorescents were introduced, placing a tube on each side of the medicine cabinet improved

Yearly Savings with Fluorescent Bulbs

Incandescent Wattage	Fluorescent Replacement (1)	Rated Fluorescent Life	Yearly Savings (2)
2-60W	1-20W Straight Tubes	9,000 Hours	$60.30
1-100W	2-20W Straight Tubes	9,000 Hours	$42.30
2-75W	1-40W Straight Tube	20,000 Hours	$196.00
2-60W	1-32W Circle Tube	12,000 Hours	$93.60
3-60W	1-32W + 1-40W Circle Tubes	12,000 Hours	$126.00
1-60W	1-13W Compact Twin	10,000 Hours	$43.00
1-100W	2-13W Compact Twins	10,000 Hours	$66.00
1-75W	1-18W Compact Quad	10,000 Hours	$53.00
1-60W	1-15W Compact Screw-In	9,000 Hours	$40.50

(1) Includes allowance for ballast wattage.
(2) Calculated @ $.10 per KWH based on deluxe warm white color.

bathroom lighting, but early fluorescents produced a harsh, yellow or greenish light.

An improved lighting strategy is to combine *several sources of lighting* — ambient, task (lighting for a specific activity), and accent lighting (to enhance room elements) — for a bright bath, especially for bathroom larger than 5' X 7'. Start the lighting plan with general lighting fixtures, then consider task lights at the mirror, tub, shower, and toilet compartment. Finally, determine the role of accent lighting in the bath.

GENERAL BATHROOM LIGHTING

Bright ideas for general lighting include:

1. Ceiling fixture, installed flush with ceiling. Reduces glare compared to ceiling fixtures that project several inches below ceiling. Select incandescent or energy-saving fluorescent lamps and a diffusing glass.

■ **Sizing**. For surface-mounted fixtures, figure 1 watt of incandescent light or $\frac{1}{3}$ to $\frac{1}{2}$ watt of fluorescent light per square foot (NKBA recommendation).

2. Recessed ceiling fixture. Also reduces glare. The spread of the light beam from the fixture varies. Consequently, the amount of floor area that is illuminated varies as well. A disadvantage is that the portion of the fixture that projects into the area above the ceiling may not be covered with insulation, according to code. (However, some recessed ceiling fixtures are fire rated to be covered with insulation. Check the fixture fire rating before you buy.) This ensures that heat from the recessed lamp will dissipate. However, it leaves a "hole" in the insulation blanket through which bathroom moisture and heat will escape.

■ **Sizing.** For recessed fixtures, allow $2\frac{1}{2}$ to 4 watts of incandescent light per square foot, or $\frac{1}{2}$ watt of fluorescent light per square foot, advises the NKBA.

3. Ceiling fixture at sink. Locate fixture over the *front edge of the sink* — not in the middle of the ceiling. Align the front edge of the fixture with the front edge of the sink; the rest of the fixture will then be positioned in front of the sink. In addition, use

cross lighting (at left and right side) at the mirror.

4. Indirect lighting. Light is directed toward the ceiling or wall; the light then bounces off that surface and illuminates the room. Conceal fluorescent tubes or incandescents behind a wide molding, or valance, located over cabinets or relatively high on the wall. Indirect lighting is very restful to the eye.

5. The small bathroom. In a small bathroom, one that is 5' X 7' or less, the mirror lighting *may* be adequate to illuminate the entire room.

TASK LIGHTING: THE MIRROR

Getting the light right at the mirror is the most critical lighting task in the bathroom. Mirror fixtures should spread light evenly over the face. That means lighting both sides of the face, under the chin, and the top of the head so no shadows are created.

Cross lighting, the technique of placing a light on each side of the mirror, is one way to provide even lighting for grooming. Placing lights on both sides of the mirror and over the top is another choice.

Fixtures that incorporate translucent milky-white plastic or glass are desirable because they diffuse the light. A lighting fixture without a translucent shielding produces uncomfortable glare. All fixtures mounted at the side of the mirror must send light not only up and down, but also to the left and right so both sides of the face will be illuminated.

Lighting techniques vary depending on the size of the mirror. For small mirrors, less than 36", two side lights are adequate; a light over the mirror is optional. For a mirror larger than 36", sidelights may be too far away to do much good, so enhanced levels of overhead lighting must be used. (See "No Shadows: Lighting the Mirror," page 160.)

Also look for vanity mirror cabinets that incorporate lighting fixtures. These one-piece designs have a very sleek appearance. Check manufacturer's recommendations for installation.

TASK LIGHTING: TUB/SHOWER

For safety's sake, plan a light for the shower or a tub/shower enclosure. Brighter light may help prevent falls and also makes bathing easier and more pleasant.

This powder room mirror (less than 36" wide) is lighted with an overhead bracket of three incandescent bulbs.

A 36" wide mirror is lighted by a decorative fluorescent fixture extending the length of the mirror and natural light from the skylight.

Select a light source designed for a wet location. These fixtures are enclosed to prevent moisture from entering. Also, remember that the switch must be located out of the wet area. (See Chapter 7, "Staying Safe.") Switch and fixture must be on a GFCI circuit to protect against electrical shock.

Select one of these fixtures for shower or tub/shower enclosure:

■ **Recessed.** An enclosed damp-location recessed fixture with diffuser; however, fixtures are usually limited to 60-watt maximum so light may be somewhat dim.

■ **Wall mounted.** Designed for wet locations; an alternative to recessed because they usually allow more wattage and therefore, help reduce shadows.

■ **Whirlpool tub lighting.** Special lighting may be desired for reading and relaxing. Consider placing lights on a dimmer for this area. Ensure that lights in other areas of the bathroom do not glare into bather's eyes. For safety, check codes for location of fixtures and switches and use GFCI circuits.

A word about heat lamp/light combinations: This fixture is often added outside of the shower for comfort and general lighting after showering. However, this light is not designed to light the shower interior.

Task Lighting: The Toilet Alcove

If a separate compartment for the toilet is part of the remodeling plan, especially in the larger bath, a separate light is needed. The most common solutions for this area are **ceiling fixtures,** or **wall sconces**.

■ **Sizing: Incandescent,** 60 watts; **fluorescent,** 30 to 40 watts.

NIGHT LIGHTS

To keep household members of all ages safe, be sure to provide night lights. The trick is to provide a low lighting level in the bath as well as on the route to the bath. Simple 7-watt lights that plug directly into an outlet are standard night lights. Sensor lights that are automatically activated when a person enters a

NO SHADOWS: LIGHTING THE MIRROR

Here's how to ensure shadowless mirror lighting.

BATHS WITH MIRRORS LESS THAN 36" WIDE:

1. **Pendants.** Place on both sides of the mirror at eye level.

■ **Sizing:** Incandescent, 75 to 100 watts on each side of mirror; place fixtures 30" apart, 60" from floor, suggests American Lighting Association (ALA).

2. **Vertical strip lights.** Place on either side of the mirror. **Strip fluorescents,** or single **incandescent bulbs in wall sconce fixtures,** provide excellent cross lighting.

■ **Sizing:** Incandescent, same as above. **Fluorescent,** 20 watts on each side of mirror, 30" apart, 60" from floor.

3. **Hollywood-type lighting strip.** A row of incandescent bulbs can do an adequate job of mirror lighting. Fixtures have been scaled down for bathroom use. Lighting strip is slimmed down to 2½"; frosted globe-shaped bulbs are 2" or less. This fixture may produce too much heat in warm climates.

■ **Sizing:** Usually four bulbs per strip.

4. **Wall bracket.** A light source over the mirror or at mirror sides, fluorescent or incandescent, with light-diffusing shield. Select a fixture as long as the mirror.

■ **Sizing: Fluorescent,** 24" 20-watt tube in each. **Incandescent,** one 75-watt or two 60-watt bulbs in each. Be aware that two 60-watt bulbs in a fixture yield as many lumens as a single 100-watt bulb but require more energy to operate.

BATHS WITH MIRRORS 36" OR WIDER:

1. **Recessed fixture in ceiling, ceiling mounted, or wall mounted.** Minimum length of fixture is 24 inches.

■ **Sizing:** Fluorescent, 36" 30-watt tube or 48" 40-watt. **Incandescent,** four to six 60-watt bulbs.

2. **Hollywood lights.**

Sizing: Strip (about 18" to 48" long) with four to six frosted globes (from 15 to 25 watts) per strip across top and down each side of mirror.

3. **Soffit lighting (overhead lighting).** Build a soffit or light box over the vanity, at a height of 78" and with one or more translucent panels. Incandescent or fluorescent bulbs are suitable; wattage depends on size of light box. The soffit also creates a custom, built-in look for the vanity.

---

room are a more contemporary type of night light; however, these sensor lights do not light the way to the bathroom.

Other night lighting options include placing the general bathroom lighting fixture on a dimmer and leaving it illuminated through the night. Or plan low-voltage lighting under wall cabinets, in the cabinet toekick, underneath a shelf or counter overhang for soft light at night. (See "Accent Lighting," below.)

ACCENT LIGHTING

The use of accent lighting to highlight features of interest in the bathroom is a growing practice. Remember that halogens are effective accent lights because of the whiteness of their light.

A greenhouse window or plant area may be highlighted with recessed or track lights. Small wall sconces in contemporary fixtures may even double as night lights. Highlight art work, a tile mural, or an interesting architectural detail.

MORE HELP

Fixtures in this chapter have been described by their location; there are too many fixture styles to enumerate. For the latest information on styles, especially for fixtures that accept halogen bulbs and compact fluorescents, visit a lighting showroom.

For additional help with lighting design, talk to a designer at the showroom with experience in bathroom lighting. Call the American Lighting Association (ALA), toll-free. (See Appendix A for the telephone number.) They will refer you to a local showroom that is a member of the ALA trade organization.

The ALA showroom may employ an ALA Certified Lighting Consultant, a staff person whose training consists of 50 hours of courses in lighting

At the double vanity, each bowl has its own mirror with two Hollywood-style brackets, positioned vertically, for cross lighting. Recessed fixtures in a narrow soffit provide overhead lighting for the mirror as well as ambient room lighting.

and design, sales training, and two years of experience. The consultant's professional credentials should also include an affidavit of competence from design professionals, submission of lighting layouts, and customer recommendations.

DAYLIGHTING

Bringing daylight into the bathroom is a job that involves:

- **Evaluating existing windows** and selecting replacement windows or options such as a skylight, greenhouse window, bow or bay window, and glass block

- **Understanding window features** such as glazing, framing, energy efficiency, and maintenance
- **Maximizing daylight**, but avoiding eye-straining brightness and overheating
- **Maintaining privacy**

Evaluate Existing Windows

During the remodeling process, consider replacing old windows for reasons of energy efficiency and aesthetics.

Inefficient windows may be costing you money. A single-glazed window, a window that allows

The double set of corner casement windows brings daylight and views to the soaking tub. A privacy curtain or shade will be needed on the right set of windows because of a housing development being built.

drafts, or one that is not properly weatherstripped and insulated are good candidates for replacement. Aesthetically speaking, windows that are damaged by bathroom moisture are an eyesore; repair or replace them.

Other window problems that you may encounter include windows that are difficult to operate, those that interfere with privacy; styles and shapes that do not blend with the new bath; or the need to use wall space for other purposes.

Another option is to improve, rather than replace, old windows. The tried-and-true techniques of caulking, weatherstripping, and reglazing old windows can reduce heat loss. Adding an indoor or outdoor storm window also improves the efficiency of older windows, for a lower cost than window replacement.

UNDERSTANDING WINDOW FEATURES

Windows have long been the weak link in the home energy system. Even the most energy-efficient types with **double-glazing** — two panes of glass with an insulating air space between — offered little resistance to the transfer of heat from the inside of the home.

The ability of a window to resist heat transfer through radiation and conduction is called its **R value;** the higher the R value, the greater the resistance, and the greater the energy savings. Double-glazed windows average an R value of 2; single glazed, an R-1.

Then along came **low-emissivity glass,** also called low-e glass, that boosted R values further. Deposited on the glass is an ultra-thin layer of a metallic compound that reduces radiant heat transfer, earning an R-3 on a double-glazed window. If the double-glazed window airspace is filled with an invisible insulating gas such as argon, it raises the expected R value to 4.

These low-emissivity coatings also reduce solar heat gain, summer and winter. In the summer, this sun-blocking action of low-e glass is a benefit; in winter, the loss of solar heat is more than offset by the low-e window's ability to reduce heat loss from the home.

Today, windows with **double the R value of early low-e windows** are coming on the market. There is no generic name for these super-windows yet. Two examples of the new window technology, rated at R-6 to R-8 include:

■ **Double-glazed window**, in which two sheets of low-e film are suspended between two panes of glass; the three air pockets created are filled with invisible insulating gas (i.e. argon).

■ **Triple-glazed window** with two low-e coatings and argon gas in the dead airspaces; a 1" thick window.

An alternate measure of energy efficiency is **U value**: $U = \frac{1}{R}$. The lower the U value, the better the performance. The American Architectural Manufacturers Association prescribes a standard test for U values — and most tested windows rank between 1.05 and 0.23 — but complying with the test is voluntary. Whether you shop for a low U value, or high R value, look for the rating of the entire window — frame and glass. Some manufacturers quote values for glass only.

And a final measure is the **air infiltration rates.** A standard national test for airtightness used by manufacturers subjects windows to the equivalent of a 25-mile-per-hour wind. Air infiltration is measured by the cubic feet of air per minute (cfm) that enter, for each linear foot of perimeter. Most windows have a rating of less than 0.35 cfm; look for a rating of 0.1 or below.

In addition to the energy efficiency of window glazing, consider these features of bathroom windows:

1. Window frame. As a rule, wood frame windows have a higher insulating value than windows with aluminum or vinyl frames. Some homeowners praise wood windows for their aesthetic value; yet wood windows require painting and are subject to water damage. A low-maintenance, energy-efficient hybrid — a wood window clad with aluminum or vinyl — is also available.

2. Weatherstripping improves airtightness. It should be flexible under temperature extremes. It should be made out of materials, like polyurethane or neoprene, and replaceable.

3. Select operable windows (windows that open) over inoperable windows, unless a combination of both is used and an adequate ventilating fan is installed. Even skylights are available with operable windows; they are opened and closed with a long pole or electronic controls.

4. Cleaning. Many window styles rotate or tip inward for easy cleaning.

5. Pricing. Stock windows are less costly than **custom.** Stock windows are available in such a variety of attractive styles and sizes that unless you have a rather unusual room, or desire a very unique design, a custom window is not needed.

A rule of thumb: The higher the energy efficiency of the window, the higher the initial price.

MAXIMIZING DAYLIGHT AND PRIVACY

For window replacement, or the addition of new daylighting options, listed are some of the products that increase daylight without reducing privacy:

■ **Skylight** (or roof window) provides about five times as much light as an ordinary window; the best option for maximizing daylight while maintaining complete privacy

■ **Glass block wall/window** provides good light transmission and privacy; very flexible design tool with many sizes and surface patterns

■ **Greenhouse window** projects beyond the house to capture additional sunlight and is glazed on top and sides; plants act as a screen to help maintain privacy; it adds a contemporary look

■ **Arched-top windows,** such as a half-round style, may be mounted relatively high in the bathroom wall to maintain privacy; a graceful arch is a pleasing alternative to the straight lines of a standard window

■ **Circular or oval windows** are good for use in the gable peak of a high-ceilinged room; adds a classical element to the bathroom design

Another option that significantly increases daylight is the traditional-style **bow or bay window** that projects beyond the house. However, these windows offer little privacy; they should be faced to the side of the house that has the least traffic and

fitted with blinds or other window treatments.

To enhance privacy, select **blinds** for bathroom windows or windows with built-in blinds. Special window glass ensures privacy too. **Opaque glass** and **etched glass** help keep bathrooms private. However, these windows admit less daylight than standard glazing, so they should be supplemented with additional windows and a carefully planned electrical lighting system.

PLANNING A SKYLIGHT

Skylights provide the most daylight per square foot of window than any other daylighting source while maintaining complete privacy. They are an excellent choice for bathroom installations. Skylights free wall space for other uses, a bonus in the small bathroom. The volume of light they admit can make a room appear to be larger than it actually is.

Skylights also work well for bathrooms that have no outside wall such as in attic remodeling. They are a substitute in those bathrooms with a window that admits too little light or causes too much glare.

Consider these skylight features:

1. Sizing. To avoid overheating and glare, skylights must be properly sized. A rule of thumb: The area of skylight glazing should equal 5 to 15 percent of the room area.

2. Location. A window on a north-facing roof provides a soft light. An east-facing window admits morning light. Shade both south- and west-facing roofs to prevent glare and uncomfortable heat gain in the summer.

3. Shaft. In cases where the ceiling is not at the roof line, a shaft to the roof must be constructed. An opening is cut in the ceiling, and the shaft is framed and finished with wallboard. The shape of the shaft — vertical, angled, or flared — determines how much light is admitted. The shaft with a flared base admits the most light.

4. Glazing. Choose an efficient glazing (such as R-3) with an optional coating to reduce heat loss in the winter for northern climates, and to reduce heat gain in the summer for warm climates. Screens and shad__ __ __ __ __ __ 1 manually with a long rod, or electronically wiu. vall-mounted controls, provide additional ways to modify the bathroom climate. Also select skylights that open to enhance bathroom ventilation.

5. Installation. Placing a skylight *between* roof rafters or trusses is the least expensive installation because the roof support system stays in place. The skylight flashing — often a metal or flexible membrane around the skylight perimeter — must be meticulously installed to prevent leaks.

DAYLIGHTING WITH GLASS BLOCK

Glass block is a very flexible design material. Both inside and outside walls or windows, curved or straight, can be formed with block. Block is available in squares, rectangles, corner units, and hexagonal shapes, as well as a variety of surface patterns.

Block is formed by fusing two pressed glass shapes. The partial vacuum created gives block sound-inhibiting qualities and an R value of about 1.8, slightly less than a standard double-glazed window.

Block for exterior applications measure $3\frac{7}{8}$" deep; those for interior uses are slimmer, $3\frac{1}{8}$" thick. Square block measures 6" X 6" to 12" X 12"; rectangular block is available in a variety of sizes.

Glass patterns are pressed onto the side of the block that faces the room interior; the exterior of the block is smooth. Surface designs include the wave-like pattern of standard glass block, as well as

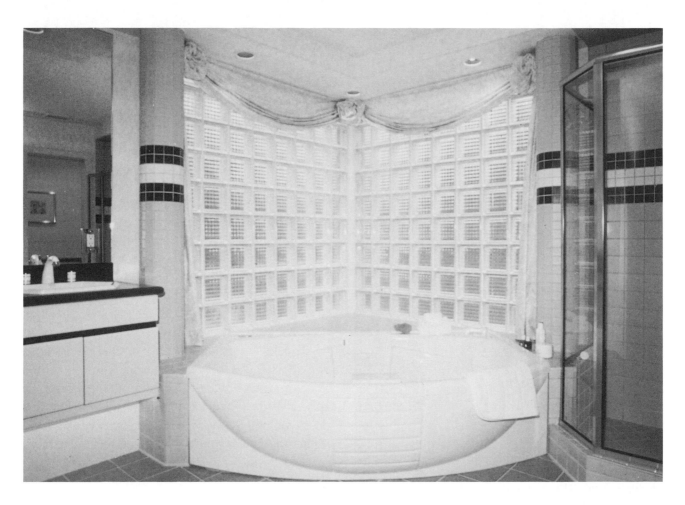

A glass block exterior wall brings in light yet provides complete privacy for this dramatic whirlpool. Overhead, recessed soffit lighting illuminates the bath at night.

Consider the exterior when locating roof windows. Placement of roof windows on two different levels is balanced on this home.

Dormers and attic bathrooms can be well lighted with double-pane roof windows. Operable styles are recommended. A sun screen is advisable for windows facing east and west to prevent glare.

striations, diamonds, and clear block. Patterns may be combined for a custom look.

Inside the bath, glass block walls create privacy, but admit light and maintain an open look — a bonus for the smaller bath. Block walls may form a floor-to-ceiling shower enclosure or a toilet compartment. They make light-transmitting walls between the bathing and grooming area in a larger bath or a wall between two adjacent baths.

Blocks are usually set in mortar and stabilized with metal ties, a job for the mason. A newer method of setting glass block in silicone with clear plastic spacers is designed for professionals or the skilled do-it-yourself homeowner. Acrylic blocks, much lighter than glass, may be installed by a carpenter.

Block may be set on a base of brick, 2X4 framing or a mortar bed. The ability of the floor to bear the load of the block must be considered. Long glass walls need expansion joints so when solar heat makes the glass expand, the blocks will not crack.

WORTH REPEATING

1. Properly lighting the mirror is one of the most critical lighting tasks in the bathroom.

2. Cross lighting, the method of lighting a mirror with fixtures on both sides to eliminate shadows on the face, may be supplemented by a wall-mounted light over the mirror.

3. For small baths, 5′ X 7′ or less, the mirror lighting may provide enough general lighting for the bath.

4. For larger baths, supplement mirror lighting with recessed or surface-mounted ceiling lights.

5. Safety lighting in the bath includes a ceiling fixture in the tub/shower area and a night light. Select fixtures designed for wet areas; controls must be on a GFCI circuit and located at least 5′ from wet areas.

6. Tungsten-halogen bulbs are tiny incandescent bulbs, about half the length of a pencil, that provide a very white light; they are especially useful at the mirror.

7. Low-voltage tungsten-halogen lamps, which operate on 12 volts, save energy. However, a transformer must be installed to make these lamps compatible with the typical 120-volt household system.

8. Fluorescent lamps require one-third to one-fifth less energy than incandescents, while producing more lumens (light) per watt. Their higher initial cost is offset by longer life and reduced operating costs.

9. Compact fluorescents come with a base that allows them to be used in fixtures with sockets for incandescent bulbs.

10. Compare window R values (resistance to heat transfer), **U values** $= \frac{1}{R}$ (propensity to conduct heat), and **air infiltration rates.** Select a product with a high R value or a low U value.

11. Double-pane windows with low-emissivity coatings, and gas-filled spaces, earn top energy efficiency ratings, about R-4.

12. Skylights supply the most daylighting per square foot of surface than any other window.

13. For privacy, skylights and glass block walls or windows are two excellent options.

16

Clearing the Air: Ventilation

Warm, moist air is soothing for showering and bathing, but it can harm bathroom walls and ceilings. The solution — ventilate.

Imagine throwing a bucket of water on your bathroom ceiling and walls, or dumping a pint or two on the attic insulation. You wouldn't do that, would you? But your bathroom may get a good soaking if a ventilating fan is not quickly exhausting the moist air produced by bathing or showering. In fact, a five-minute shower dumps one-half pint of water into the air, according to University of Minnesota tests.

Humid air causes damage in three ways:

1. It harms the bathroom walls, ceilings, fixtures, the framing in walls and attics, and the exterior paint and siding

2. High humidity levels may reduce home energy efficiency during the cooling season

3. Mold, mildew, and unvented aerosol sprays may affect family health

Without adequate ventilation, moisture from showering or bathing condenses on the cool surface of walls and ceiling, and water droplets form. This condensation traps dirt, making frequent cleaning and painting necessary.

Mildew appears on painted walls, tile, and grout, making cleaning tougher yet. Prolonged exposure to high humidity causes paint to crack, shortens the life of wallcoverings and tile adhesives, and rusts metal fixtures and hardware. Ultimately, dampness in a bathroom may result in rotting wallboard, deteriorating woodwork, and warped doors.

What's more, moisture also affects areas that cannot be seen. As steam builds up in a bathroom, the increased pressure pushes moist air into cracks in walls and into electrical and plumbing penetrations in walls and ceiling. Humid air then escapes into wall cavities and attics where it may damage joists, framing, and roof sheathing.

MORE MOISTURE PROBLEMS

Not only is the inside of a home vulnerable to moisture damage, but the exterior may suffer also. Hot, steamy air may escape through walls or cracks around bathroom windows. Outside, that moisture is capable of discoloring paint and causing it to peel. Siding may be damaged too.

Energy efficiency may also be reduced. When attic insulation becomes damp, its insulating value is drastically reduced. Humid air from bathing and showering may burden the cooling system in the summer.

And there is another effect of hot, humid bathrooms — family health problems. First of all, high humidity promotes the growth of bacteria, mold, and mildew and that may affect people with respiratory ailments or allergies. Secondly, irritants such as aerosol sprays, as well as odors, linger in the air in an unventilated bathroom.

Living in one of today's well-insulated homes multiplies the damage from high levels of humidity. The insulation that makes the home nearly airtight also reduces the number of air changes that occur each hour. Therefore, pollutants and moisture become concentrated in the home unless proper ventilation is supplied.

Damage to the bathroom, attic, insulation, and exterior walls may cost hundreds of dollars to repair. But the cost of a ventilating fan is modest. Economy models, suitable for small bathrooms, cost about $25. The powerful models, which combine fan, light, and heater, cost $150 to $200. That's a relatively small investment to protect a home from damaging tropical bathroom air.

BENEFITS

The cure for bathroom humidity problems is simple — expel warm, moist air with an efficient exhaust fan. The fan acts on a muggy bathroom in three ways:

1. Drastically reduces humidity levels
2. Helps control bathroom temperatures
3. Cuts water vapor pressure, which propels moist air into cracks in bathroom walls

Fans Help to Reduce Humidity

It is **not** enough to open a bathroom window or door to get rid of muggy air. Tests comparing moisture levels in a ventilated and an unventilated bathroom were conducted at the Texas Engineering Experiment Station at Texas A & M University, a recognized authority on air movement. The tests showed that, after running a shower for five minutes, moisture levels in the bathroom with an exhaust fan were reduced **ten times faster** than levels in the room with no fan.

Humidity in the unventilated bathroom reached 99 percent during the shower and remained at 98 percent for 25 minutes after the shower. In contrast, the ventilated bathroom humidity level peaked at 97 percent and fell to 79 percent in 25 minutes. To put it another way: Just **two minutes** after the shower, the humidity was lower in the ventilated bathroom than it was after **twenty minutes** in the unventilated bath.

Fans Help to Reduce Water Vapor Pressure

The Texas tests also showed that water vapor pressure was quickly reduced in the ventilated bathroom.

The pressure in the unventilated bathroom rose faster and remained much higher than in the bathroom with an exhaust fan operating. Within ten minutes after the shower, the exhaust fan had cut the pressure to half the amount found in the unventilated bath.

Fans Help to Reduce Temperature

What's more, temperatures in the bathroom with the exhaust fan fell quickly to more comfortable levels. Within 20 minutes after the shower, temperatures had dropped to a normal 70 degrees in the ventilated bathroom; the unventilated room measured a sweltering 85 degrees.

The conclusion: Install a ventilating fan to reduce humidity, temperature, and water vapor pressure. The fan is insurance against moisture damage inside — and outside — the home.

A FAN THAT FITS

Buying a fan is something like buying clothing — the fan must "fit" the room it ventilates. Fan sizes are determined by the **cubic feet of air** the fan exhausts in one minute (**cfm**).

Here's the story behind cfm sizing. A bathroom fan should provide eight air changes per hour, according to guidelines specified by the Federal De-

...ment of Housing and Urban Development and the Home Ventilating Institute (HVI), a voluntary organization of manufacturers of home ventilating equipment. This air-change frequency is effective in controlling moisture.

Calculating Fan Size

Bathroom fans manufactured in the U.S. have cfm capacities of 50, 60, 70, 80, 90, 100, and 110. A few manufacturers produce ventilators for the bath with capacities up to 160 cfm.

To determine the correct size fan for a bath, follow this formula from HVI: Multiply the room's length (in feet) and width (in feet) by the factor 1.1 (assume an 8′ ceiling). For a 6′ X 10′ bath, for example, the calculation is:

$$6 \text{ X } 10 \text{ X } 1.1 = 66.0$$

This bathroom requires a fan of at least 60 cfm; a 70 cfm fan will ensure proper ventilation.

CFM Ratings Are Tested

The HVI verifies cfm rates claimed by manufacturers. A manufacturer voluntarily submits an exhaust fan to HVI for testing. HVI tests products at independent laboratories, where accurate measurements of the fan's capacity to move air are taken. The product is then labeled by HVI with its certified cfm rating. These ratings are reported in the annual *Home Ventilating Institute Certified Home Ventilating Products Directory*. To obtain a copy, see Appendix A.

And what about today's large bathrooms? Will fans certified by HVI still do the job? Yes, according to HVI, the rate of eight air changes per hour is as effective today as it was in the mid-50s when the average bathroom measured 5′ X 7′ and used the standard 50 cfm fan. The simple formula for fan size — room length X width X 1.1 — provides effective ventilation for today's large bathrooms.

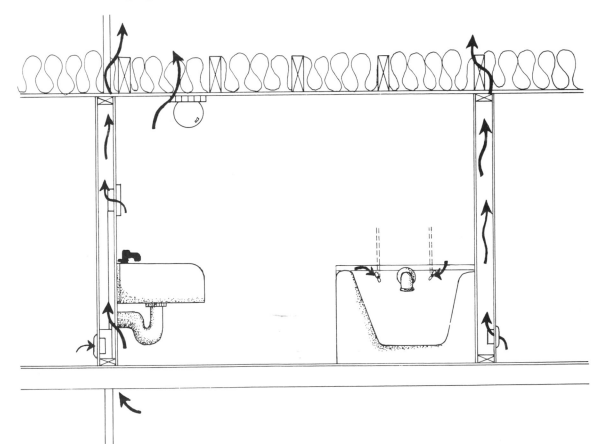

Moist air from bathing and showering may be forced into cracks where electrical and plumbing fixtures penetrate walls and ceiling (arrows). As a result, the framing in walls and attic may be damaged. The solution: Install and use a ventilating fan to remove moist air before it can do damage.

A typical ventilating fan has three components: a housing with a damper and cylindrical duct connector (left), a motor and wheel assembly (center), and a grill (right).

NOT TOO NOISY, PLEASE

Ventilating fans are rated not only by cfm capacity, but also by the amount of noise they produce. The noise they produce is measured in **sones**. The lower the sone rating, the quieter the fan. A bathroom ventilating fan rated at 3 sones, for example, makes half the noise of a fan rated at 6 sones. HVI-tested fans carry a **sone rating** on the certification label along with the cfm rating.

What exactly is a sone? Technically speaking, a sone is an internationally recognized unit of loudness. In everyday terms, one sone is equivalent to the sound of a quiet refrigerator in a quiet kitchen, according to HVI. The HVI maximum is 6.5 sones for bathroom fans. But an analysis of HVI test results for 1991 showed that most fans were rated from 2.5 to 4.0 sones.

Quiet Fans

Fans that are powerful and quiet are manufactured today. The use of insulation in the fan housing, quieter blowers, and improved motors have reduced fan noise.

A wide variety of fans are available. For example, one manufacturer offers a 110 cfm ventilator with a 1.5 sone level; the same manufacturer offers an 80 cfm fan rated at 3.5 sones. Generally speaking, quieter fans with more power have a higher cost.

INSTALLATION FACTS

To work properly, a fan must be installed properly. It is important to understand:

- **The best fan location**
- **The steps in an installation**
- **The hallmarks of an expert installation**

Motion and Humidity Sensor

A new venting product is available. It features a fan with a motion and humidity sensor that automatically ventilates the bathroom. First, on entering the shower, the motion sensor turns on the light. Next, the humidity sensor turns on the venting fan. When the shower is ended, the lack of motion turns off the light. Stabilized humidity turns off the fan.

Location

Installing the fan directly over the shower is the most effective way to exhaust humid air. Some fans are manufactured expressly for this purpose. These fans must carry an Underwriters Laboratory (UL) label indicating that they are safe for over-shower installation. This type of fan also requires wiring with a ground fault interrupter branch circuit (GFCI). If the joists above the ceiling or another obstacle interferes with the installation, select a location as close to the shower as possible.

Step-by-Step Installation

The first step in a fan installation is to install the electrical wiring for the motor/blower assembly and the controls. This stage of the work is completed when other electrical work is done in the bathroom project.

Next an opening is cut in the ceiling for the fan housing, and it is attached to joists through adjustable mounting brackets or stationary mounting ears. The duct connector and damper are snapped into place on the housing. Then the motor/blower assembly is added, electrical connections are made, and the grill is put in place. The wallboard is also cut around the wiring for the controls, and the control plate cover is installed.

Finally, rigid metal duct work is attached to the duct connector. The rigid metal offers less resistance to air than the flexible plastic ducting. The duct is

---

FAN FEATURES

There are five important ventilator features to evaluate:

1. Function. The most common fans are designed for **a single purpose** — exhausting moist air. Other fans are **multipurpose**, combining venting capacity with an attractive light, a heater and/or a 7 watt night light. If adequate lighting and heating have been included in the bathroom plan, an exhaust fan is probably the best choice. In other projects, the multipurpose fan may provide an inexpensive method of adding supplemental lighting and heating.

2. Placement. Fans may be installed in the **ceiling** or the **exterior wall**. The ceiling fan is the most common. When joists or other obstructions interfere with ceiling fan installation, a wall fan must be used. Exterior wall fans exhaust air directly to the outside; no ducting is used. A wall fan must have an effective **damper** to prevent outside air from entering the home. Wall fans may detract from the bathroom decorating scheme, but some models have a front panel that may be painted or finished with wallcovering.

3. Controls. In addition to conventional toggle switch controls, **electronic wall controls** are available. **Multiple-speed** controls provide two or three operating levels; **solid state variable-speed** controls provide an almost unlimited number of settings. **Automatic controls** include **timers**, which turn the fan off after a preset period, and **humidistats**, which operate the fan when humidity reaches a certain level. Both may be useful to people who must leave before the fan has completed its ventilating cycle.

4. Finish. Say goodbye to that plain aluminum fan. Attractive fans framed with **rich wood**, **antique brass**, and **polished brass** are available. Fans with **white polymeric** framing and white grills are also available.

5. Ducting. A **ducted** ventilating fan discharges bathroom air outside the home. On the other hand, a **nonducted** fan draws air through an activated charcoal filter, then recirculates it. This type of fan is **not** suitable for moisture removal; it may be used for freshening air in a bathroom.

Ducted fans discharge air either **vertically** through a duct 6" to 7" in diameter or through a **side discharge**, using a duct 3" to 4" in diameter. The side discharge vent is more common; the ducting is vented through the wall, roof, or soffit. The vertical discharge fan is usually vented through the roof.

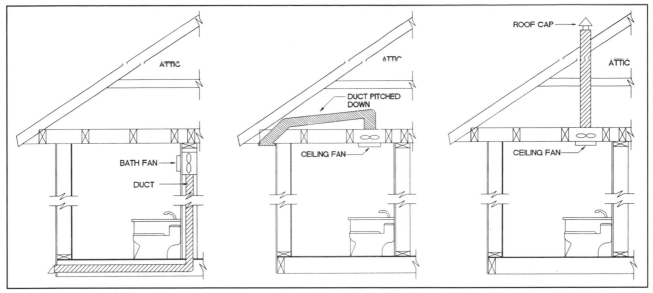

A wall fan is ducted through the wall framing and floor joists (left). A fan on an exterior wall may be vented directly through the wall. A ceiling fan is ducted above the ceiling and down through the eave (middle). A ceiling fan is ducted vertically through the attic to the roof (right).

vented to the outside through the roof, soffit, or wall. A cap with a damper is placed on the exterior.

A Quality Installation

The installation of the duct work is crucial for the fan to work effectively. Rigid metal duct work of the recommended diameter should be used. To enhance air flow, the ducting run should be as short as possible with the least number of elbows. And the exterior cap — at the roof, soffit, or wall — must be designed for the duct size used. The exterior cap

should be fitted with a damper to prevent the passage of outside air.

Energy concerns affect installation too. All duct connections should be sealed with duct tape; the duct work itself should be insulated. Also, caulking is recommended where the fan housing penetrates the ceiling. This prevents humid air from passing into the area above the ceiling.

Finally, to get the most from a quality installation, learn to operate the fan effectively. Turn the unit on before entering the shower or bath, and allow

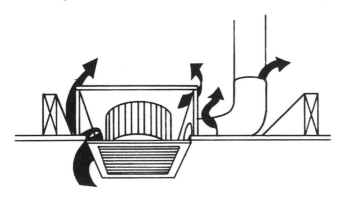

Arrows indicate where warm, moist air can escape through cracks between the ventilating fan and ceiling, and through gaps in the fan housing. The escaping air reduces fan efficiency and may cause damage to framing members above the ceiling.

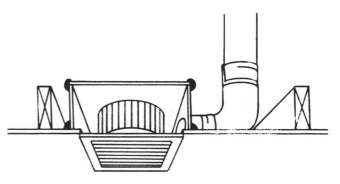

Caulking joints where the fan meets the ceiling increases fan efficiency and prevents humid air from escaping. Apply caulk to the fan housing and duct tape or caulk at duct connections.

it to run 10 to 20 minutes afterwards. That is the best and most efficient way to get rid of the visible moisture on mirrors and walls as well as hidden moisture in wall cavities or attics. Using the fan the right way stops hot, humid air from damaging the newly remodeled bathroom.

WORTH REPEATING

1. A ventilating fan ducted to the outside of the home is the only fan capable of removing moist bathroom air; do not install a nonducted fan that simply recirculates air.

2. Calculate the proper size fan for your bathroom, expressed in cubic feet of air moved per minute (cfm), with the formula **room length X width X 1.1. = cfm.**

3. The lower the sone rating, the quieter the fan; sone ratings range from 1.5 to 6.5 (upper limit set by testing agency, the Home Ventilating Institute).

4. The HVI label on a fan certifies cfm and sone ratings claimed by the fan manufacturer; HVI tests of cfm and sone levels are accepted as the industry standard.

5. Install fan above shower for greatest efficiency; for safety, use only UL listed fans installed with a GFCI circuit.

6. Improve lighting levels and safety with a fan/light combination; select a fan with a night light too.

7. To efficiently exhaust bathroom air, use rigid metal duct and install the shortest possible duct run; for energy efficiency, tape all metal joints, insulate ducting, and caulk the fan housing; check to make sure that the duct damper and cap damper operate.

17

Bathroom Heating and Cooling

*Proper heating and cooling
systems will boost bathroom comfort.*

Have you ever stepped from the shower, dripping wet and shivering from an inadequately heated bathroom? Or, perhaps, you've tried to apply makeup in front of a foggy mirror steamed-up from a hot, humid bathroom. Certainly, you can appreciate the advantage of a bathroom that is not too hot, not too cold, and not too humid.

Getting bathroom temperatures just right is tricky. First of all, the trend in bathroom design is towards larger spaces. If these bigger baths and master suites are going to be comfortable, especially if a home addition is built, they may require a source of heat that supplements the central heating system.

Second, the location of old and new heating ducts, pipes, radiators, and registers must be considered in every remodeling project, no matter how big or small. For example, would it be feasible and economical to eliminate an existing tub and add a corner whirlpool where a register is located? Is it possible to expand the bath by breaking through a wall that contains pipes for a hot water heating system? What is the best location for new registers?

Third, supplemental heating systems are limited to *permanently installed* wall or ceiling heaters. That's because portable heaters are too dangerous around water. What's more, the likelihood of burns on bare skin is increased in the bathroom.

Finally, humans tolerate only a very narrow range of temperature and humidity, called the *comfort zone*. And bathroom temperatures may be most comfortable at 3 to 5 degrees warmer than the rest of the house, suggests the NKBA, because a person's activity level in the bathroom is low and they also may be soaking wet. The elderly require elevated temperatures for comfort too.

FINDING A SOLUTION

The best heating/cooling options depend primarily upon:

■ **Scope of the remodeling project**, specifically the change in the volume of the bathroom. Volume is important because heating/cooling systems are sized by heating/cooling capacity per cubic foot.

■ **The location of the bath in relation to the central heating system equipment.** The nearer the central heating equipment, the more heat delivered to the bath, as a general rule.

■ **The age and efficiency of the existing heating/cooling system** and the ease with which it can be modified.

A bathroom undergoing a face lift or minor remodeling (projects in which the volume is usually unchanged) may benefit from a small-capacity supplemental heat source such as a built-in electric heater. However, the installation of a new household heating system will not be warranted. On the other hand, a major remodeling that enlarges the bathroom through an addition may require a secondary bathroom heating system or the replacement of the current system.

But whether the remodeling project is a face lift or a room addition, it is essential that the designer/contractor check the walls during the first visit to the home to identify the location of ducts, hot water heating pipes, vents and registers, radiators and other heating equipment. The location of this equipment is critical to locating fixtures in the new plan. To minimize costs, the bathroom is planned for the minimum disruption to heating/cooling equipment.

HEATING AND COOLING: MINOR REMODELING

In the face lift or minor remodeling improving the heating/cooling system may include:

■ **Improving the energy efficiency of the bathroom**

■ **Modifying existing equipment to meet new demands**

■ **Adding a supplemental heating unit**

The bathroom will benefit from **improving the energy efficiency of windows,** including the addition of interior or exterior storm windows and caulking to reduce air infiltration. Aging windows may require replacement with energy-efficient models, which will decrease heat loss. (See Chapter 15, "Good Looks with Lighting," for details on windows.) Any other source of air leaks, such as those around ventilating fans, should be eliminated.

Modifying existing heating is somewhat difficult with hot water and radiant heating systems. But with forced-air furnaces, a rule of thumb is that two additional registers per house may be added without unbalancing the system, provided that the furnace is *centrally located.* Remember that increasing the distance from the furnace reduces the temperature of warm air. Usually a duct is split, and an opening

is made in the wall for a new register.

SUPPLEMENTAL HEATING

There are two basic types of supplemental heating:

■ **Radiant heat**

■ **Convection heat**

The basic formula for sizing both radiant and convection heat sources, for wall and the ceiling installations, is to allow $1\frac{1}{2}$ watts per cubic foot of space. Heaters less than 1,500 watts usually operate on a 120-volt circuit, so they can be used with the existing electrical system. Over 1,500 watts, the heater will require a 240-volt circuit.

Radiant heat

Radiant heaters transfer heat in waves from an energy source, such as a heat lamp; the radiant energy strikes an object or person and is absorbed as heat. Radiant heaters are good alternatives for spot heating, rather than heating an entire room. Two options:

1. **Infrared heat lamp**
2. **Radiant heater with a metal heating element**

An **infrared ceiling lamp** can be installed near the shower/tub, either as a separate unit or combined with a fan and light. The heat lamp has an interior reflective surface that directs heat waves downward. It is designed to be placed near the tub/shower. It should be UL (Underwriters Laboratory) listed as safe for these locations.

The radiant heater with a metal heating element (such as a baseboard heater) outputs more heat than the infrared lamp, generally speaking. It also is quieter than methods that use a fan to force the heated air into the room. Radiant wall heaters are also available. The NKBA advises they should not be installed on the side of a vanity or next to a toilet where someone could accidentally bump into the them and get burned.

Convection Heat

While radiant heaters transmit heat via waves, convection heaters transmit heat via a fan. First the air is heated by an element, then it is moved by a fan to cooler objects. Convection fans are manufactured to be mounted in either the wall or the ceiling.

One advantage of the fan is that air is distributed evenly and quickly throughout the space. However, convection fans are not appropriate for locations near the shower or bathtub because when air blows across the body, it produces a "windchill" effect. Moving air feels cool to wet skin.

A disadvantage of convection heat is that the fan operation may be noisy. To overcome this drawback, select a unit with a fan that moves the required volume of air, but at a very low motor speed.

HEATING AND COOLING: ENLARGING THE BATH

To select the best heating/cooling option in cases in which the bathroom will be enlarged, follow these three steps:

1. Evaluate the existing heating/cooling system. Can the present system be modified or extended? Is it efficient? Should it be replaced? Can the present system provide adequate heating/cooling for additional volume?

2. **Estimate new heating/cooling needs.** How much volume will be added to the existing bath? Will the plan require relocation of ducts, pipes, registers, radiators, or other heating/cooling equipment? Where is the bathroom in relation to the central heating/cooling equipment?

3. **Identify new and supplemental heating/cooling systems that will be adequate for the remodeling project.** What are the options for adding a heating/cooling system? What are recommended supplemental systems?

EVALUATING THE EXISTING SYSTEM

Of the three major types of heating systems — *forced-air, water (or hydronic) and electric* — forced-air systems are generally the least expensive *and* the most adaptable. A forced-air system in a home built on a slab is an exception. Duct work is embedded in concrete rather than installed over a basement or crawl space.

Forced-Air Heat

Forced-air heating systems, whether gas or oil, distribute heat from the furnace via a plenum and a system of ducts and registers. Modifying the existing equipment will involve adding duct work and/or registers. To add registers, it is necessary to split a duct to deliver air to old and new registers. Adding new duct work may be required. This work is done by a specialist, the heating-ventilating-air conditioning (HVAC) contractor.

Hydronic Heating

Hydronic systems circulate water heated in a boiler to the home via a system of pipes. The pipes supply hot water to radiators, fan-coil units, or convectors. One example is radiant-floor heating, a system in which hot water lines may be embedded in concrete in a home built on a slab. This system provides a very comfortable floor in cold climates, but it is not possible to add to this kind of heating system.

A common convector unit is the baseboard convector. Hot water heats a core and metal fins which warm the air passing over them. Fan-coil units operate in a similar fashion, but a fan pushes the heated air into the room.

Rearranging any of these components to accommodate a new bathroom design will involve changes in piping. An HVAC contractor should be consulted about the feasibility of moving or rearranging this equipment.

Electric Resistance Heat

Electric resistance heating systems are somewhat flexible, primarily because they do not rely on a central furnace for the heat source. Instead, electric current is converted into heat. Electric resistance heat may be provided by baseboard units, which resemble hot water baseboard heaters.

Electric units have several advantages. They are the least expensive to install, but circuits must be added to handle the heating load. They also allow the user to control the temperature of each room separately, which is called *zoned heating*. On the other hand, electric heat usually results in the biggest heating bills.

HEATING EFFICIENCY

Efficiency involves several factors:

■ **The age of the system**

■ **The efficiency rating when purchased**

■ **Adequacy for current heating needs**

■ **Results of a professional energy efficiency audit**

Since the late '70s and early '80s, furnace and boiler efficiencies have been increasing in response to concerns over energy costs and the availability of energy resources. An energy efficiency rating, called the Annual Fuel Utilization Efficiency (AFUE), was developed. It gives two kinds of information:

■ **The amount of fuel available** to heat the home

■ **A measure of heat output**, expressed in BTU

For example, if a forced-air furnace has a rating of 92, then 92 percent of the fuel burned is available for heating; the other 8 percent escapes up the chimney. In 1992, new furnace energy efficiency standards went into effect. A base efficiency rate of 78 percent was established. Therefore, 78 percent of the fuel burned is used to heat the home.

The higher the energy efficiency of your heating equipment and the newer the system, the less likely you will need to replace it. Re-examine the rating on your equipment, and identify its age, make, and model. Present this information to your designer or contractor for discussion during the design stage of the remodeling project.

And the tighter the house, the less air will infiltrate from the outside. Consider getting a *heat loss analysis* by an energy auditor or HVAC contractor. The analysis includes measuring the wall, ceiling, floor, and window areas; the depth and type of insulation; and the amount of air infiltration around doors, windows, and other penetrations in the shell. From this analysis, the auditor can determine if the existing furnace is large enough to handle the greater volume created by a bathroom addition.

The audit will also indicate which energy improvements can be made to boost heating efficiency. Improvements such as adding attic insulation or caulking windows to reduce infiltration may be recommended. In the case of an addition, the contractor is responsible for following the *minimum* requirements for energy-efficient building, which are detailed in the building code. Discuss upgrading the basic insulation requirements with the design professional or contractor.

ESTIMATING NEW HEATING DEMAND

Factors to consider in estimating the new heating demand are:

■ **The increase in volume of the bath** (cubic feet)

■ **Proximity of bathroom to the furnace**

The first option to consider is adding a supplemental heating unit, especially if the additional volume is small. For example, a bathroom that has been enlarged by extending it into an existing linen closet or a bedroom closet is a good candidate for supplemental heating. The heaters mentioned above in "Supplemental Heating," pages 176 to 177, will probably be the best options in this case.

But if a room is enlarged significantly, or a room is added, a secondary system may be necessary. A rule of thumb: If the enlarged room is more than 40 feet from the central heating unit, the system may not be able to deliver adequate heat.

One answer is zoned heat, in which different parts of the home are controlled by separate heating sources. Some electrical heating units, such as electric baseboard heaters, operate without a central control; instead, several heaters are controlled on one circuit. Adding an electrical heater simply requires the addition of a circuit. And adding a second circuit allows the homeowner to control the heat independently of the first circuit.

A home that is very long is a good candidate for zoned heating. So is an L-shaped addition.

COOLING

The **bathroom ventilating fan** plays an important role in cooling. Its job is not only to reduce moisture and vapor pressure, but to lower bathroom temperatures. (See Chapter 16, "Clearing the Air: Ventilation.") In a moderate climate, a ventilating fan of the appropriate size may provide all the cooling necessary.

Like the ventilating fan, **air conditioners** remove heat and humidity. The basic types include:

- **Room air conditioners**
- **Central systems**
- **Heat pumps**

In all cases, the air conditioner must be located so cool air does not blow directly on people. For example, a heating duct may be located in the toekick of a vanity cabinet, but a cooling outlet in the same location will blow cold air onto people's feet, making them uncomfortable.

A room air conditioner must be sized for the room it will cool. These units may be noisy and create fluctuations in temperatures. They are also highly visible. When installed in a window, they may interfere with the bathroom design.

A central air conditioning system may be added if a central forced-air heating system is in place. Both systems share duct work. Although it is much more expensive, the central cooling system is quieter than the room air conditioner, and the cooling unit is out of sight.

Heat pumps are used for both heating and cooling. In the heating mode, the heat pump extracts heat from outside air and moves it into the house. In the cooling mode, it extracts heat from the house and draws it outside. Operating somewhat like a refrigerator, a refrigerant fluid in the heat pump changes from a liquid to a vapor to alternately extract heat from the outside air and heat from the house.

Heat pumps are suitable for climates in which temperatures are moderate and do not vary widely. At freezing, for example, there is no excess heat outside for the pump to capture. Also heat pumps deliver air at about 90 degrees, which is lower than air from a furnace, but they compensate by delivering air at a higher velocity. However, the blowing air may make a bather uncomfortably cool.

Heat pumps can be mounted just about anywhere; if space is tight, this feature is an advantage. However, they are somewhat noisy, so a heat pump should not be located by a bedroom.

COOLING SYSTEM SIZE AND EFFICIENCY

Most air conditioners are rated in BTUs per hour; central cooling systems and heat pumps are rated by cooling capacity by tons, where one ton equals 12,000 BTUs. The Air Conditioning and Refrigeration Institute certifies capacity ratings of many air conditioning systems.

Air conditioner costs are proportional to size; if the cooling output is double, the cost of the unit is nearly doubled. For example, a two-ton air conditioner costs about twice that of a one ton unit.

Room air conditioner efficiency is measured by the **Energy Efficiency Rating (EER)**, which is the rate of the cooling output in BTUs per hour divided by the power consumption in watts. A room air conditioner with an EER over 9.5 is considered efficient. The Association of Home Appliance Manufacturers (AHAM) annually publishes EER ratings of room air conditioners. (See Appendix A, AHAM.)

Central air conditioners and heat pumps carry a different type of energy efficiency rating, called a **Seasonal Energy Efficiency Rating or SEER.** The seasonal cooling output in BTUs per hour is divided by the seasonal energy input in watt hours for the average U.S. climate. A minimum SEER of 10 was required by the 1992 National Appliance Efficiency Standard for central air conditioners.

OTHER COOLING OPTIONS

Whole house fans and attic fans, in moderate climates, may help cool the entire home, and thereby reduce bathroom temperatures. The whole house fan is mounted in the ceiling of the upper floor, usually in a hallway. It draws the warm air out of the home through the attic and vents it to the outside. Adequate vents and louvers must be included in the attic to accommodate the increased quantity of air.

Fans with two speeds are useful; manual controls are advised for safety reasons. The highest speed should be capable of changing the entire volume of air in the house every three minutes. The NKBA offers the example of a 1,500 square foot house with 8' ceilings, containing 12,000 cubic feet. The fan should be rated at 4,000 cubic feet per minute.

Attic fans should be standard home equipment as they can substantially reduce the temperature of attic air and the home itself at night. Make sure the attic vents are large enough for the fan. Attic temperatures may reach 140 degrees or higher on a hot day. This heat is transferred into the living areas below, which increases the house's cooling load.

Consult the designer/HVAC contractor for the correct vent sizing. Roof vents should be mounted high in the gable to discharge hot air; vents in the eaves or soffits draw in cool air.

Ceiling fans cool by circulating air; they do not vent warm air. They are not generally recommended for bathroom use because they will chill the bather when cool air blows on a wet body.

WORTH REPEATING

1. Plan heating/cooling at the beginning of the project. On the first home visit, the planner should check walls for location of heating ducts, hot-water heating pipes, registers, radiators, and other heating equipment.

2. The need for a supplemental heating or cooling system depends upon the extent to which the *volume* of the bathroom has been increased. Major remodeling projects and additions are more likely to require supplemental heating/cooling equipment than a face lift or minor remodeling.

3. Location affects heating/cooling too. In a central heating system, the farther the heat source, the less heat is available. If the new bathroom is located more than 40 feet from the central heating source, a secondary furnace may be installed.

4. Zoned heating provides independently controlled heat sources for different areas of the home. Adding a secondary heater for a master suite addition is an example.

5. For safety, supplemental heating should be limited to permanently installed equipment located so there is no danger of bumping into the equipment and getting burned; portable heaters are extremely dangerous in wet areas and in compact spaces such as the bathroom.

6. Energy efficiency labels are carried on heating and cooling equipment to assist the buyer.

APPENDIX A:

RESOURCES

CODES & STANDARDS

**AMERICAN NATIONAL
STANDARDS INSTITUTE (ANSI)**
1430 Broadway Avenue
New York, NY 10018
(212) 354-3300
Members include industrial firms, trade associations, technical societies, labor organizations, consumer organizations, and government agencies. Clearinghouse for nationally coordinated voluntary standards for many industries, including the construction industry. Develops standards and designates them as American National Standards when all ANSI members agree on parameters. Founded in 1918; 1,250 members.

Publication: *Catalog of American National Standards.* Lists about 8,000 current ANSI-approved standards, including those that apply to bathroom remodeling and construction ($20). Contact the library for a reference copy.

**BUILDING OFFICIALS AND CODE
ADMINISTRATORS INTERNATIONAL
(BOCA)**
4051 West Flossmoor Road
Country Club Hills, IL 60477-5795
(708) 799-2300
(800) 323-1103

Government officials and agencies that administer or formulate building, zoning, or housing codes. Promotes establishment of minimum, unbiased building codes and provides services for keeping them up to date. Founded in 1915; 9,500 members.

Publications: BOCA National Codes, including *Basic Building Code*. Contact the library for a reference copy or municipal building inspection department.

**COUNCIL OF AMERICAN BUILDING
OFFICIALS (CABO)**
5203 Leesburg Pike, Suite 708
Falls Church, VA 22041
(703) 931-4533
Three model code organizations — BOCA, ICBO, and International Association of Plumbing and Mechanical Officials — with membership of building officials in cities, counties, and states. Founded in 1972; about 8,000 members.

Publication: *Model Energy Code, One- and Two-Family Dwelling Code.* Contact library for reference copy or municipal building inspection department.

**INTERNATIONAL ASSOCIATION OF
PLUMBING AND MECHANICAL
OFFICIALS (IAPMO)**
20001 Walnut Drive South

Walnut, CA 91789

(714) 595-8449

Members are government agencies, administrative officials, sales representatives, manufacturers, and associations related to the plumbing field. Sponsors and writes the Uniform Plumbing Code; sponsors the Uniform Mechanical Code. Founded in 1926; 4,000 members.

Publications: *Uniform Plumbing Code, Uniform Mechanical Code.* Contact the library for reference copies or municipal building inspection department.

INTERNATIONAL CONFERENCE OF BUILDING OFFICIALS (ICBO)

5360 South Workman Mill Road

Whittier, CA 90601

(213) 699-0541

Representatives of local, regional, and state governments who publish, promote, and maintain the Uniform Building Code.

Publication: *The Uniform Building Code.* Contact library for reference copy or municipal building inspection department.

CONFLICT RESOLUTION

AMERICAN ARBITRATION ASSOCIATION

140 West 51st Street

New York, NY 10020

(212) 484-4100

Dedicated to the resolution of disputes of all kinds through arbitration, mediation, democratic elections, and other voluntary methods. Members are businesses, unions, trade and educational associations, law firms, and arbitrators. Founded 1926; 7,000 members.

Publications: pamphlets on arbitration practices; write for catalog.

COUNCIL OF BETTER BUSINESS BUREAUS, INC.

4200 Wilson Boulevard, Suite 800

Arlington, VA 22203

(703) 276-0100

(800) 334-2406

Supported by 200 local autonomous Better Business Bureaus, and 240,000 business and professional firms in all fields. Assists in settlement of consumer complaints through alternative dispute resolution (ADR), which are alternatives to legal remedies. ADR includes arbitration (binding or nonbinding) and mediation.

Call the toll-free ADR Answerline for answers to questions on the ADR process.

Publications: Three clearly written pamphlets explain the ADR process: *Alternative Dispute Resolution: The Commonsense Alternative; Alternative Dispute Resolution: Arbitration (Binding);* and *Alternative Dispute Resolution: Mediation.* All are free.

Also request the *Better Business Bureau Consumer Information Series Order Form,* which lists free booklets on buying products and services, including energy saving, supplemental heating systems, home equity loans, home improvements, hot tubs and spas, and water quality. Write to the address above or contact the local Better Business Bureau.

U.S. OFFICE OF CONSUMER AFFAIRS

Washington, D.C. 20405

One of the most popular books ever published by the federal government is the U.S. Office of Consumer Affairs' *Consumer's Resource Handbook.*

This ninety-seven page book has two useful sections. *How to Be a Smart Consumer* includes tips on getting the most for your money, handling a complaint, and writing a complaint letter. *Consumer Assistance Directory* lists state and federal offices to contact for help with consumer problems, as well as a four page section on dispute resolution programs.

For ordering information, request the *Consumer Information Catalog* from the Consumer Information Center, Pueblo, CO 81006, or call 719-948-4000.

CONSTRUCTION

HOME OWNERS WARRANTY CORPORATION (HOW)
1110 North Glebe Road
Arlington, VA 22201
(703) 516-4100
Administers the Remodeler Program which provides up to ten years of warranty/insurance on remodeling work performed by its remodeling members. Client receives a limited written warranty for each enrolled job. The Remodeler Program was introduced in 1983; HOW was formed in 1974.

Publication: *The How-to Guide to Remodeling.* Overview of remodeling process, including selecting a contractor, contracts, codes, and the HOW program. Free.

NATIONAL ASSOCIATION OF HOME BUILDERS (NAHB) REMODELORS™ COUNCIL
15th and M Streets, NW
Washington, D.C. 20005
(202) 822-0200
(800) 368-5242
Works to unify, represent, and serve the professional remodeling and rehabilitation industry. Provides information and educational opportunities to improve business and technical skills of members. Furthers consumer awareness of the industry and the professionalism of its members.

Publication: *How to Choose a Remodeler Who's on the Level.* How to select a contractor, contracts, working together, zoning and codes, financing. Requires a self-addressed, stamped envelope plus $.25 cents.

NATIONAL ASSOCIATION OF THE REMODELING INDUSTRY® (NARI®)
4301 North Fairfax Drive, Suite 310
Arlington, VA 22203-1627
(703) 276-7600
(800) 966-7601
A not-for-profit trade association representing all segments of the professional remodeling service industry. Members include remodeling contractors, wholesalers and manufacturers of building supplies and remodeling products, among others. Purpose is to develop and sustain programs that expand and unite the remodeling industry and to encourage ethical conduct. NARI® Certification Program developed in 1983. Founded in 1941; 5,800 members.

Publications: *Selecting a Professional Remodeling Contractor.* Remodeling planning, specifications, building codes and permits, contracts, financing, and NARI® code of ethics. Free.

Annual Membership Roster & Consumer Guide. Free. Write or call local chapter.

NATIONAL ASSOCIATION OF WOMEN IN CONSTRUCTION (NAWIC)
327 South Adams Street
Fort Worth, TX 76104
(817) 877-5551
(800) 552-3506
Professional women in the construction industry. Educates members in new construction techniques. Sponsors educational programs and distributes scholarships.

Call toll-free number for local member firms.

DESIGN

THE AMERICAN INSTITUTE OF ARCHITECTS (AIA)
1735 New York Avenue, NW
Washington, DC 20006
(202) 626-7461
Membership consists of architects who have passed

the licensing examination required in every state, plus allied members who are completing architectural training but have not yet taken the state examination. Includes architects with specialties in residential or commercial architecture. Nationwide organization with chapters in every state.

Consult the local phone book for chapters in your area.

Publication: *A Beginner's Guide to Architectural Services.* The benefits of hiring an architect, how to select an architect, and an overview of the design process. Free.

AMERICAN SOCIETY OF INTERIOR DESIGNERS (ASID)

608 Massachusetts Avenue, NE
Washington, D.C. 20002-6006
(202) 546-3480

Promotes a professional code of ethics, supports interior design licensing at the state level, and institutes educational standards for all designers. Aims to protect and inform the public, advance the design profession, strengthen interaction with industry and allied professionals, and promote design excellence. Sponsors continuing education for members. Founded in 1931; over 33,000 members and 49 chapters in the U.S.

Call or write for chapter in your area.

Publication: *Hire An Interior Designer . . . Explore the Possibilities.* Helps homeowners, apartment dwellers, and do-it-yourselfers determine if they need professional design help, suggests how to find a qualified designer, and explains how design professionals charge for services. A checklist assists consumers with the selection and design process. Free.

INTERIOR DESIGN SOCIETY (IDS)

P.O. Box 2396
High Point, NC 27261
(800) 888-9590

Retail designers, independent designers, design-oriented firms, and design service firms.

Grants accreditation and recognition to qualified interior designers. Conducts educational courses in management, design, sales training, and marketing. Founded in 1973; about 2,600 members.

Call toll-free number for information on IDS members in your area and current consumer publications.

INTERNATIONAL ASSOCIATION OF LIGHTING DESIGNERS

18 East 16th Street, Suite 208
New York, NY 10003
(212) 206-1281

Professionals, educators, students, and others working in lighting design in five countries. Promotes lighting as a design medium and emphasizes its role in enhancing environmental quality. Provides training, education; promotes licensing and professional certification standards. Maintains biographical archives and speakers' bureau. Founded in 1969; about 450 members.

Call or write for information on members in your area and current consumer publications.

INTERNATIONAL SOCIETY OF INTERIOR DESIGNERS (ISID)

433 South Spring Street, 10th Floor
Los Angeles, CA 90013
(213) 680-4240

Organization of professional designers, assistant designers, educators, and students with the purpose of establishing and maintaining professional standards for the field of design. Maintains biographical archives and operates a speakers' bureau. Founded in 1979; about 3,500 members.

Call or write for members in your area and current consumer publications.

NATIONAL KITCHEN & BATH ASSOCIATION (NKBA)

687 Willow Grove Street
Hackettstown, NJ 07840

(908) 852-1695
(800) 367-6522
A national trade association formed by the kitchen and bath industry for the benefit of kitchen and bath retailers, distributors, manufacturers, manufacturers' representatives, and those associated with the industry. Publishes the Kitchen Industry Technical Manuals, the Bathroom Industry Technical Manuals, and sponsors in-depth education. Certifies qualified designers as a Certified Kitchen Designer (CKD) and/or Certified Bathroom Designer (CBD). Chapters throughout the U.S.; international groups. Originally named American Institute of Kitchen Dealers, founded in 1963.

Call toll-free number for information on CKD, CBD, or member firm in your area.

Publications: *Annual Directory of Certified Kitchen Designers and Certified Bathroom Designers*. A state-by-state listing of kitchen and bath designers, plus description of credentials and code of professional conduct. Free.

From Inspiration to Sensation: Creating Your Dream Kitchen or Bathroom. Full-color booklet with samples of kitchen and bathroom designs. Describes the planning process, the design conference, and contains checklists and work sheets to aid in planning a kitchen or bath. Free.

RESIDENTIAL SPACE PLANNERS INTERNATIONAL (RSPI)
20 Ardmore Drive
Minneapolis, MN 55422
(no phone inquiries)
An organization of independent design practitioners who specialize in residential, rather than commercial, space planning.

Write for information on members in your area.

MECHANICAL/PLUMBING SYSTEMS

AMERICAN GAS ASSOCIATION
1515 Wilson Boulevard

Arlington, VA 22209-2470
(703) 841-8400
Utilities and pipeline companies involved with natural, manufactured, and liquified gas. Compiles a wide variety of industry statistics. Founded in 1918; 4,760 members.

Publications: *Buyer's Guide: Efficient Gas Water Heating*. Operating, venting, and sizing of gas water heaters. Free.

The Right Choice: Energy-Efficient Gas Water Heaters. Free.

Hot Water by Gas. Full-color booklet on uses of hot water throughout the home. Free.

HOME VENTILATING INSTITUTE (HVI)
Division of Air Movement and Control Association, Inc.
30 West University Drive
Arlington Heights, IL 60004
(708) 394-0150
Tests home ventilating products at independent laboratories to obtain accurate measurements of air movement. Manufacturers voluntarily submit products to HVI for testing. Affixes HVI certification label to products which pass tests. Recognized as a quality control agency by the International Conference of Building Officials. Founded in 1955.

Publications: *Home Ventilating Guide (Publication 15)*. Detailed look at home ventilating products. Free.

Bathroom Ventilation. In-depth look at bathroom moisture problems and how to prevent them. Free.

Annual Certified Home Ventilating Products Directory. Manufacturer, model, cfm, and sone ratings for tested fans. Free.

NATIONAL SAFE KIDS CAMPAIGN
111 Michigan Avenue, NW
Washington, D.C. 20010-2970
(202) 939-4993

The first nationwide childhood injury prevention campaign. First headed by Dr. C. Everett Koop, former U.S. Surgeon General. Dedicated to preventing unintentional childhood injury, which is the number one child killer in the country. Sponsors an aggressive campaign against hot water burns that occur in the bathroom. A program of the Children's National Medical Center in Washington, D.C.; major corporate sponsorship from the Johnson & Johnson Company. Founded in 1988; supported by over ninety national organizations, one hundred state local coalitions in forty states.

Publication: *How to Protect Your Child From Injury.* Includes bathroom accident prevention strategies. Call (900) 446-SAFE to receive a copy. (Each call costs $2.95 and will be billed through your phone company.)

WATER QUALITY ASSOCIATION

National Headquarters and Laboratory
4151 Naperville Road
Lisle, IL 60532
(708) 505-0160

International trade association representing 2,500 dealers and manufacturers of point-of-use water quality improvement technologies. Mission is to assure the right of users to modify or enhance the quality of water to meet a specific need or desire. The focus is on industry issues, education, and idea exchange. Receives consumer complaints.

Tests products and affixes Water Quality Association seal.

Publications: *Water Quality Answers.* Detailed look at water purification processes. Free.

Look for This Seal and Buy With Confidence. The industry testing program. Free.

A trio of brochures on drinking water treatment: *Quality Drinking Water Through Point-of-Use Distillation; Quality Drinking Water Through Reverse Osmosis; Quality Drinking Water Through Activated Carbon Filtration.* Free.

PRODUCTS

AMERICAN LIGHTING ASSOCIATION (ALA)

435 North Michigan Avenue
Chicago, IL 60611-4067
(312) 644-0828
(800) 274-4484

A not-for-profit organization for the residential and commercial lighting industry, including manufacturers, wholesale and retail showroom distributors, and manufacturers' representatives. Its mission is to expand public knowledge of lighting design and products. Establishes standards for certification of qualified lighting consultants and recognizes them as Certified Lighting Consultants. Works to improve the quality, safety, and energy efficiency of lighting products. Founded in 1945; 825 member firms.

Call toll-free number for ALA lighting showrooms in your area.

Publication: *Lighting Your Life.* A twenty-four page brochure that covers types of lighting, energy savings, energy efficiency, and lighting designs for each room in the house. Free.

ASSOCIATION OF HOME APPLIANCE MANUFACTURERS (AHAM)

20 North Wacker Drive
Chicago, IL 60606
(912) 984-5816

Trade association of appliance manufacturers; covered appliances are refrigerators, freezers, dishwashers, air conditioners, microwaves, ranges, ovens. Recently has added small electric goods to its product concerns. Conducts ongoing consumer education effort with annual guides to appliance selection. Collects and analyzes data on consumer preferences, consumer appliance use, and sales of appliances.

Publications: *Annual Consumer Selection Guide.* One issued for each product category mentioned above. Tips on how to select appliances, appliance features, and a directory of makes and models. Free.

CERAMIC TILE INSTITUTE
700 North Virgil Avenue
Los Angeles, CA 90029
(213) 660-1911
Tile contractors, setters, finishers, manufacturers, and distributors; individuals interested in the tile industry or working in a related field. Promotes the use of tile and disseminates information on the development and improvement of tile and its installation; seeks to upgrade the industry through research and development; provides industry training.

Publications: Ask for Order Form CTI-60-2, *Table of Publications*.

Trade and consumer publications are both listed on order forms. Such titles as *Marble Tile: You Must Understand It* ($.75); *Guides for a Homeowner in Contracting for Ceramic Tile Installation* ($.75); *Care of Ceramic Tile* ($1.75); *How to Select Ceramic Tile for Flooring* ($.75).

CULTURED MARBLE INSTITUTE
435 North Michigan Avenue, Suite 1717
Chicago, IL 60611
(312) 644-0828
Companies that manufacture cultured marble products and the firms that supply them. Develops and promotes industry-wide standards of product quality and acceptability for the protection of purchasers of cultured marble products.

Founded in 1974; about 310 member firms.

Publications: *Annual Cultured Marble Institute-Membership/Product Directory*. ($10 to non-members.) Write for current consumer publications.

KITCHEN CABINET MANUFACTURERS ASSOCIATION (KCMA)
1899 Preston White Drive

Reston, VA 22091-4326
(703) 264-1690
Principal trade association for the cabinet manufacturing industry. Members include manufacturers of kitchen cabinets and bathroom vanities, and cabinet suppliers to the industry. Administers a Certification Program in which manufacturers voluntarily submit cabinets to testing under standards set by the American National Standards Institute; products may earn KCMA Certification label. Promotes code of ethics, education, and research in the industry. Responds to consumer complaints on certified cabinets. Established in 1955. Formerly the National Kitchen Cabinet Association.

No current consumer publications, but consumers with questions may contact the association at the phone number or address above.

MARBLE INSTITUTE OF AMERICA
33505 State Street
Farmington, MI 48024
(313) 476-5558
Trade association that represents marble finishers, installers, and fabricators of marble products.

Call or write for current consumer information.

NATIONAL ASSOCIATION OF MIRROR MANUFACTURERS
9005 Congressional Court
Potomac, MD 20854
(301) 365-4080
Manufacturers of mirrors. Founded in 1958.

Publication: *Mirrorscapes*. Complete guide to using mirrors in the home ($1).

NATIONAL DECORATING PRODUCTS ASSOCIATION (NDPA)
1050 North Lindbergh Boulevard
St. Louis, MO 63132-2994
(314) 991-3470
Retailers of decorating products, including paint, wallcovering, draperies, window treatments,

carpeting. Purpose is to enhance professionalism of retail salespeople, maintain good customer relations with thorough product knowledge and customer service.

Publications: *How to Hang Wallcoverings.* An illustrated step-by-step guide to materials and procedures. Covers basic wallcovering techniques as well as special applications such as doors, cabinets, ceilings, and stairways ($.75).

Decorating With Confidence. A full-color booklet with dozens of room settings that illustrate the dynamics of color, pattern, setting a mood, and decorating with coordinates ($1).

Annual NDPA Products Catalog. Publications for members, but also includes comprehensive reference books on caring for, and decorating with, carpeting, paint, window treatments, and wallcoverings. Free.

NATIONAL SPA AND POOL INSTITUTE (NSPI)

2111 Eisenhower Avenue
Alexandria, VA 22314
(703) 549-0493
(800) 323-3996

An association of pool, spa, and hot tub industries. Commitment to public health and safety in the installation, maintenance, and operation of pools, spas, and hot tubs. Establishes voluntary uniform design and construction standards. Offers member training programs, as well as consumer education. Founded in 1956; 4,300 member firms.

Call toll-free number for information on an NSPI dealer in your area and for other free publications.

Publications: NSPI covers spa and hot tubs for both indoor and outdoor use; somewhat more emphasis is placed on outdoor use so not all information is applicable to spas in the bathroom.

The Sensible Way to Enjoy Your Spa or Hot Tub. Fourteen-page booklet with tips on using the spa or hot tub for exercise and entertaining, plus safety and maintenance tips ($1.75).

Maintaining Your Spa or Hot Tub. Mechanical systems, use of chemicals in the water, and maintenance. Free.

Enjoying Your Spa or Hot Tub. Ideas for health and relaxation. Free.

TILE COUNCIL OF AMERICA INC.

P.O. Box 326
Princeton, NJ 08542-0326
(609) 921-7050

A national trade association of domestic manufacturers of ceramic tile; associate members supply raw material and equipment to domestic manufacturers. Acts as industry information source. Cooperates with governments in applying installation and product standards through membership and support of the American National Standards Institute. Provides education for members. Founded in 1945.

Publications: *How to Decorate with Ceramic Tile.* Full-color brochure with room settings that illustrate tile design in bathrooms, kitchens, and sun spaces. Free.

How to Install and Maintain Ceramic Tile. Color illustrations. How to shop for tile, installation tools, and tiling procedures for floors, countertops, and walls. Free.

WALLCOVERING INFORMATION BUREAU

P.O. Box 1708
Grand Central Station
New York, NY 10163-1708

Publications: *Transformations.* A twenty-four page brochure that describes the goal of ten design challenges and the results ($1).

Work Wonders With Wallcoverings. A sixteen-page booklet of tips on how to choose and use wallcoverings, how to personalize space, mix patterns, and create special effects ($.50).

NOTE: Information for Appendix A was adapted from the Encyclopedia of Associations, 26th Edition, 1992, and from information provided by trade associations.

APPENDIX B:

ADAPTABLE LIVING RESOURCES FOR THE PHYSICALLY CHALLENGED

ABLEDATA
Adaptive Equipment Center
Newington Children's Hospital
181 East Cedar Street
Newington, CT 06111
(800) 344-5405
Maintains data bank of manufacturers and provides printouts by category with product descriptions.

ACCENT ON LIVING
P.O. Box 700
Bloomington, IL 61702-9956
(309) 378-2961
Catalog: *Accent Buyer's Guide*. Annual catalog of publications, products, services, and organizations.

ACCESS TO INDEPENDENCE INC.
1954 East Washington Avenue
Madison, WI 53704
(608) 251-7575
Publication: *The Accessible Bathroom*. Written by the Design Coalition, a community design and planning center of Madison, Wisconsin. Includes illustrations, detailed dimensions, and construction tips on building an accessible bathroom or modifying an existing bath. Ask for current price.

**ADAPTIVE
ENVIRONMENTS CENTER**
374 Congress Street, Suite 301
Boston, MA 02210

(617) 695-1225 (voice and TDD)
Publication: *A Consumer's Guide to Home Adaptation*. Recommended by Courage Center. (See below.) $9.50 + postage and handling.

**AMERICAN ASSOCIATION OF
RETIRED PERSONS (AARP)**
Consumer Affairs Department
601 East Street NW
Washington, D.C. 20049
(202) 434-6031 (request line)
Publication: *The Do-Able Renewable Home*: *Making Your Home Fit Your Needs*. Tips on making the entire home, including the bathroom, accessible. Free.

COURAGE CENTER
Accessibility by Design Program
3915 Golden Valley Road
Golden Valley, MN 55422
(612) 520-0518
Assistance with accessible design planning (for Minnesota residents), information on financing, general information on accessibility.
   Publication: *Home Modification Products Catalog*. Includes bathroom, kitchen, doors, walls, and lifts. Free.

**EASTERN PARALYZED
VETERANS ASSOCIATION**
75-20 Astoria Boulevard

Jackson Heights, NY 11370-1178
(718) 803-3782
Publications: *Building Design Requirements for the Physically Handicapped* and *Wheelchair House Designs.* Ask for current price.

**INSTITUTE FOR
TECHNOLOGY DEVELOPMENT**
Advanced Living Systems Division
428 North Lamar Boulevard
Oxford, MS 38655
(601) 234-0158
Publication: *Enabling Products: A Sourcebook.* Ask for current price.

MADDAK INC.
Pequannock, NJ 07440-1993
(201) 628-7600
Catalog: *Ableware.* Hundreds of products to help the physically challenged individual perform daily activities with a greater degree of independence. Includes bathroom products. Free.

**NATIONAL ASSOCIATION
OF HOME BUILDERS**
National Research Center
400 Prince George Boulevard
Upper Marlboro, MD 20772-8731
(301) 249-4000
Publications: *Fire-Safe, Adaptable Demonstration House; Home Modifications for the Elderly;* and *Directory of Accessible Building Products.* Ask for current prices.

NATIONAL COUNCIL ON THE AGING
Consumer Affairs
600 Maryland Avenue SW
Washington, D.C. 20024
(202) 479-1200
Ask for current publications list.

STATE OF CALIFORNIA
Department of Rehabilitation

Topanga, CA 90290
Publication: *Housing Adaptability Guidelines: A Concept to Make All Housing Accessible.* Free.

**U.S. DEPARTMENT OF HOUSING
AND URBAN DEVELOPMENT**
Office of Fair Housing and Equal Opportunity
451 Seventh Street SW, Room 5116
Washington, D.C. 20410-2000
(800) 424-8590
In Washington, D.C. (202) 708-2878
(800) 543-8294 TDD for hearing impaired.
Information on the Fair Housing Act which prohibits discrimination in housing because of handicap, race or color, national origin, religion, sex, or familial status.

For the disabled, HUD offers interpreters, tapes and Braille materials, and assistance in reading and completing forms.

Publication: *Fair Housing: It's Your Right.* Details the provisions of the Fair Housing Act, from individual rights to filing a complaint. Free.

From regional HUD offices (consult telephone book under "U.S. Government"): *Adaptable Housing.* Free. *Universal Design — Housing for the Lifespan of All People,* HUD 1156-PA, August 1988. Ask for current price.

WHIRLPOOL CORPORATION
Administrative Center
Benton Harbor, MI 49022-2692
(616) 926-3164
Publications: *Designs for Independent Living: Kitchen and Laundry Designs for Disabled Persons,* Form No. 1B310, Appliance Information Service. May be helpful to those considering a bathroom laundry. Free.

Tools for Independent Living: Suggestions for Installing and Operating Major Home Appliances for Easier Use by Disabled Persons, Form No. 1B314, Appliance Information Service. Includes photos. Free.

CREDITS

American Lighting Association, Chicago, Illinois; illustration, page 156 and chart, page 157, adapted from ALA *Lighting Your Life*; photos, pages 64, 159.

Bill Armsted, contractor, Signature Properties, Dallas, Texas; **Clint Visnick**, tile contractor, Dallas, Texas; **Robbie Fusch**, architect, Fusch Seroid Partners, AIA, Dallas Texas; **Gerald Tomlin, ASID**, interior designer, Dallas, TX; bathroom design, page 52.

Ralph J. Cerino, interior designer, Philadelphia, Pennsylvania; **James Levin**, photographer, New York, New York; bathroom design, page 61 (top and bottom).

Stu Dettelbach, CKD, CR, SD Kitchens, Baltimore, Maryland; Sample Design and Consultation Agreement, page 30.

Joan Eisenberg, CKD, CBD, CHE, JME Consulting, Inc., Baltimore, Maryland; bathroom designs, pages 36, 44, 71.

Joan Eisenberg, designer; **Edward R. Stough**, designer, Stevenson Village Center, Stevenson, Maryland; bathroom design, page 43.

Gay Fly, CKD, CBD, ASID, Gay Fly Interior Designs, Houston, Texas; bathroom design, **Global Design Challenge**, pages 54-55.

Elly Hartmanis, PHD Environments, Inc., Kitchens & Baths, Ithaca, New York; bathroom design, page 53; Sample Specification Sheet 2, page 104.

Michelle Heaton-Rolens, CBD, Neil Kelly Designers/Remodelers, Beaverton, Oregon; **Pat Burt**, photographer; bathroom design, **1992 National Kitchen and Bath Association Design Competition winner;** page 147.

Home Improvement Costs for Interior Projects (1991), R. S. Means Company, Inc., Kingston, Massachusetts; illustrations and charts, pages 16-19.

Linder Jones, Linder Design/Build, Mountain View, California, designer/contractor; **Shelley Patterson**, Linder Design/Build, designer; **Debra Jones**, Linder Design/Build, photographic stylist; **Michael C. Lewis**, photographer; bathroom design, **1992 National Kitchen and Bath Association Design Competition winner,** pages 48-49.

Journal of Light Construction, Hanley-Wood Partners, Richmond, VT; illustrations, page 173 (top).

Leo H. Kelsey, CKD, European Country Kitchens, Far Hills, New Jersey; bathroom design, **Global Design Challenge,** pages 68-69, 143.

Kitchen Cabinet Manufacturers Association, Reston, Virginia; photos, pages 138-139.

Colleen B. Langston, CKD, Euro-American Kitchens & Baths, Santa Ana Heights, California; bathroom designs, pages 57, 65.

Loree L. Lord, architect, Northwest Home Designing, Inc., Tacoma, Washington; **Stephen Mead,** interior designer, Stephen Mead Associates, Des Moines, Iowa; accessible bathroom design, page 75.

Stuart Margol, CR, Stuart Margol Companies, Dallas, Texas; bathroom design and construction, pages 6-7.

Stuart Margol, CR, contractor; **Gary Covert**, architect, Covert and Associates, Dallas, Texas; **Mark Miller**, designer, M2 Designs, Dallas, Texas; **J. Benoist**, photographer, Dallas, Texas; accessible bathroom, **1991 National Association of the Remodeling Industry Cot/Y Award, National winner,** pages 80-81.

Minnesota Department of Public Service, Energy Division, St. Paul, Minnesota; illustrations, pages 170, 173 (bottom).

National Kitchen and Bath Association, Hackettstown, New Jersey, illustrations on the following pages, reprinted with permission from the NKBA Bathroom Industry Technical Manuals (BITMs): page 41, BITM, Volume 2, figure 2.3; page 38, BITM, Volume 2, figure 2.10; page 89, BITM, Volume 4, figures 4.41 (left), 4.40 (right); page 136, BITM, Volume 3, figure 3.118; page 137, BITM, Volume 3, figure 3.119.

National SAFE KIDS Campaign, Washington, D.C.; illustration, page 86.

Joseph E. Nicolini, Alladin Remodelers, Inc., Massapequa Park, New York; **Gary Denys**, photographer; accessible bathroom design, **1992 National Kitchen and Bath Association Design Competition winner,** pages 77, 82.

Mike Palkowitsch, CKD, CBD, Kitchens by Krengel, Inc., St. Paul, Minnesota; bathroom design, pages 66-67 and Sample Specification Sheet, page 102.

Gordon Schroll, Deborah Schroll, ABC Kitchens & Baths, Des Plaines, Illinois; **bathroom design, 1991 National Kitchen and Bath Association Design Competition winner,** pages 58-59.

Ann M. Schwalm, Lamperti Associates, San Rafael, California; designer, **1992 National Kitchen and Bath Association Design Competition winner,** page 150.

Carolyn B. Thomas, Allied ASID, Town & Country Baths, Washington, D.C.; **Walter Smalling**, photography; bathroom design (for **Melvin C. Keller Co.**, Washington, D.C.), **1992 National Kitchen and Bath Association Design Competition winner;** pages 62-63.

Gladys Tobey, designer, Forum Industries, San Mateo, California; cultured marble bathtub, page 152.

Marie Vos Owens, Concept II Building Corporation, West Allis, Wisconsin, designer/contractor, with **Terry Anderson,** homeowner, and **Bruce Jackson**, architect; bathroom design, **1991 National Association of the Remodeling Industry Cot/Y Awards, Regional winner,** pages 42, 50-51.

Gary White, CBD, Kitchen Design, Newport Beach, California; bathroom design (for the **Safe Bath Project**); pages 56, 90.

Joni Zimmerman, CKD, Kitchen Encounters, Annapolis, Maryland; bathroom design, page 165.

Credentials: AIA, American Institute of Architects; ASID, American Society of Interior Designers; CBD, Certified Bath Designer; CHE, Certified Home Economist; CKD, Certified Kitchen Designer; CR, Certified Remodeler.

INDEX